CHRIS **MISKIEWICZ**   PALLE **SCHMIDT**

TH⊙MAS ALS⊙P

THE **HAND** OF THE **ISLAND**

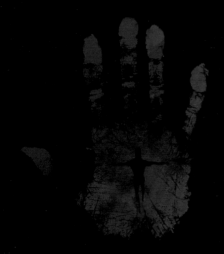

BOOM!
STUDIOS

BOOM! STUDIOS

THOMAS ALSOP Volume One, May 2015. Published by BOOM! Studios, a division of Boom Entertainment, Inc. Thomas Alsop is ™ & © 2015 Boom Entertainment, Inc. Originally published in single magazine form as THOMAS ALSOP No. 1-4. ™ & © 2014 Boom Entertainment, Inc. All rights reserved. BOOM! Studios™ and the BOOM! Studios logo are trademarks of Boom Entertainment, Inc., registered in various countries and categories. All characters, events, and institutions depicted herein are fictional. Any similarity between any of the names, characters, persons, events, and/or institutions in this publication to actual names, characters, and persons, whether living or dead, events, and/or institutions is unintended and purely coincidental. BOOM! Studios does not read or accept unsolicited submissions of ideas, stories, or artwork.

A catalog record of this book is available from OCLC and from the BOOM! Studios website, www.boom-studios.com, on the Librarians Page.

BOOM! Studios, 5670 Wilshire Boulevard, Suite 450, Los Angeles, CA 90036-5679. Printed in China. First Printing.

ISBN: 978-1-60886-684-7, eISBN: 978-1-61398-355-3

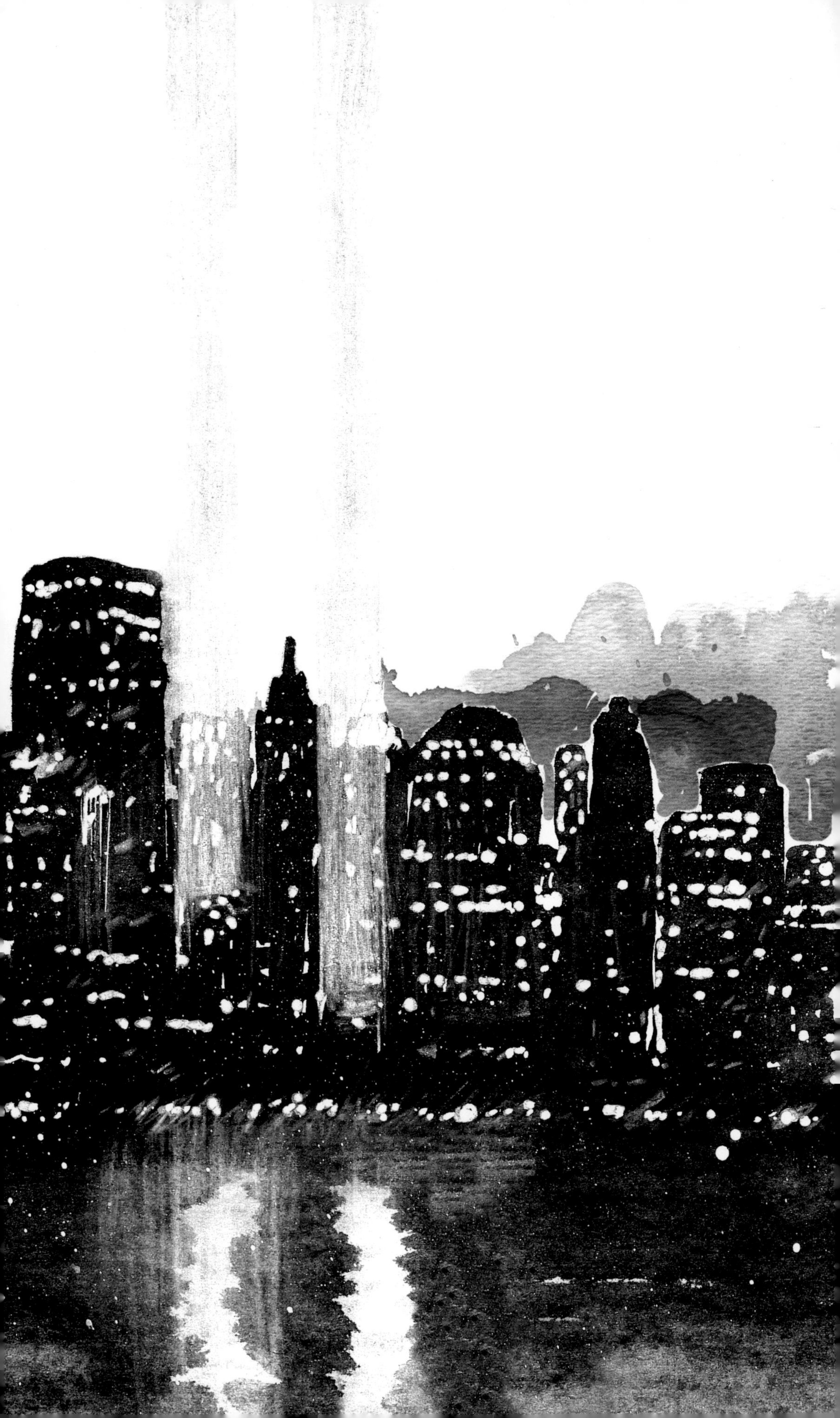

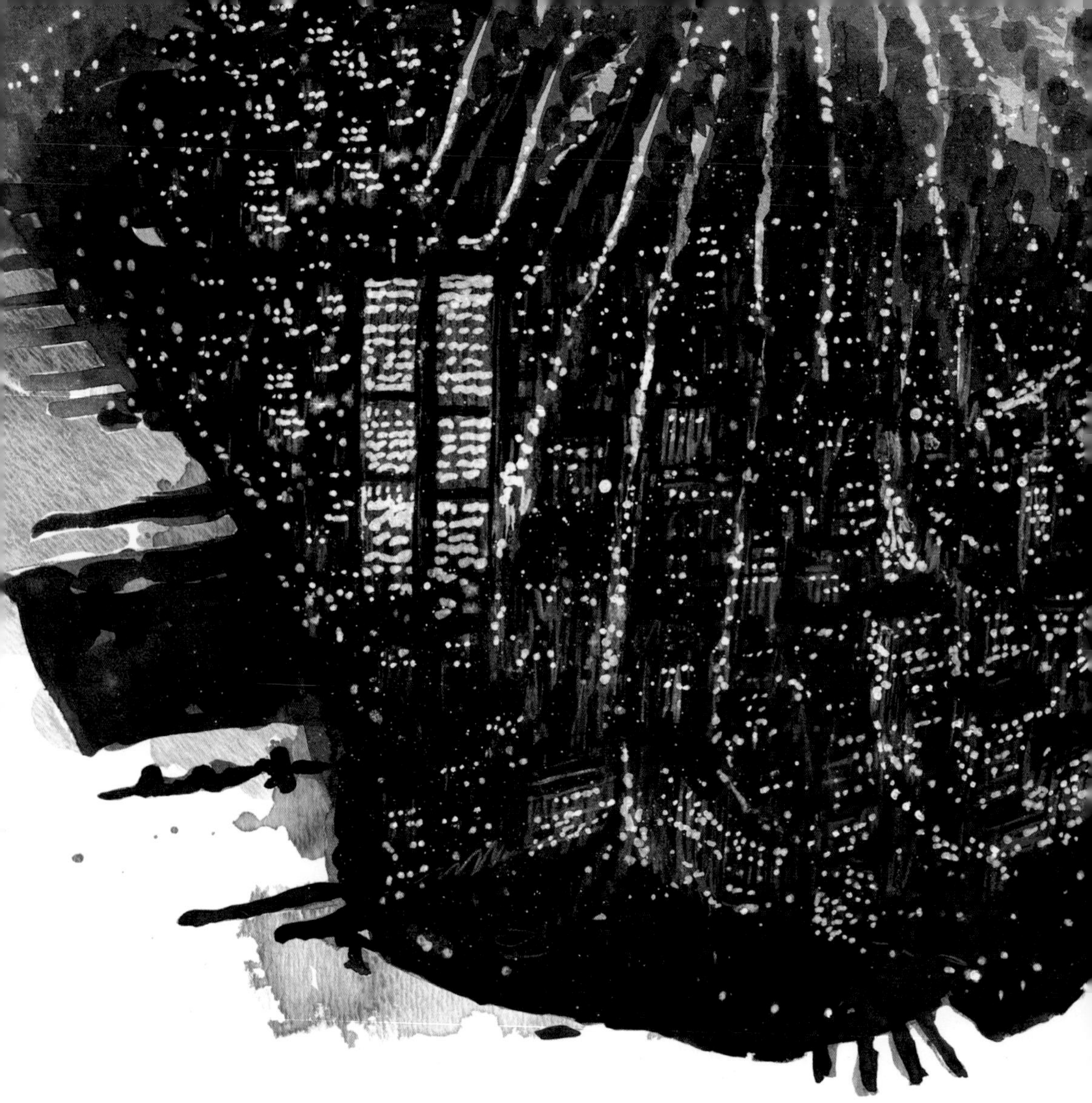

THOMAS ALSOP
THE HAND OF THE ISLAND

CREATED BY
CHRIS **MISKIEWICZ** AND PALLE **SCHMIDT**

WRITTEN BY
CHRIS **MISKIEWICZ**

ILLUSTRATED BY
PALLE **SCHMIDT**

LETTERING BY
DERON **BENNETT**

DESIGNER
SCOTT **NEWMAN**

COVER BY
PALLE **SCHMIDT**

ASSISTANT EDITOR
JASMINE **AMIRI**

EDITOR
IAN **BRILL**

SPECIAL THANKS TO
CHIP **MOSHER**   MATT **GAGNON**   DAFNA **PLEBAN**   PAUL **BOSCHE**

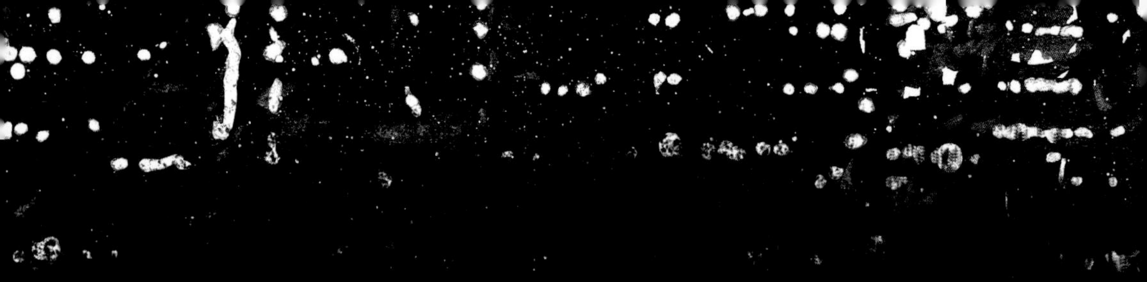

I love New York. I also have a thing for cemeteries, abandoned buildings, industrial waterways, and places from generations past that are still hanging on in crumbling defiance against the lackluster glass and steel towers of the modern age.

As a teenager it was common to find me wandering along the decrepit shores of Brooklyn's broken bottle coastline and the collapsing piers of the East River. I'd climb fences, trespassing, just so I could get to a new section of the shore to sit alone and stare at the towers of Manhattan.

But this aspect of my personality isn't limited to NYC. I do a similar walk in every city I visit. And no matter what city it is, I always have a way of finding a cemetery.

The initial idea for ***Thomas Alsop*** came to me while I was on one of my cemetery walks. I was watching a friend's dog when my local park had been invaded by a group of hipsters who set up a game of croquet in the main field. So I thought about where I could go to let him off the leash for a run. I ended up going to Calvary Cemetery just a mile away from where I live in Greenpoint, Brooklyn. I figured it was as close to a park as we were going to get.

Calvary is one of the oldest cemeteries in the United States covering 365 acres, as well as being the final resting place to over three million souls. It's massive, located on a hilltop that overlooks Greenpoint, the East River, and Manhattan.

On this particular day I walked through an area that's famous for the amount of mobsters buried there, where I came upon a smaller gated family cemetery that I had never seen. Each of the remaining headstones dated back to the 1700's. They were in disrepair, as you would expect, but there sunken into the ground was one that caught my eye. I moved the dead grass away to read the name. *Richard Alsop – One Month Old. 1701*. Stunned by the date, I tried to imagine what the surrounding area must of looked like, amazed that something so old could be situated there.

Weeks passed and I couldn't get *Richard Alsop's* name out of my head. So, I began my research. The Alsop Farm was purchased in 1845 with an adjoining 115 acres. I researched how Newtown Creek was once wild with game, Indians, and wolves. I delved deeply into the history of NYC, its waterways, and hidden corners, and once again found myself walking along forgotten shorelines looking for traces of what had been. Only this time, every bit of it felt like magic, with this Dutch figure staring back prodding me to tell a story.

Several days later, I read an article about the hull of a ship that was uncovered at Ground

WELCOME, STRANGE CITIZENS

AN INTRODUCTION BY CHRIS MIŚKIEWICZ

Zero. Once again, my imagination soared. Initial reports claimed that it had the same design as slave ships used to bring Africans to the America's as forced labor. I was floored. How could this be real and buried beneath the World Trade Center?

I came up with the plot for Thomas Alsop soon after when a simple question went through my head, *"Where would the highest concentration of ghosts be located in Manhattan right now?"*

The answer filled me with an eerie silence.

I labored over the 9/11 plotline of Thomas Alsop for months while writing this story. I couldn't see how to avoid it and still craft a believable tale that was as entrenched in the history of New York City as this is. But why bring a topic like 9/11 to a story so ripe with possibilities and spin-offs?

Well, we all had that question, and so internal discussions began about the weight of 9/11 over hours of conference calls between Los Angeles, Brooklyn, and Copenhagen, where we cited examples of other media that had already used 9/11 as a plot point, while trying to understand if Thomas Alsop needed this event.

I felt like we did. Nothing else had the weight that the book demanded. And I kept wandering back to the same question,

"If we're building the myth of this noble cursed family who protected Manhattan for three hundred years, then how would the current Hand of the Island miss such a major event?"

I couldn't see a way around it. Instead, I decided that it would be a moment that would define Thomas Alsop as much as it defined the version of New York City that continued into the twenty-first century. The event would have to be intrinsically interwoven into the fabric of who our character is, and who he would later become, while treating the actual topic with the utmost possible care the entire time.

In the end, Editor-in-Chief, Matt Gagnon felt comfortable with how we were handling the delicate subject matter and decided to go forward with our plot.

Due to the sensitive nature of 9/11 I feel as though I need to say that I mean no disrespect to any who suffered a loss. I hope to tell the story of an unlikely hero who climbed out of that day in the same way that my city, and our nation have done since. Hopefully, Strange Citizens, you'll come along with Palle and me to find out exactly what that means.

Respectfully yours,
CHRIS **MISKIEWICZ**

CHAPTER ONE
WHO IS THOMAS ALSOP?

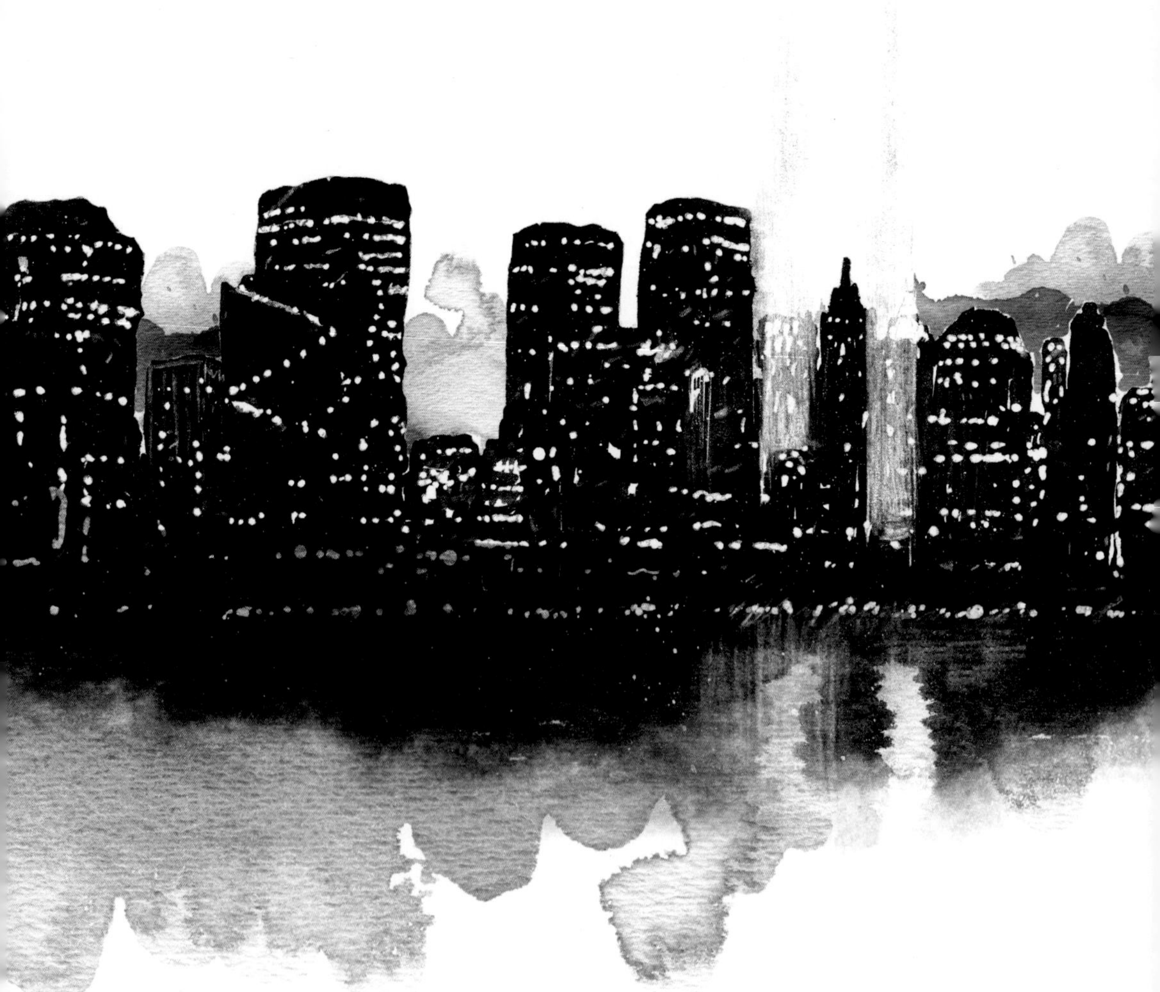

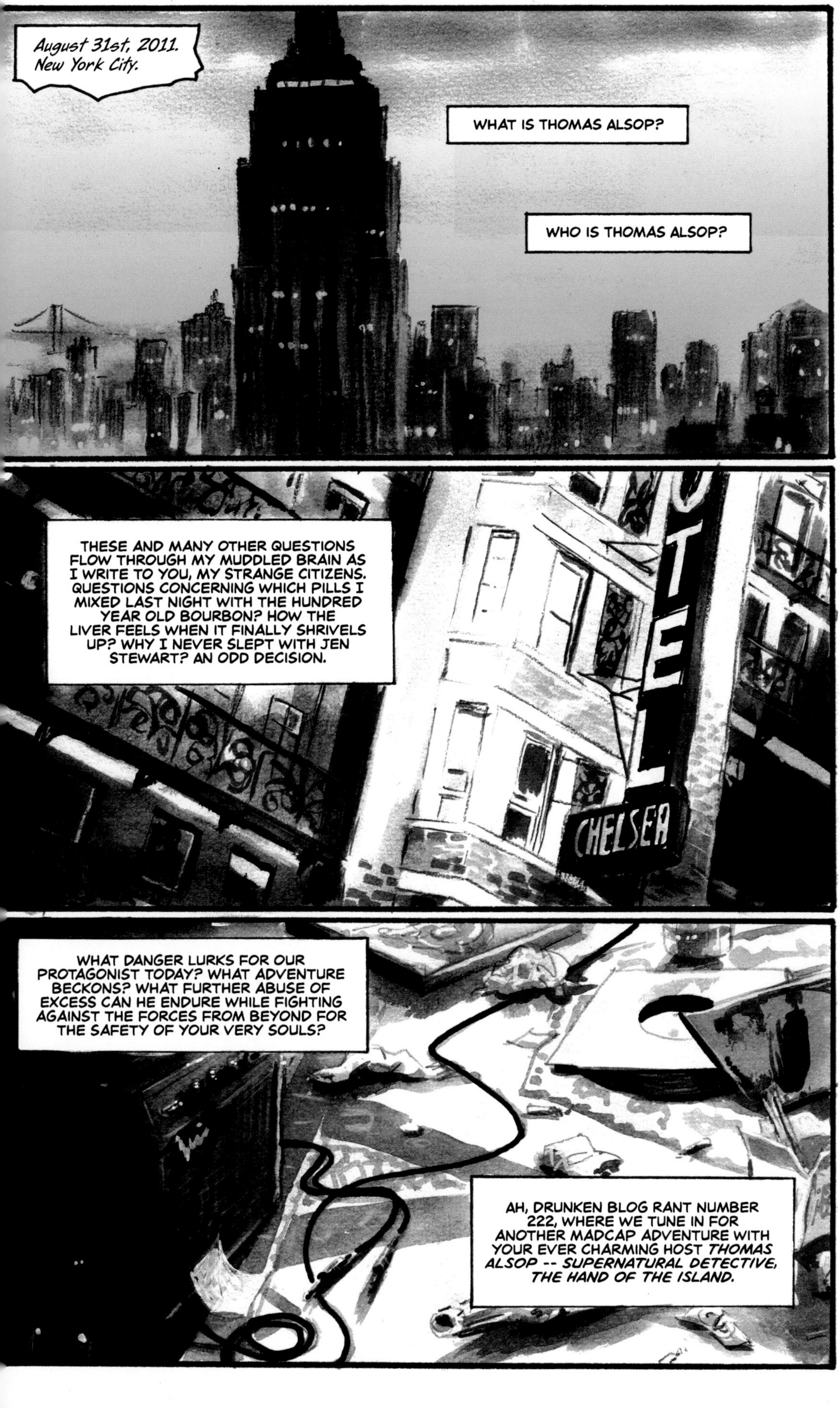
August 31st, 2011. New York City.
WHAT IS THOMAS ALSOP?
WHO IS THOMAS ALSOP?
THESE AND MANY OTHER QUESTIONS FLOW THROUGH MY MUDDLED BRAIN AS I WRITE TO YOU, MY STRANGE CITIZENS. QUESTIONS CONCERNING WHICH PILLS I MIXED LAST NIGHT WITH THE HUNDRED YEAR OLD BOURBON? HOW THE LIVER FEELS WHEN IT FINALLY SHRIVELS UP? WHY I NEVER SLEPT WITH JEN STEWART? AN ODD DECISION.
CHELSEA
WHAT DANGER LURKS FOR OUR PROTAGONIST TODAY? WHAT ADVENTURE BECKONS? WHAT FURTHER ABUSE OF EXCESS CAN HE ENDURE WHILE FIGHTING AGAINST THE FORCES FROM BEYOND FOR THE SAFETY OF YOUR VERY SOULS?
AH, DRUNKEN BLOG RANT NUMBER 222, WHERE WE TUNE IN FOR ANOTHER MADCAP ADVENTURE WITH YOUR EVER CHARMING HOST *THOMAS ALSOP -- SUPERNATURAL DETECTIVE, THE HAND OF THE ISLAND.*

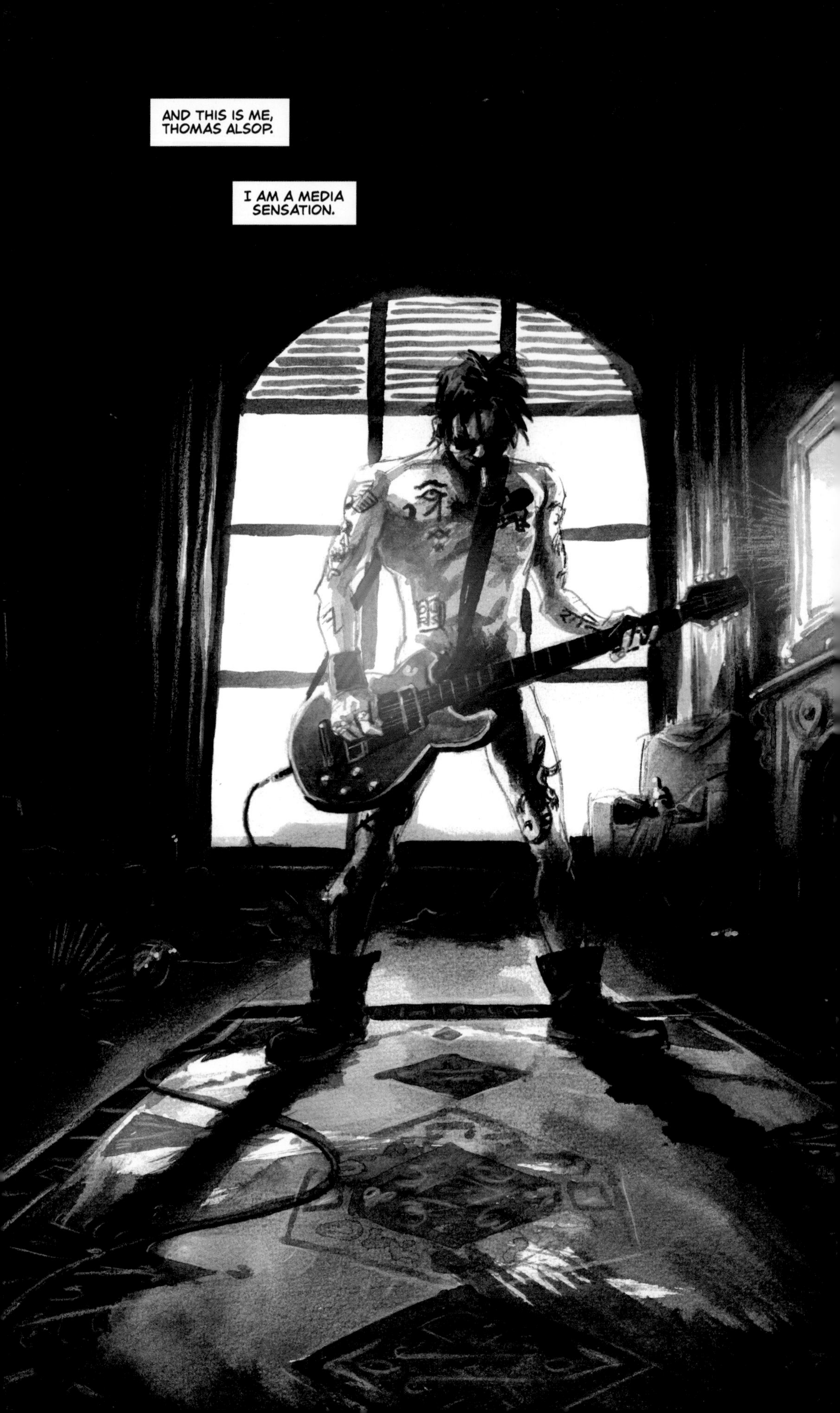
AND THIS IS ME, THOMAS ALSOP.
I AM A MEDIA SENSATION.

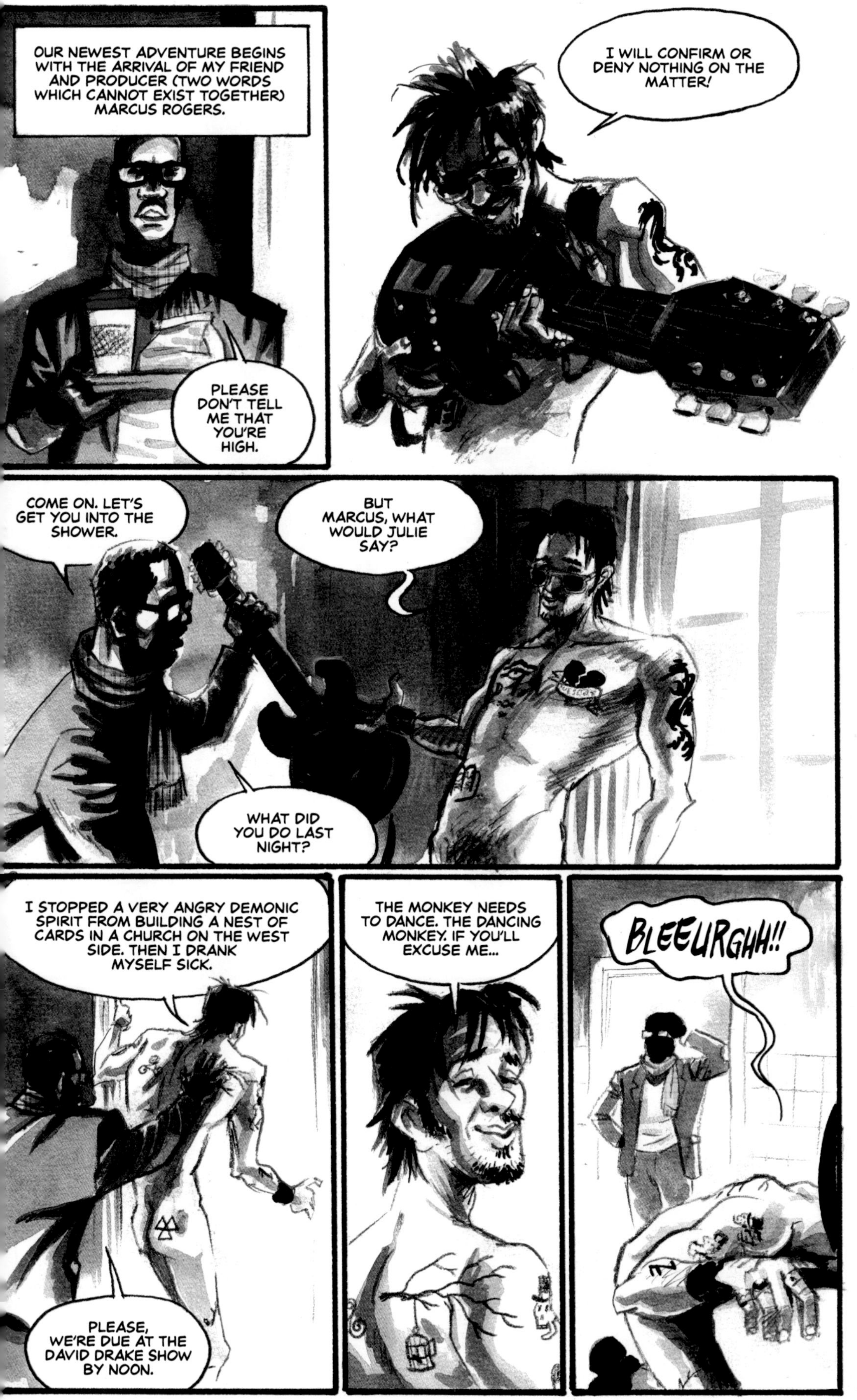
OUR NEWEST ADVENTURE BEGINS WITH THE ARRIVAL OF MY FRIEND AND PRODUCER (TWO WORDS WHICH CANNOT EXIST TOGETHER) MARCUS ROGERS.
PLEASE DON'T TELL ME THAT YOU'RE HIGH.
I WILL CONFIRM OR DENY NOTHING ON THE MATTER!
COME ON. LET'S GET YOU INTO THE SHOWER.
BUT MARCUS, WHAT WOULD JULIE SAY?
WHAT DID YOU DO LAST NIGHT?
I STOPPED A VERY ANGRY DEMONIC SPIRIT FROM BUILDING A NEST OF CARDS IN A CHURCH ON THE WEST SIDE. THEN I DRANK MYSELF SICK.
PLEASE, WE'RE DUE AT THE DAVID DRAKE SHOW BY NOON.
THE MONKEY NEEDS TO DANCE. THE DANCING MONKEY. IF YOU'LL EXCUSE ME...
BLEEURGHH!!

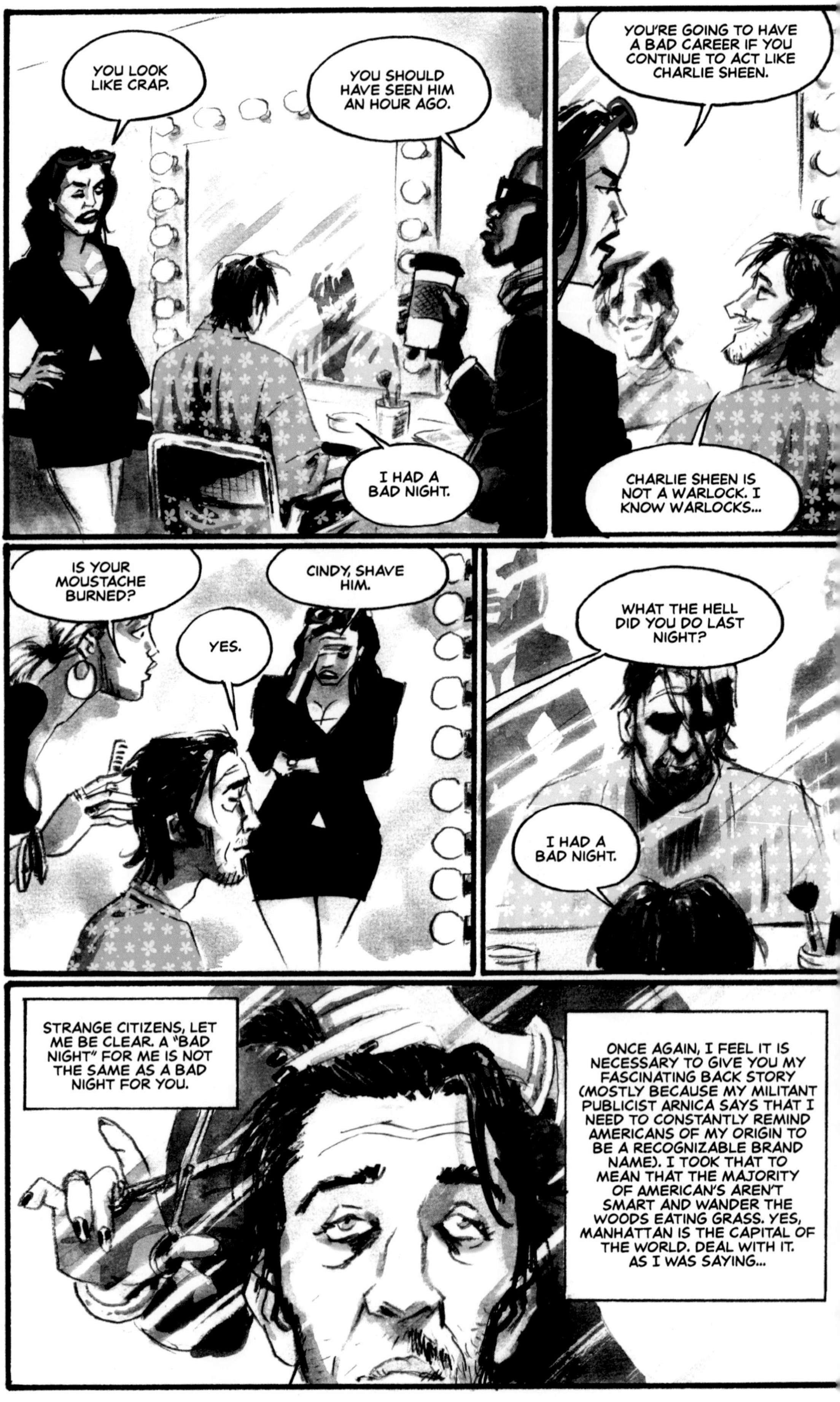
YOU LOOK LIKE CRAP.
YOU SHOULD HAVE SEEN HIM AN HOUR AGO.
I HAD A BAD NIGHT.
YOU'RE GOING TO HAVE A BAD CAREER IF YOU CONTINUE TO ACT LIKE CHARLIE SHEEN.
CHARLIE SHEEN IS NOT A WARLOCK. I KNOW WARLOCKS...
IS YOUR MOUSTACHE BURNED?
YES.
CINDY, SHAVE HIM.
WHAT THE HELL DID YOU DO LAST NIGHT?
I HAD A BAD NIGHT.
STRANGE CITIZENS, LET ME BE CLEAR. A "BAD NIGHT" FOR ME IS NOT THE SAME AS A BAD NIGHT FOR YOU.
ONCE AGAIN, I FEEL IT IS NECESSARY TO GIVE YOU MY FASCINATING BACK STORY (MOSTLY BECAUSE MY MILITANT PUBLICIST ARNICA SAYS THAT I NEED TO CONSTANTLY REMIND AMERICANS OF MY ORIGIN TO BE A RECOGNIZABLE BRAND NAME). I TOOK THAT TO MEAN THAT THE MAJORITY OF AMERICAN'S AREN'T SMART AND WANDER THE WOODS EATING GRASS. YES, MANHATTAN IS THE CAPITAL OF THE WORLD. DEAL WITH IT. AS I WAS SAYING...

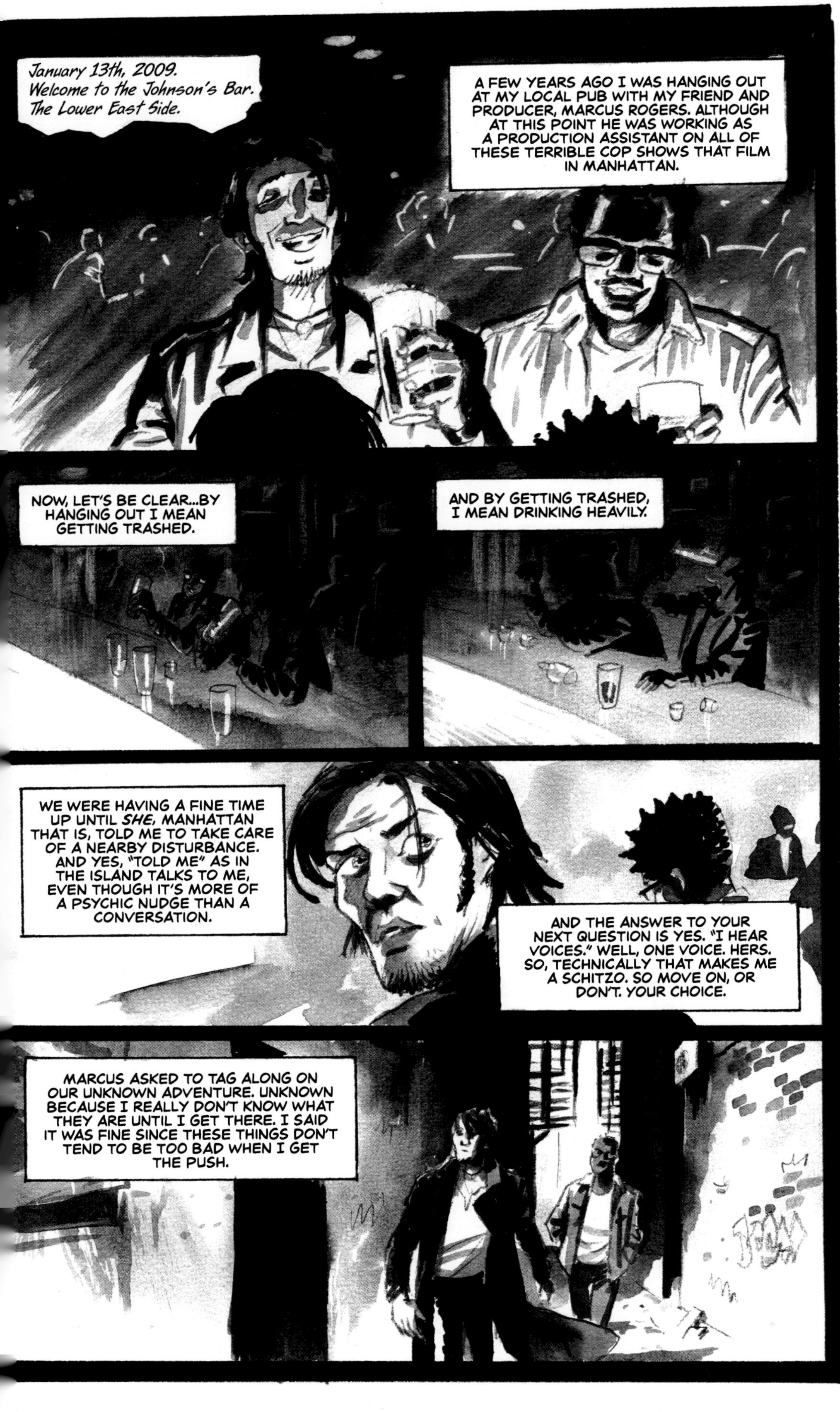
January 13th, 2009. Welcome to the Johnson's Bar. The Lower East Side.
A FEW YEARS AGO I WAS HANGING OUT AT MY LOCAL PUB WITH MY FRIEND AND PRODUCER, MARCUS ROGERS. ALTHOUGH AT THIS POINT HE WAS WORKING AS A PRODUCTION ASSISTANT ON ALL OF THESE TERRIBLE COP SHOWS THAT FILM IN MANHATTAN.
NOW, LET'S BE CLEAR...BY HANGING OUT I MEAN GETTING TRASHED.
AND BY GETTING TRASHED, I MEAN DRINKING HEAVILY.
WE WERE HAVING A FINE TIME UP UNTIL *SHE*, MANHATTAN THAT IS, TOLD ME TO TAKE CARE OF A NEARBY DISTURBANCE. AND YES, "TOLD ME" AS IN THE ISLAND TALKS TO ME, EVEN THOUGH IT'S MORE OF A PSYCHIC NUDGE THAN A CONVERSATION.
AND THE ANSWER TO YOUR NEXT QUESTION IS YES. "I HEAR VOICES." WELL, ONE VOICE. HERS. SO, TECHNICALLY THAT MAKES ME A SCHITZO. SO MOVE ON, OR DON'T. YOUR CHOICE.
MARCUS ASKED TO TAG ALONG ON OUR UNKNOWN ADVENTURE. UNKNOWN BECAUSE I REALLY DON'T KNOW WHAT THEY ARE UNTIL I GET THERE. I SAID IT WAS FINE SINCE THESE THINGS DON'T TEND TO BE TOO BAD WHEN I GET THE PUSH.

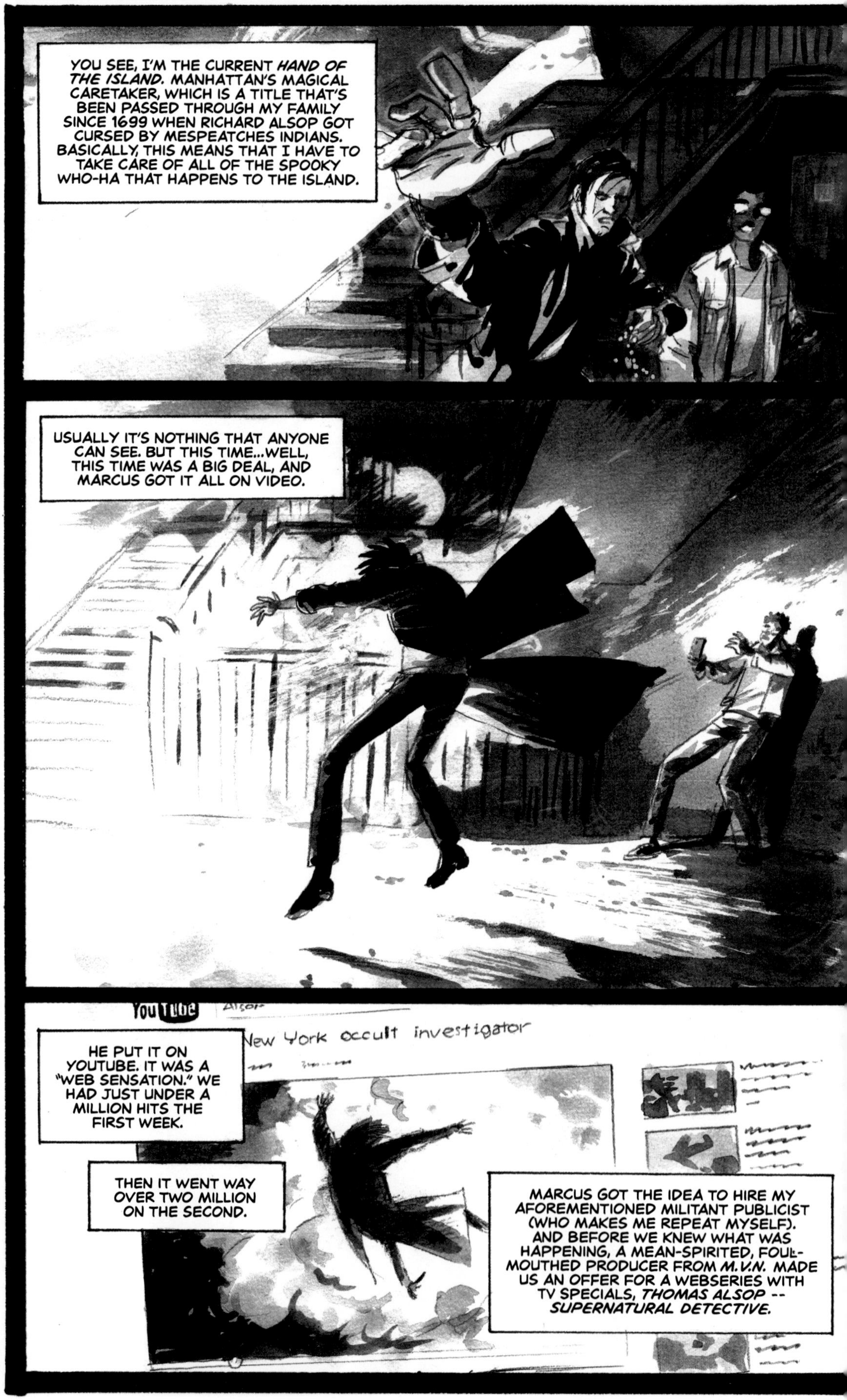
YOU SEE, I'M THE CURRENT HAND OF THE ISLAND. MANHATTAN'S MAGICAL CARETAKER, WHICH IS A TITLE THAT'S BEEN PASSED THROUGH MY FAMILY SINCE 1699 WHEN RICHARD ALSOP GOT CURSED BY MESPEATCHES INDIANS. BASICALLY, THIS MEANS THAT I HAVE TO TAKE CARE OF ALL OF THE SPOOKY WHO-HA THAT HAPPENS TO THE ISLAND.
USUALLY IT'S NOTHING THAT ANYONE CAN SEE. BUT THIS TIME...WELL, THIS TIME WAS A BIG DEAL, AND MARCUS GOT IT ALL ON VIDEO.
YouTube
New York occult investigator
HE PUT IT ON YOUTUBE. IT WAS A "WEB SENSATION." WE HAD JUST UNDER A MILLION HITS THE FIRST WEEK.
THEN IT WENT WAY OVER TWO MILLION ON THE SECOND.
MARCUS GOT THE IDEA TO HIRE MY AFOREMENTIONED MILITANT PUBLICIST (WHO MAKES ME REPEAT MYSELF). AND BEFORE WE KNEW WHAT WAS HAPPENING, A MEAN-SPIRITED, FOUL-MOUTHED PRODUCER FROM M.V.N. MADE US AN OFFER FOR A WEBSERIES WITH TV SPECIALS, THOMAS ALSOP -- SUPERNATURAL DETECTIVE.

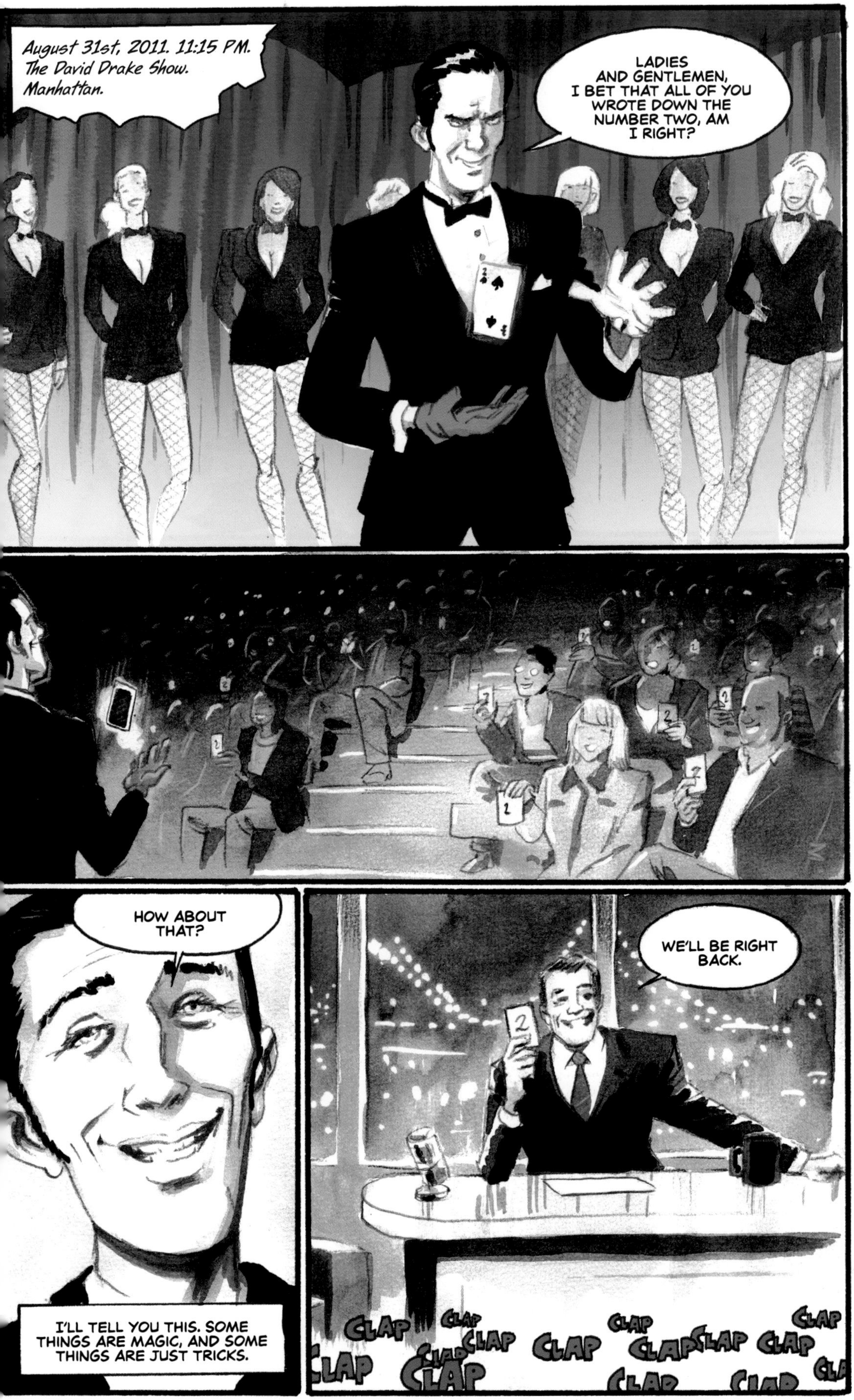
August 31st, 2011. 11:15 PM. The David Drake Show. Manhattan.
LADIES AND GENTLEMEN, I BET THAT ALL OF YOU WROTE DOWN THE NUMBER TWO, AM I RIGHT?
HOW ABOUT THAT?
I'LL TELL YOU THIS. SOME THINGS ARE MAGIC, AND SOME THINGS ARE JUST TRICKS.
WE'LL BE RIGHT BACK.
CLAP CLAP CLAP CLAP CLAP CLAP CLAP CLAP CLAP CLAP CLAP CLAP CLAP

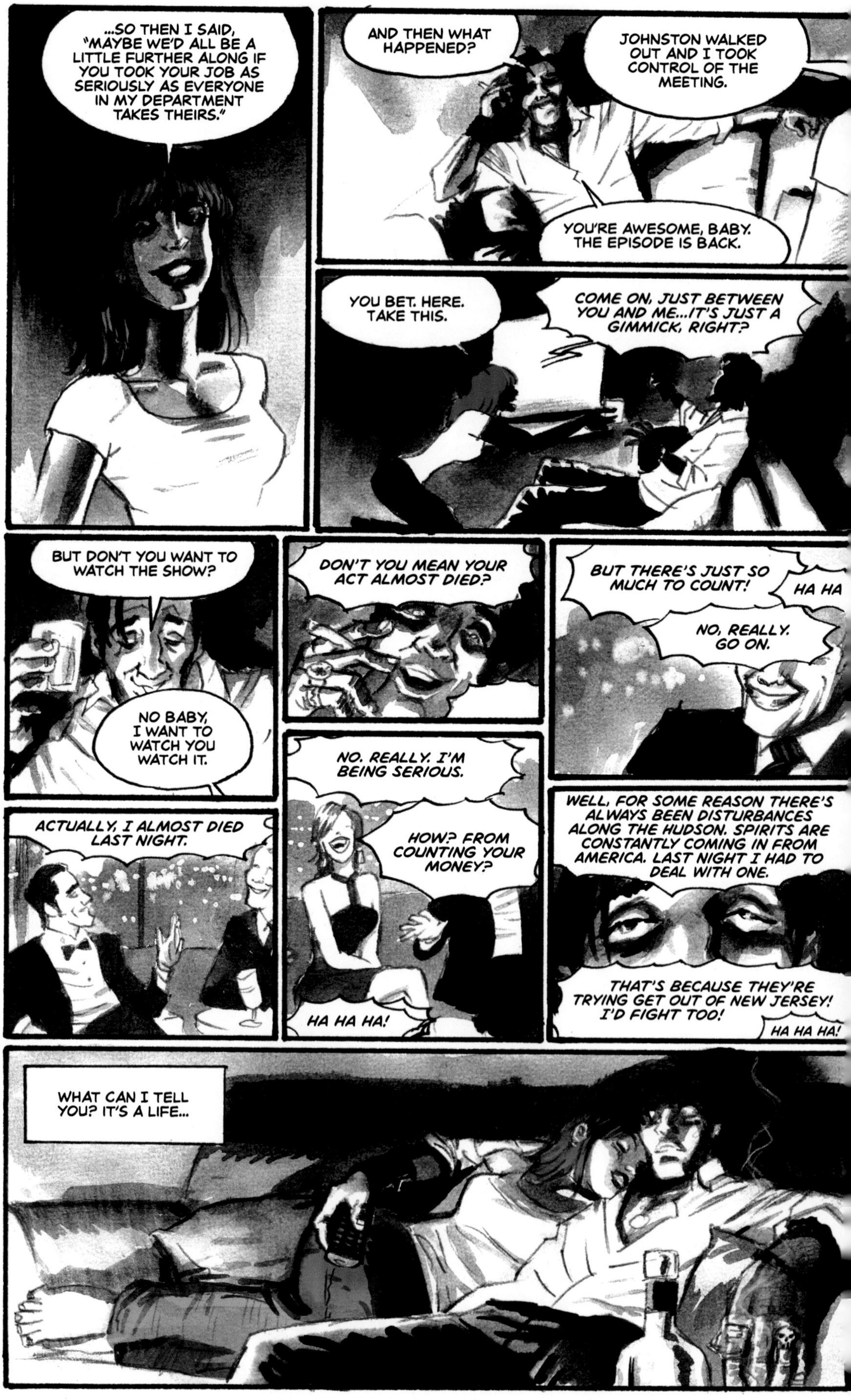
...SO THEN I SAID, "MAYBE WE'D ALL BE A LITTLE FURTHER ALONG IF YOU TOOK YOUR JOB AS SERIOUSLY AS EVERYONE IN MY DEPARTMENT TAKES THEIRS."
AND THEN WHAT HAPPENED?
JOHNSTON WALKED OUT AND I TOOK CONTROL OF THE MEETING.
YOU'RE AWESOME, BABY. THE EPISODE IS BACK.
YOU BET. HERE. TAKE THIS.
COME ON, JUST BETWEEN YOU AND ME...IT'S JUST A GIMMICK, RIGHT?
BUT DON'T YOU WANT TO WATCH THE SHOW?
NO BABY, I WANT TO WATCH YOU WATCH IT.
ACTUALLY, I ALMOST DIED LAST NIGHT.
DON'T YOU MEAN YOUR ACT ALMOST DIED?
NO. REALLY. I'M BEING SERIOUS.
HOW? FROM COUNTING YOUR MONEY?
HA HA HA!
BUT THERE'S JUST SO MUCH TO COUNT!
HA HA
NO, REALLY. GO ON.
WELL, FOR SOME REASON THERE'S ALWAYS BEEN DISTURBANCES ALONG THE HUDSON. SPIRITS ARE CONSTANTLY COMING IN FROM AMERICA. LAST NIGHT I HAD TO DEAL WITH ONE.
THAT'S BECAUSE THEY'RE TRYING GET OUT OF NEW JERSEY! I'D FIGHT TOO!
HA HA HA!
WHAT CAN I TELL YOU? IT'S A LIFE...

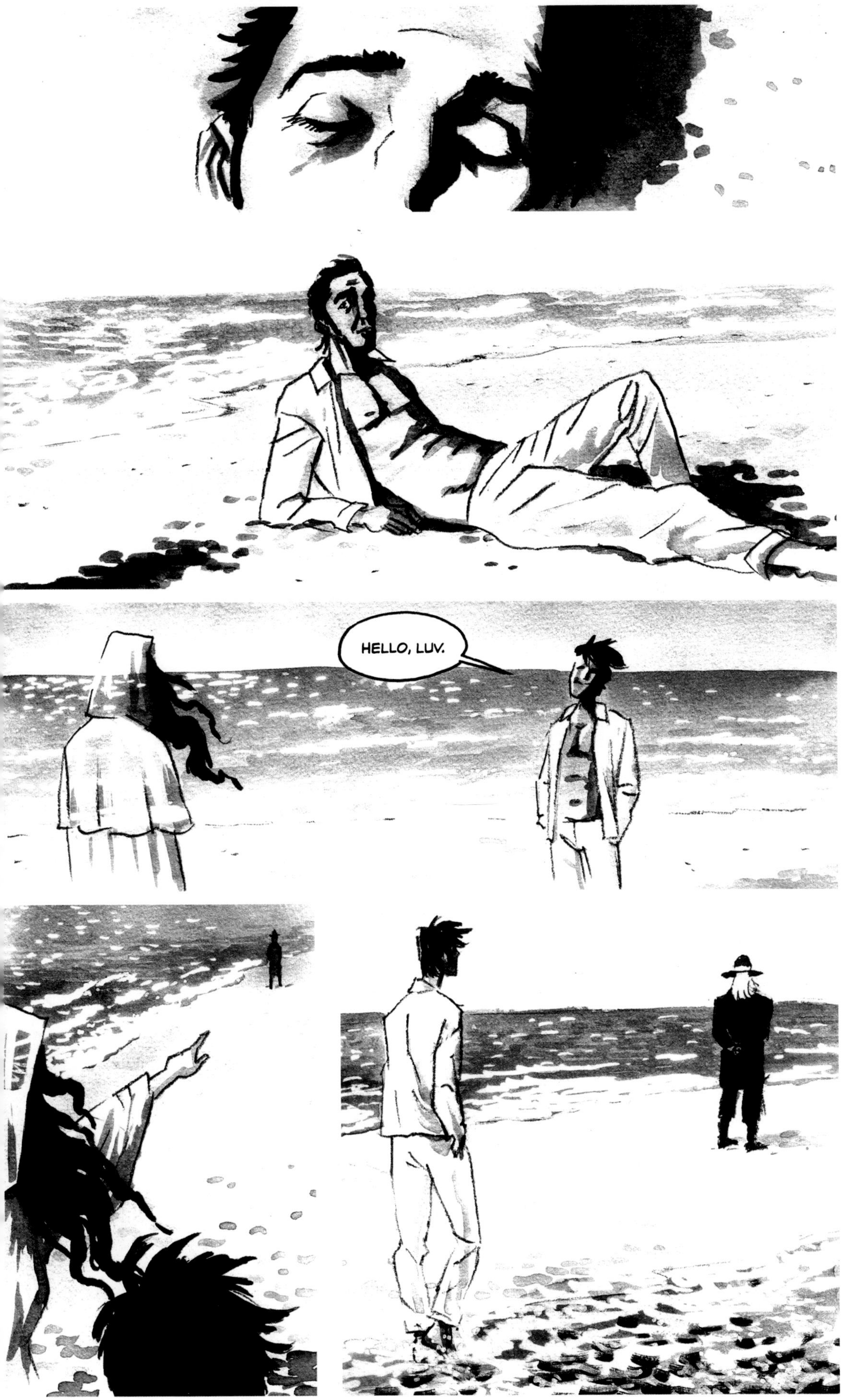
HELLO, LUV.

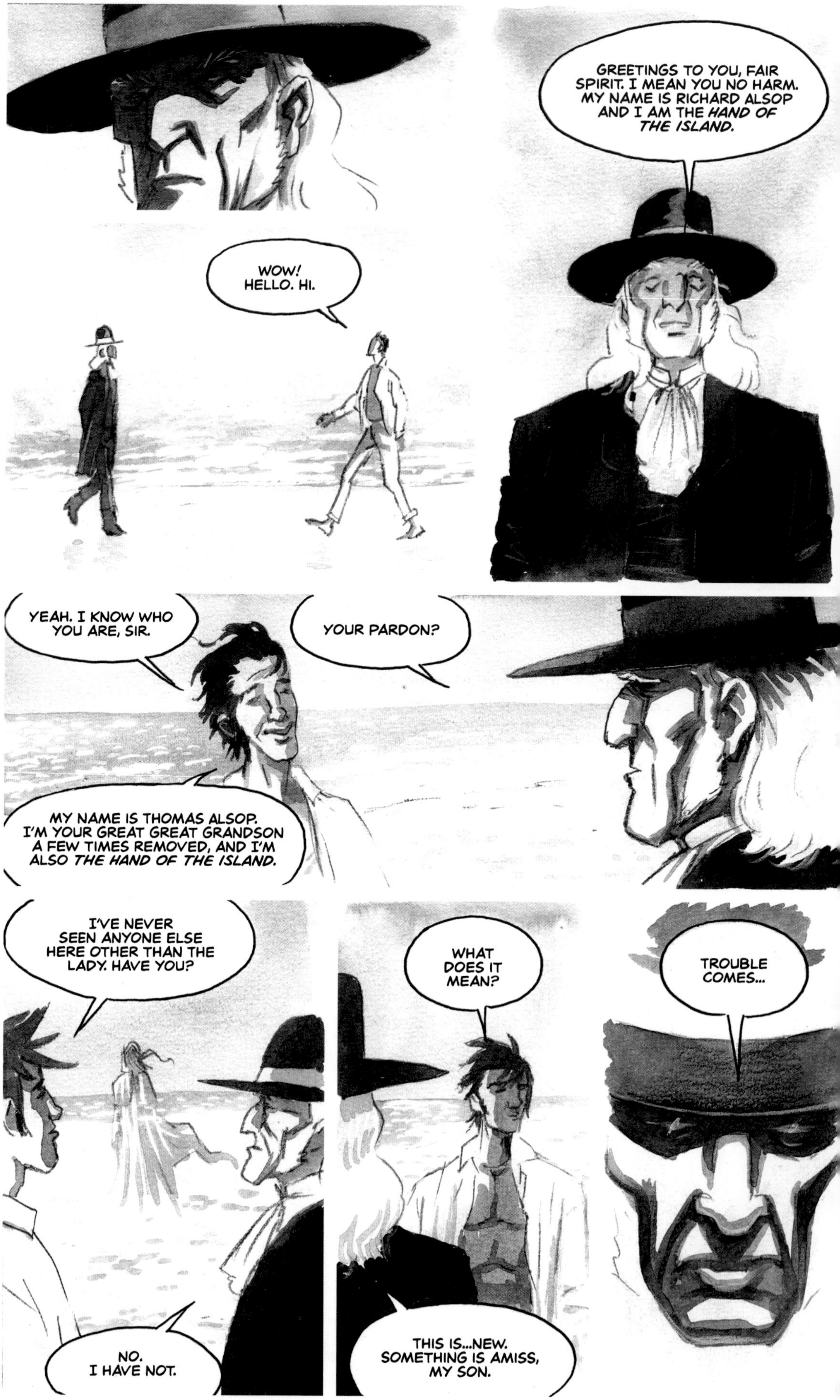
GREETINGS TO YOU, FAIR SPIRIT. I MEAN YOU NO HARM. MY NAME IS RICHARD ALSOP AND I AM THE *HAND OF THE ISLAND.*
WOW! HELLO. HI.
YEAH. I KNOW WHO YOU ARE, SIR.
YOUR PARDON?
MY NAME IS THOMAS ALSOP. I'M YOUR GREAT GREAT GRANDSON A FEW TIMES REMOVED, AND I'M ALSO *THE HAND OF THE ISLAND.*
I'VE NEVER SEEN ANYONE ELSE HERE OTHER THAN THE LADY. HAVE YOU?
NO. I HAVE NOT.
WHAT DOES IT MEAN?
THIS IS...NEW. SOMETHING IS AMISS, MY SON.
TROUBLE COMES...

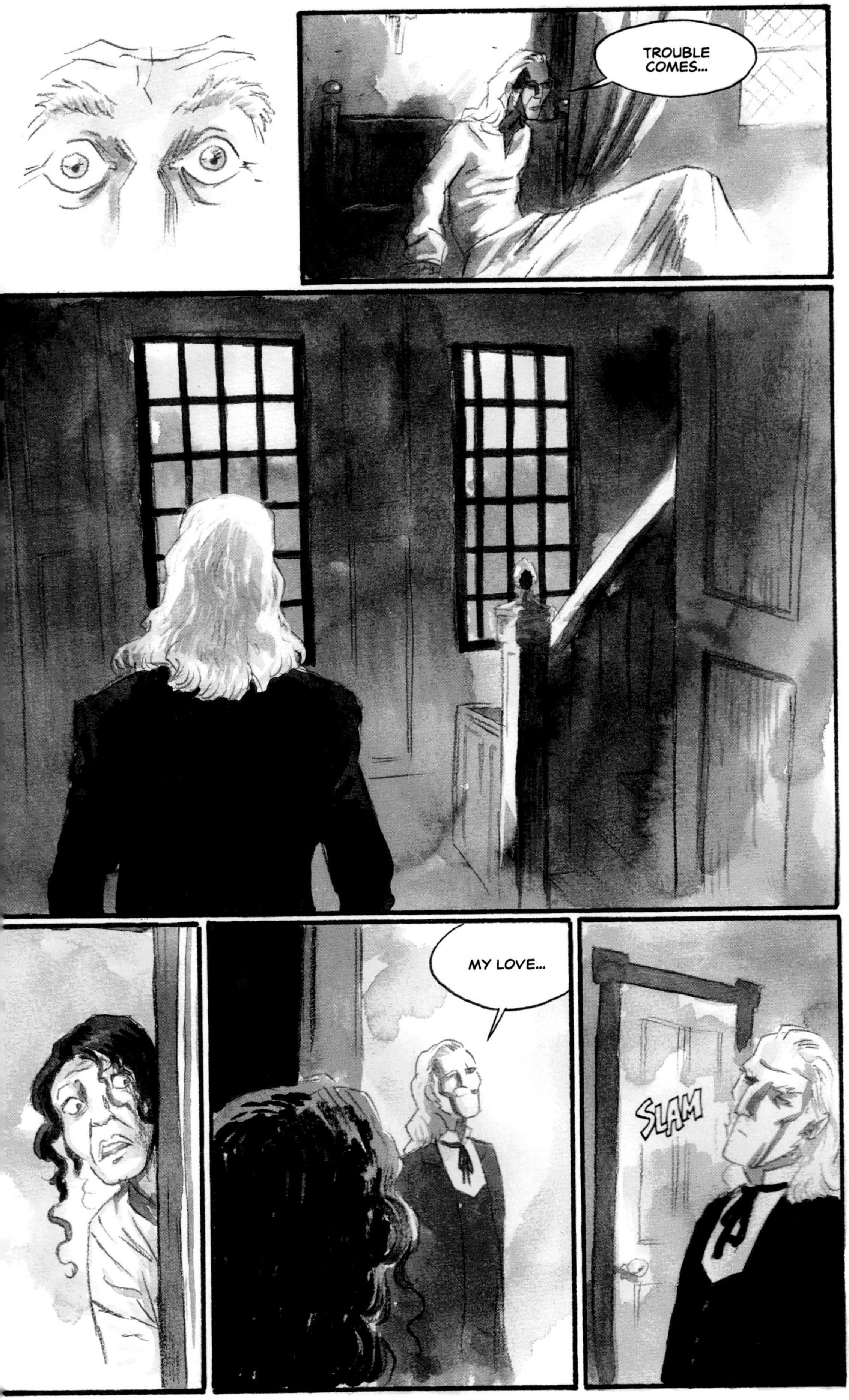
TROUBLE COMES...
MY LOVE...
SLAM

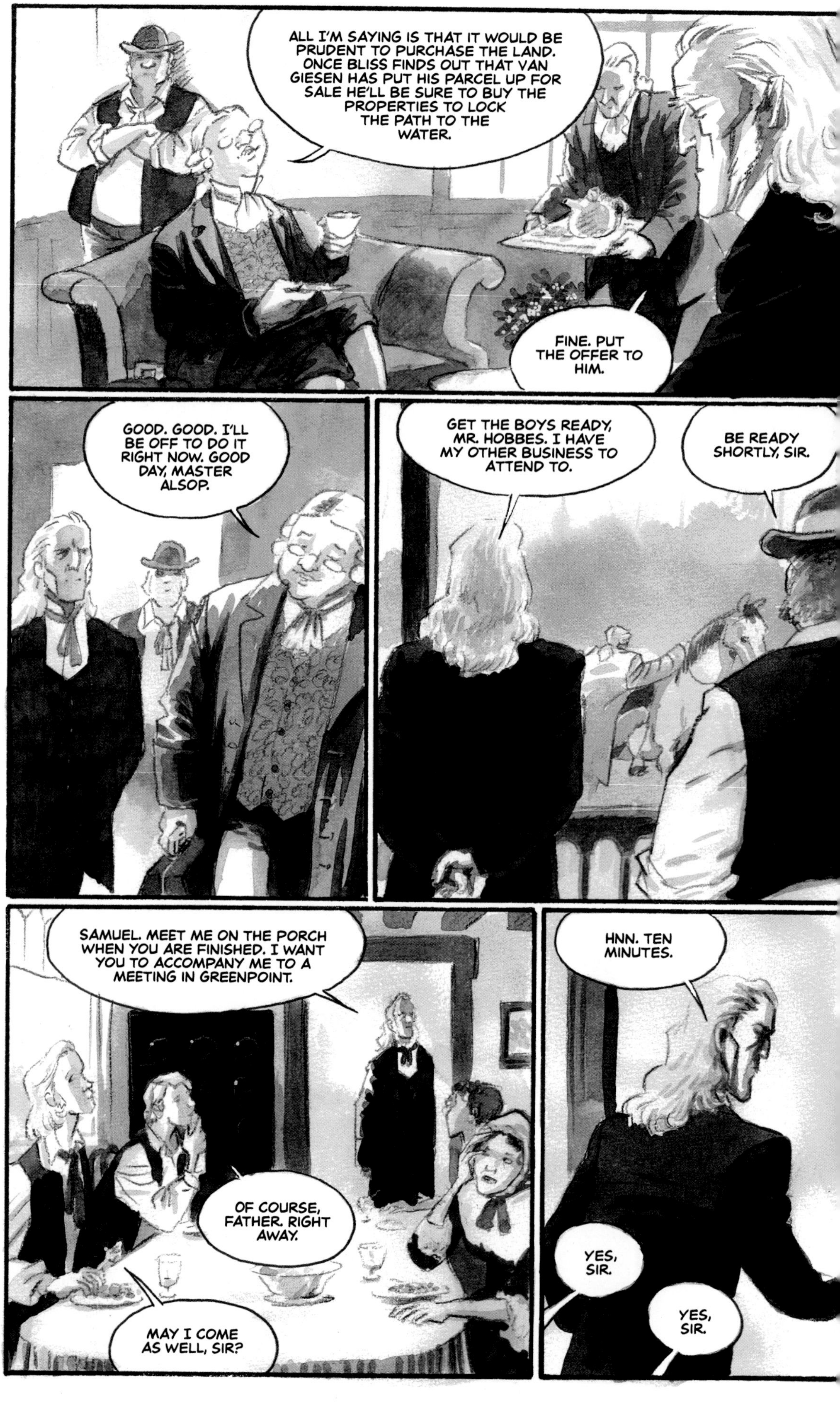
ALL I'M SAYING IS THAT IT WOULD BE PRUDENT TO PURCHASE THE LAND. ONCE BLISS FINDS OUT THAT VAN GIESEN HAS PUT HIS PARCEL UP FOR SALE HE'LL BE SURE TO BUY THE PROPERTIES TO LOCK THE PATH TO THE WATER.
FINE. PUT THE OFFER TO HIM.
GOOD. GOOD. I'LL BE OFF TO DO IT RIGHT NOW. GOOD DAY, MASTER ALSOP.
GET THE BOYS READY, MR. HOBBES. I HAVE MY OTHER BUSINESS TO ATTEND TO.
BE READY SHORTLY, SIR.
SAMUEL. MEET ME ON THE PORCH WHEN YOU ARE FINISHED. I WANT YOU TO ACCOMPANY ME TO A MEETING IN GREENPOINT.
OF COURSE, FATHER. RIGHT AWAY.
MAY I COME AS WELL, SIR?
HNN. TEN MINUTES.
YES, SIR.
YES, SIR.

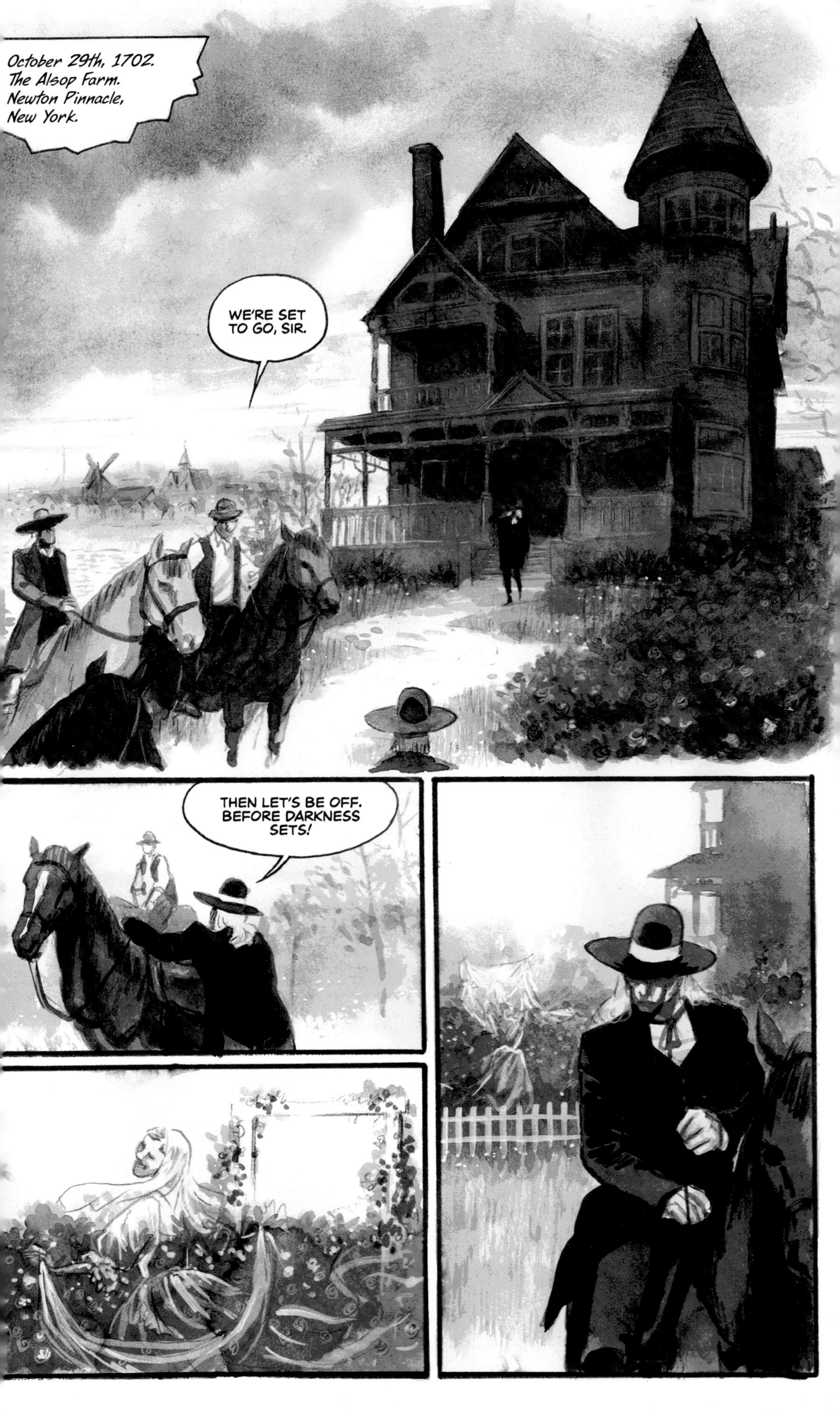
October 29th, 1702.
The Alsop Farm.
Newton Pinnacle,
New York.
WE'RE SET TO GO, SIR.
THEN LET'S BE OFF. BEFORE DARKNESS SETS!

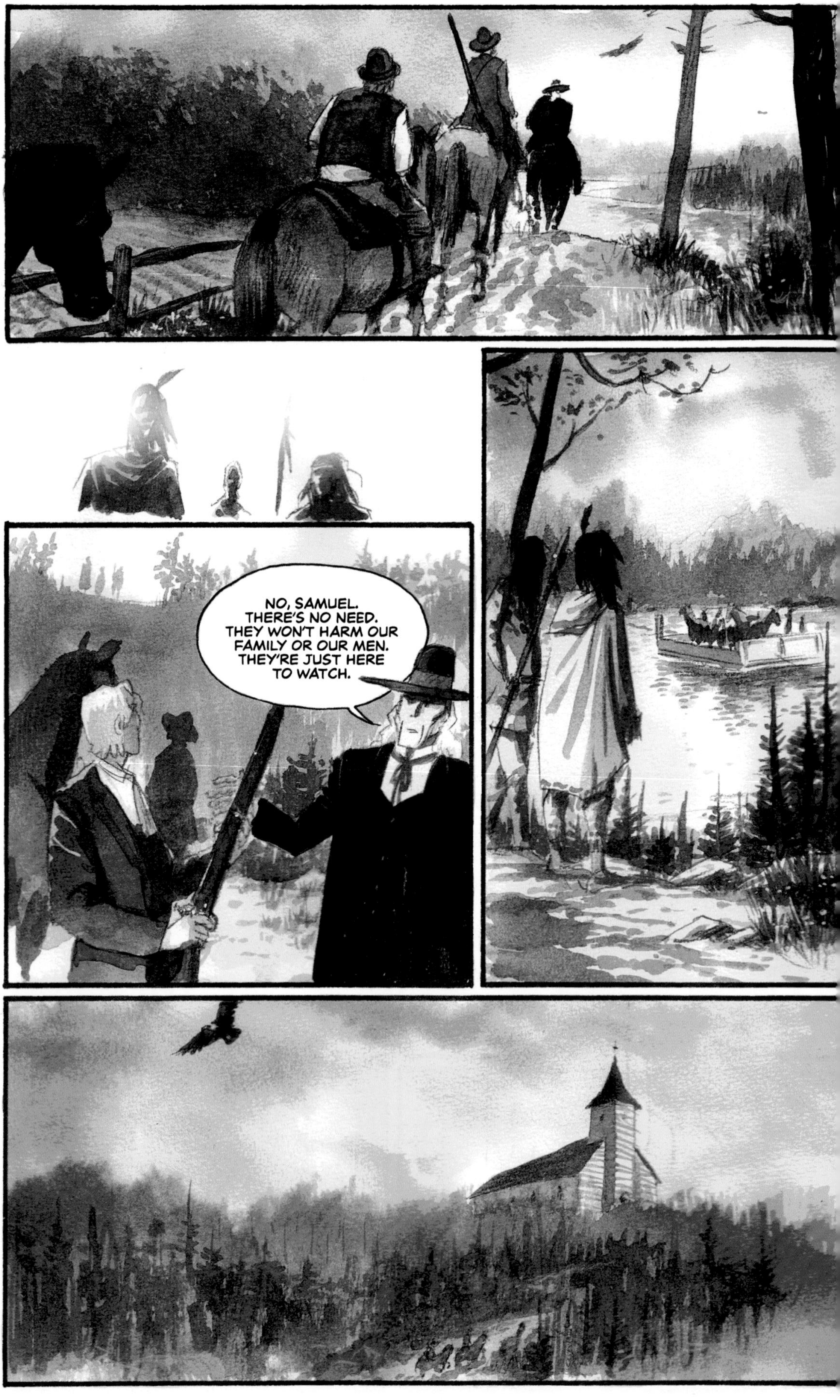
NO, SAMUEL. THERE'S NO NEED. THEY WON'T HARM OUR FAMILY OR OUR MEN. THEY'RE JUST HERE TO WATCH.

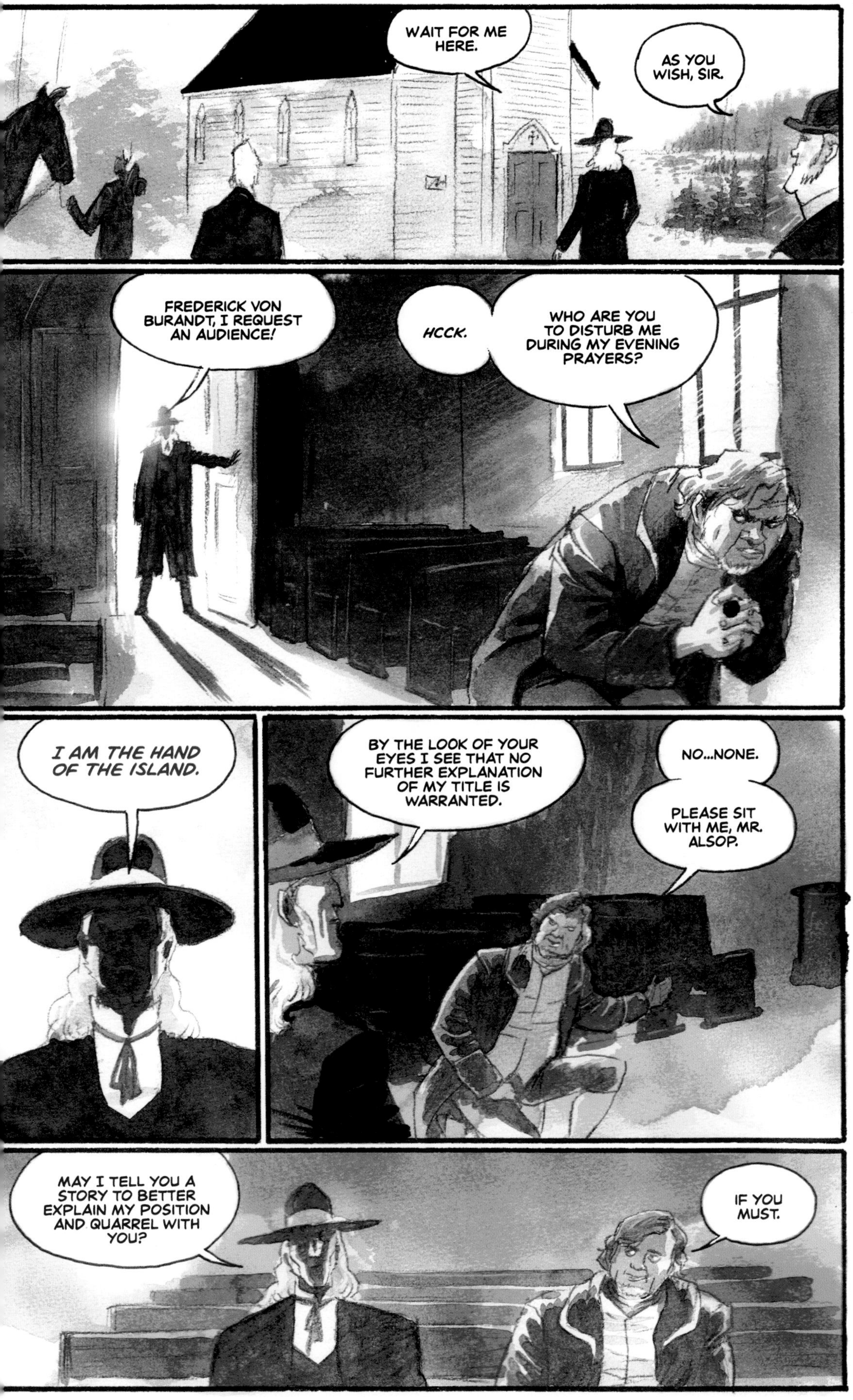
WAIT FOR ME HERE.
AS YOU WISH, SIR.
FREDERICK VON BURANDT, I REQUEST AN AUDIENCE!
HCCK.
WHO ARE YOU TO DISTURB ME DURING MY EVENING PRAYERS?
I AM THE HAND OF THE ISLAND.
BY THE LOOK OF YOUR EYES I SEE THAT NO FURTHER EXPLANATION OF MY TITLE IS WARRANTED.
NO...NONE.
PLEASE SIT WITH ME, MR. ALSOP.
MAY I TELL YOU A STORY TO BETTER EXPLAIN MY POSITION AND QUARREL WITH YOU?
IF YOU MUST.

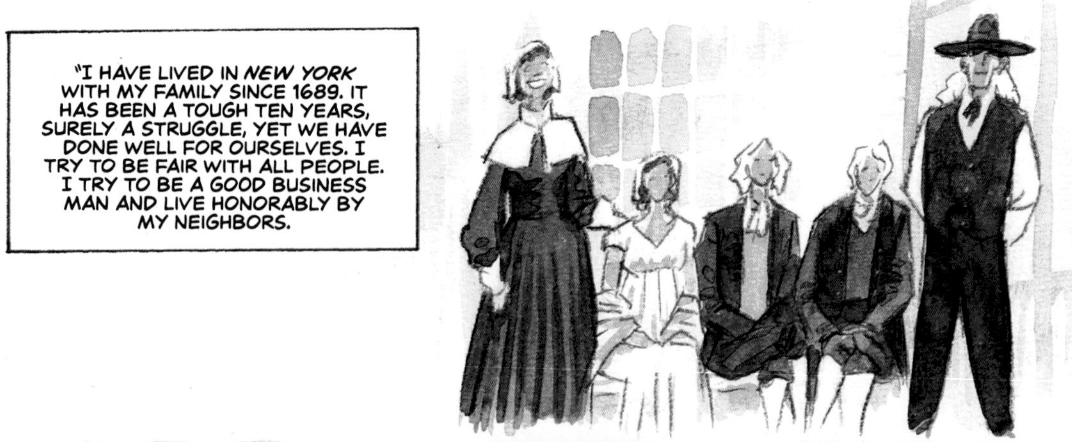
"I HAVE LIVED IN *NEW YORK* WITH MY FAMILY SINCE 1689. IT HAS BEEN A TOUGH TEN YEARS, SURELY A STRUGGLE, YET WE HAVE DONE WELL FOR OURSELVES. I TRY TO BE FAIR WITH ALL PEOPLE. I TRY TO BE A GOOD BUSINESS MAN AND LIVE HONORABLY BY MY NEIGHBORS.

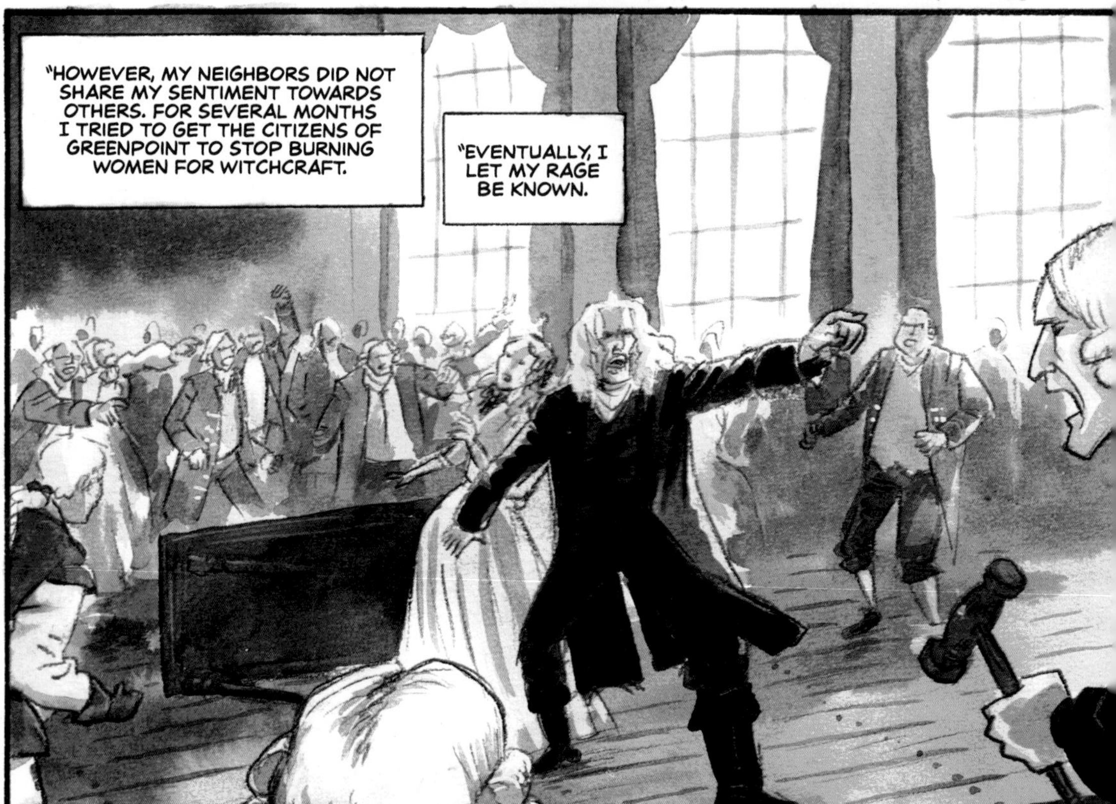
"HOWEVER, MY NEIGHBORS DID NOT SHARE MY SENTIMENT TOWARDS OTHERS. FOR SEVERAL MONTHS I TRIED TO GET THE CITIZENS OF GREENPOINT TO STOP BURNING WOMEN FOR WITCHCRAFT.
"EVENTUALLY, I LET MY RAGE BE KNOWN.

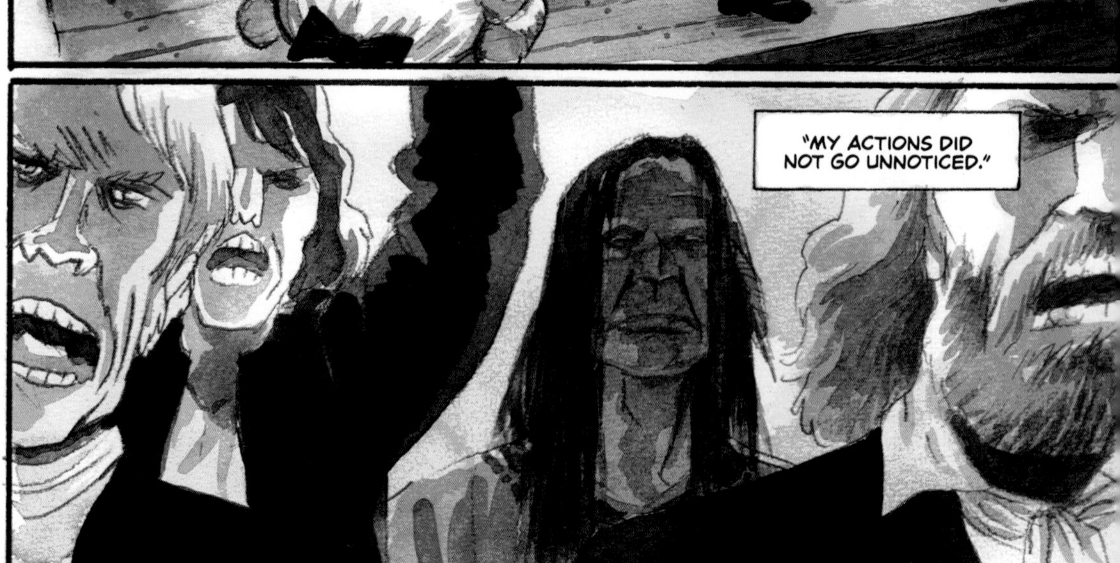
"MY ACTIONS DID NOT GO UNNOTICED."

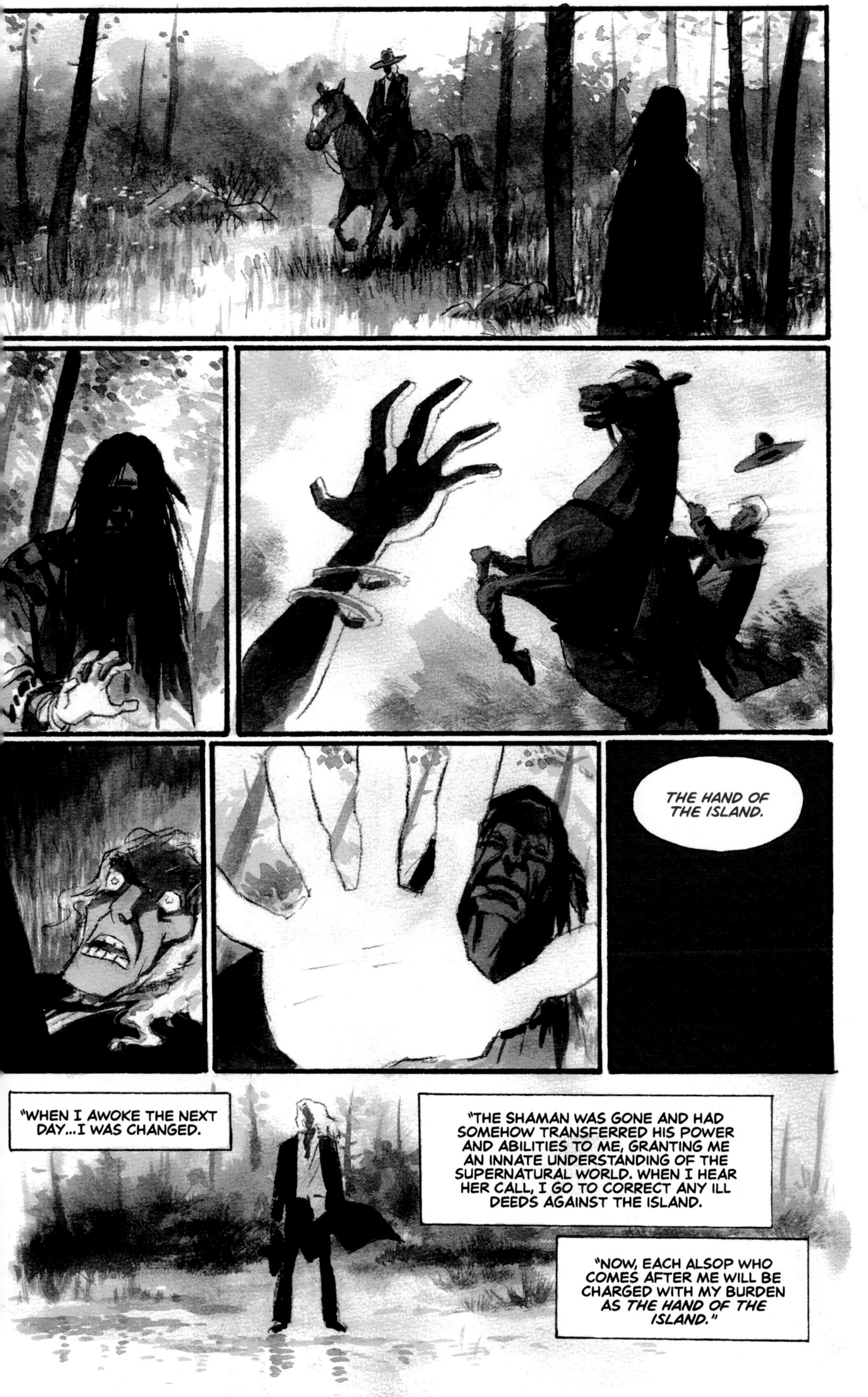
THE HAND OF THE ISLAND.
"WHEN I AWOKE THE NEXT DAY...I WAS CHANGED.
"THE SHAMAN WAS GONE AND HAD SOMEHOW TRANSFERRED HIS POWER AND ABILITIES TO ME, GRANTING ME AN INNATE UNDERSTANDING OF THE SUPERNATURAL WORLD. WHEN I HEAR HER CALL, I GO TO CORRECT ANY ILL DEEDS AGAINST THE ISLAND.
"NOW, EACH ALSOP WHO COMES AFTER ME WILL BE CHARGED WITH MY BURDEN AS THE HAND OF THE ISLAND."

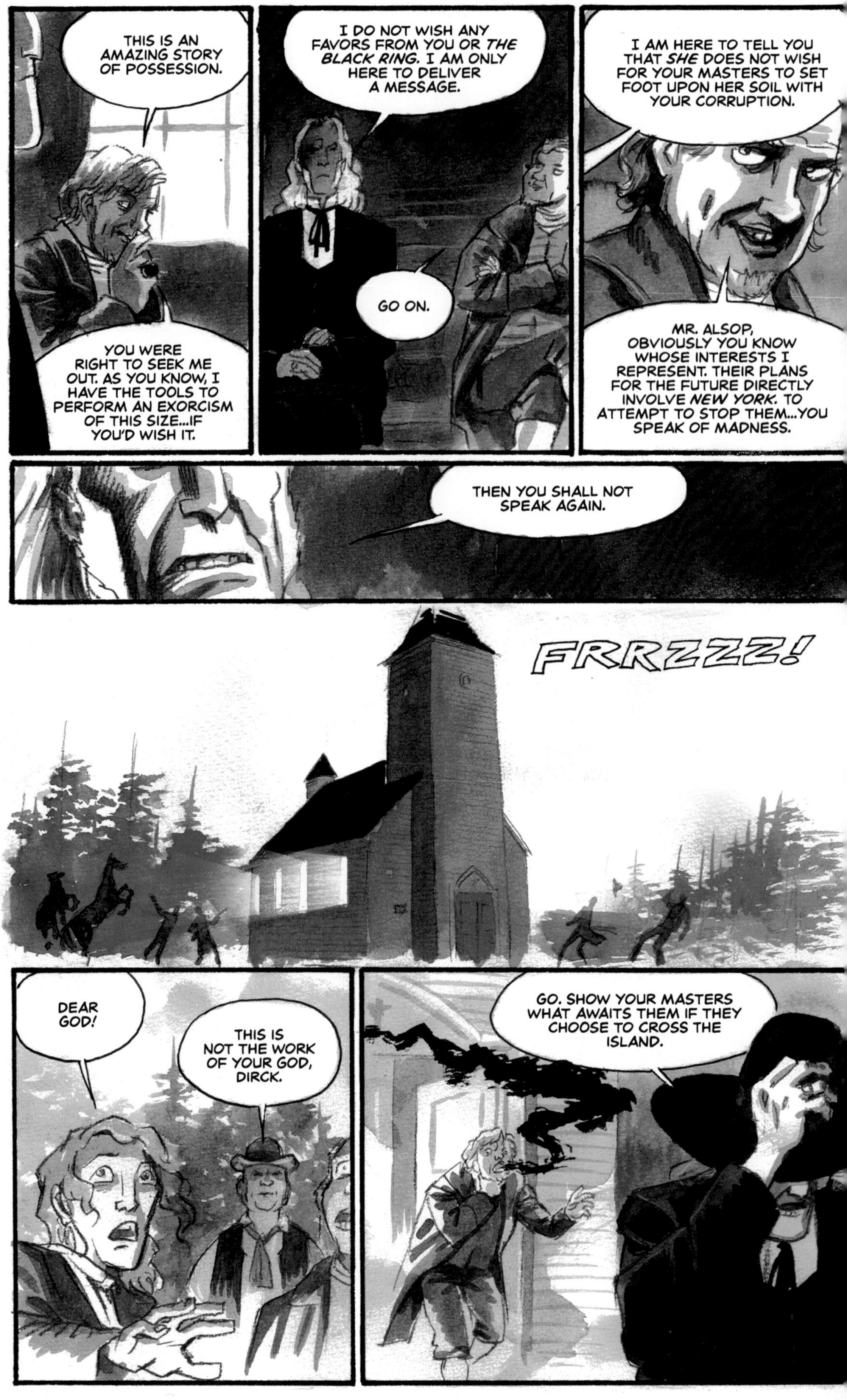
THIS IS AN AMAZING STORY OF POSSESSION.
YOU WERE RIGHT TO SEEK ME OUT. AS YOU KNOW, I HAVE THE TOOLS TO PERFORM AN EXORCISM OF THIS SIZE...IF YOU'D WISH IT.
I DO NOT WISH ANY FAVORS FROM YOU OR *THE BLACK RING.* I AM ONLY HERE TO DELIVER A MESSAGE.
GO ON.
I AM HERE TO TELL YOU THAT *SHE* DOES NOT WISH FOR YOUR MASTERS TO SET FOOT UPON HER SOIL WITH YOUR CORRUPTION.
MR. ALSOP, OBVIOUSLY YOU KNOW WHOSE INTERESTS I REPRESENT. THEIR PLANS FOR THE FUTURE DIRECTLY INVOLVE *NEW YORK.* TO ATTEMPT TO STOP THEM...YOU SPEAK OF MADNESS.
THEN YOU SHALL NOT SPEAK AGAIN.
FRRZZZ!
DEAR GOD!
THIS IS NOT THE WORK OF YOUR GOD, DIRCK.
GO. SHOW YOUR MASTERS WHAT AWAITS THEM IF THEY CHOOSE TO CROSS THE ISLAND.

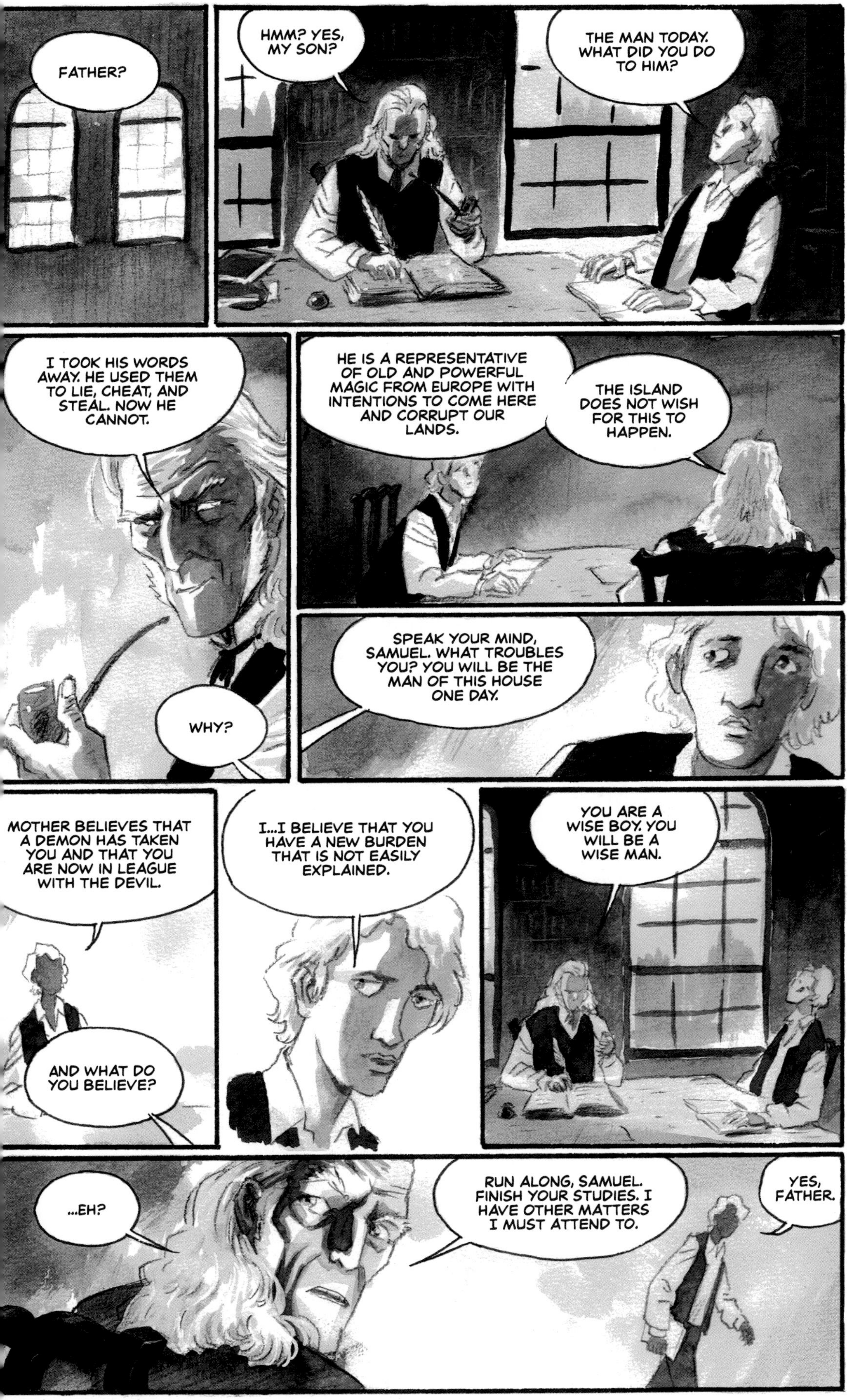
FATHER?
HMM? YES, MY SON?
THE MAN TODAY. WHAT DID YOU DO TO HIM?
I TOOK HIS WORDS AWAY. HE USED THEM TO LIE, CHEAT, AND STEAL. NOW HE CANNOT.
WHY?
HE IS A REPRESENTATIVE OF OLD AND POWERFUL MAGIC FROM EUROPE WITH INTENTIONS TO COME HERE AND CORRUPT OUR LANDS.
THE ISLAND DOES NOT WISH FOR THIS TO HAPPEN.
SPEAK YOUR MIND, SAMUEL. WHAT TROUBLES YOU? YOU WILL BE THE MAN OF THIS HOUSE ONE DAY.
MOTHER BELIEVES THAT A DEMON HAS TAKEN YOU AND THAT YOU ARE NOW IN LEAGUE WITH THE DEVIL.
AND WHAT DO YOU BELIEVE?
I...I BELIEVE THAT YOU HAVE A NEW BURDEN THAT IS NOT EASILY EXPLAINED.
YOU ARE A WISE BOY. YOU WILL BE A WISE MAN.
...EH?
RUN ALONG, SAMUEL. FINISH YOUR STUDIES. I HAVE OTHER MATTERS I MUST ATTEND TO.
YES, FATHER.

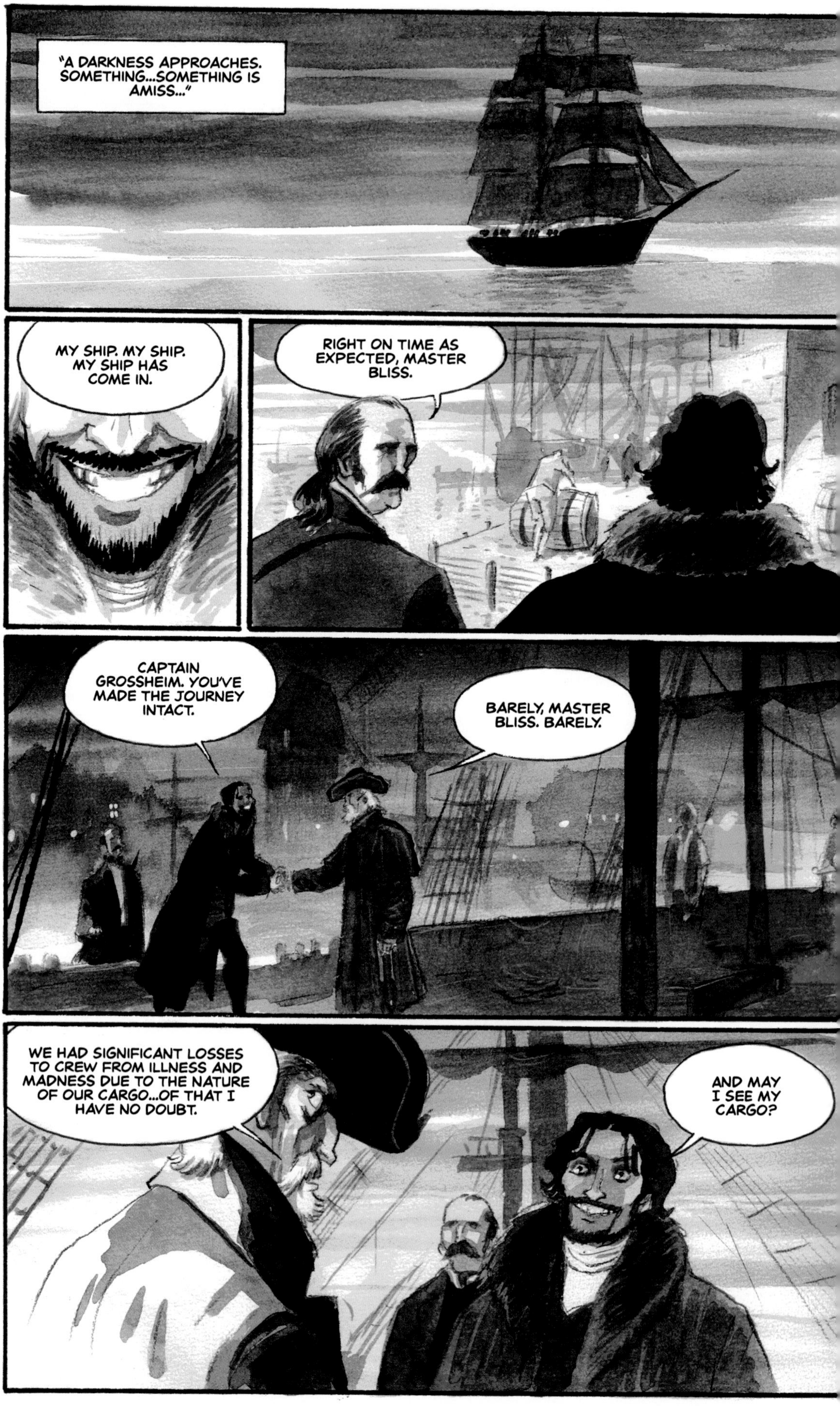
"A DARKNESS APPROACHES. SOMETHING...SOMETHING IS AMISS..."
MY SHIP. MY SHIP. MY SHIP HAS COME IN.
RIGHT ON TIME AS EXPECTED, MASTER BLISS.
CAPTAIN GROSSHEIM. YOU'VE MADE THE JOURNEY INTACT.
BARELY, MASTER BLISS. BARELY.
WE HAD SIGNIFICANT LOSSES TO CREW FROM ILLNESS AND MADNESS DUE TO THE NATURE OF OUR CARGO...OF THAT I HAVE NO DOUBT.
AND MAY I SEE MY CARGO?

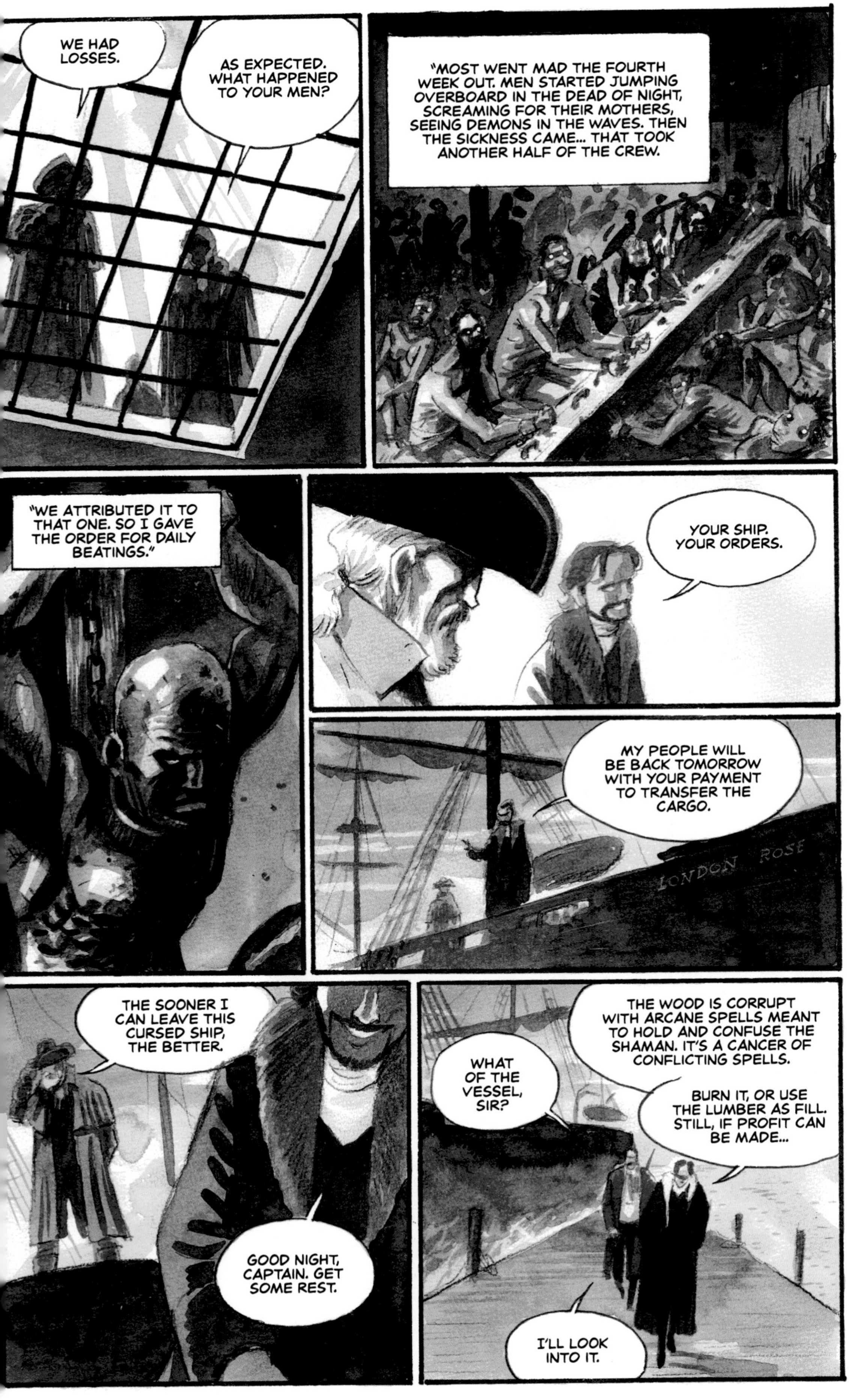
WE HAD LOSSES.
AS EXPECTED. WHAT HAPPENED TO YOUR MEN?
"MOST WENT MAD THE FOURTH WEEK OUT. MEN STARTED JUMPING OVERBOARD IN THE DEAD OF NIGHT, SCREAMING FOR THEIR MOTHERS, SEEING DEMONS IN THE WAVES. THEN THE SICKNESS CAME... THAT TOOK ANOTHER HALF OF THE CREW.
"WE ATTRIBUTED IT TO THAT ONE. SO I GAVE THE ORDER FOR DAILY BEATINGS."
YOUR SHIP. YOUR ORDERS.
MY PEOPLE WILL BE BACK TOMORROW WITH YOUR PAYMENT TO TRANSFER THE CARGO.
LONDON ROSE
THE SOONER I CAN LEAVE THIS CURSED SHIP, THE BETTER.
GOOD NIGHT, CAPTAIN. GET SOME REST.
WHAT OF THE VESSEL, SIR?
THE WOOD IS CORRUPT WITH ARCANE SPELLS MEANT TO HOLD AND CONFUSE THE SHAMAN. IT'S A CANCER OF CONFLICTING SPELLS.
BURN IT, OR USE THE LUMBER AS FILL. STILL, IF PROFIT CAN BE MADE...
I'LL LOOK INTO IT.

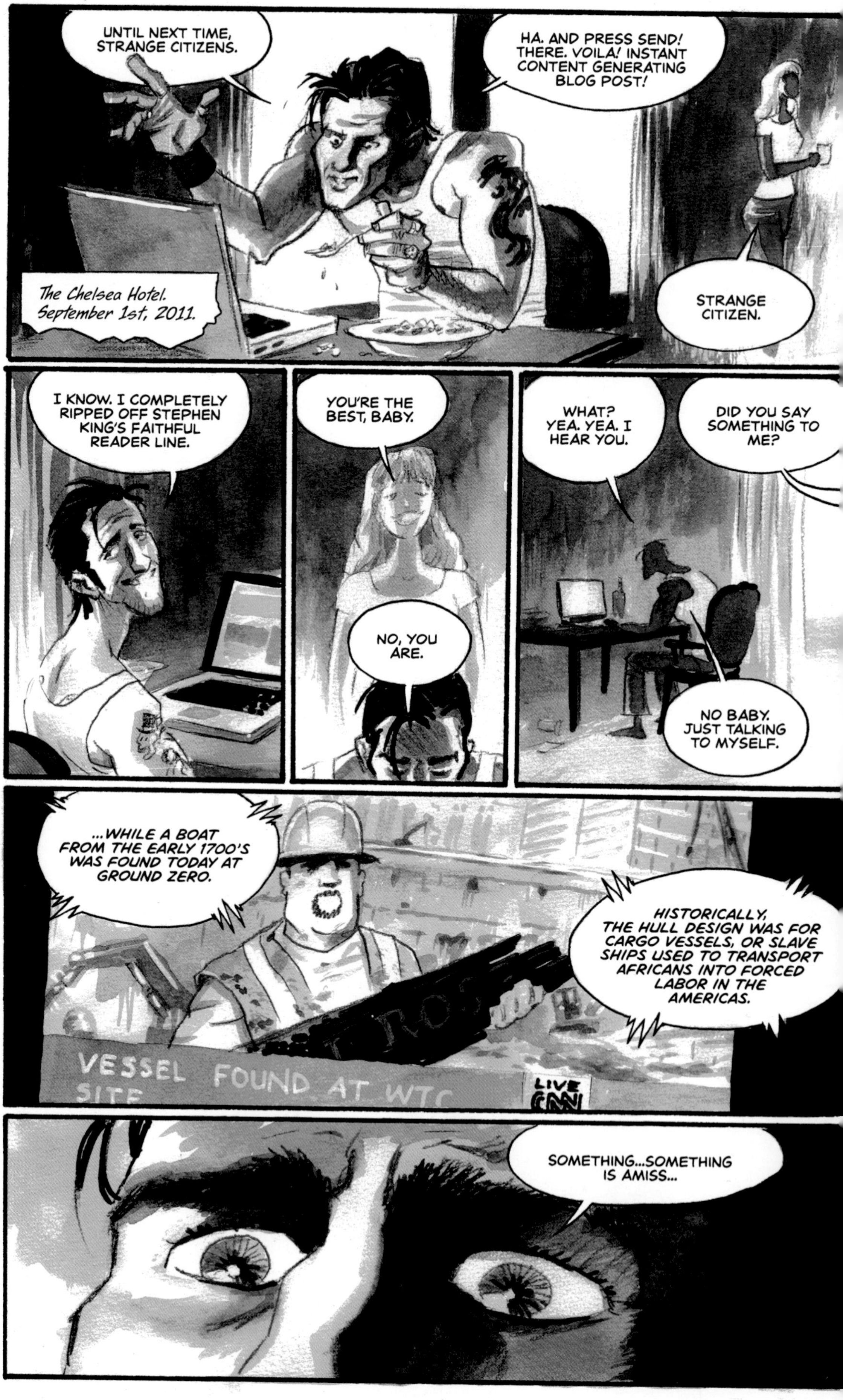
UNTIL NEXT TIME, STRANGE CITIZENS.
HA. AND PRESS SEND! THERE. VOILA! INSTANT CONTENT GENERATING BLOG POST!
The Chelsea Hotel. September 1st, 2011.
STRANGE CITIZEN.
I KNOW. I COMPLETELY RIPPED OFF STEPHEN KING'S FAITHFUL READER LINE.
YOU'RE THE BEST, BABY.
NO, YOU ARE.
WHAT? YEA. YEA. I HEAR YOU.
DID YOU SAY SOMETHING TO ME?
NO BABY. JUST TALKING TO MYSELF.
...WHILE A BOAT FROM THE EARLY 1700'S WAS FOUND TODAY AT GROUND ZERO.
HISTORICALLY, THE HULL DESIGN WAS FOR CARGO VESSELS, OR SLAVE SHIPS USED TO TRANSPORT AFRICANS INTO FORCED LABOR IN THE AMERICAS.
VESSEL FOUND AT WTC SITE
LIVE CNN
SOMETHING...SOMETHING IS AMISS...

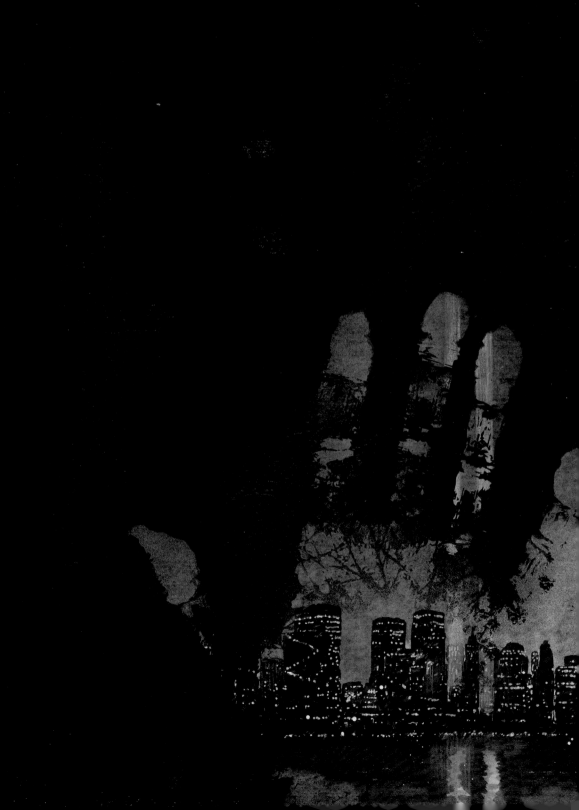

CHAPTER TWO
THE LEGEND OF BUSHWICK MANOR

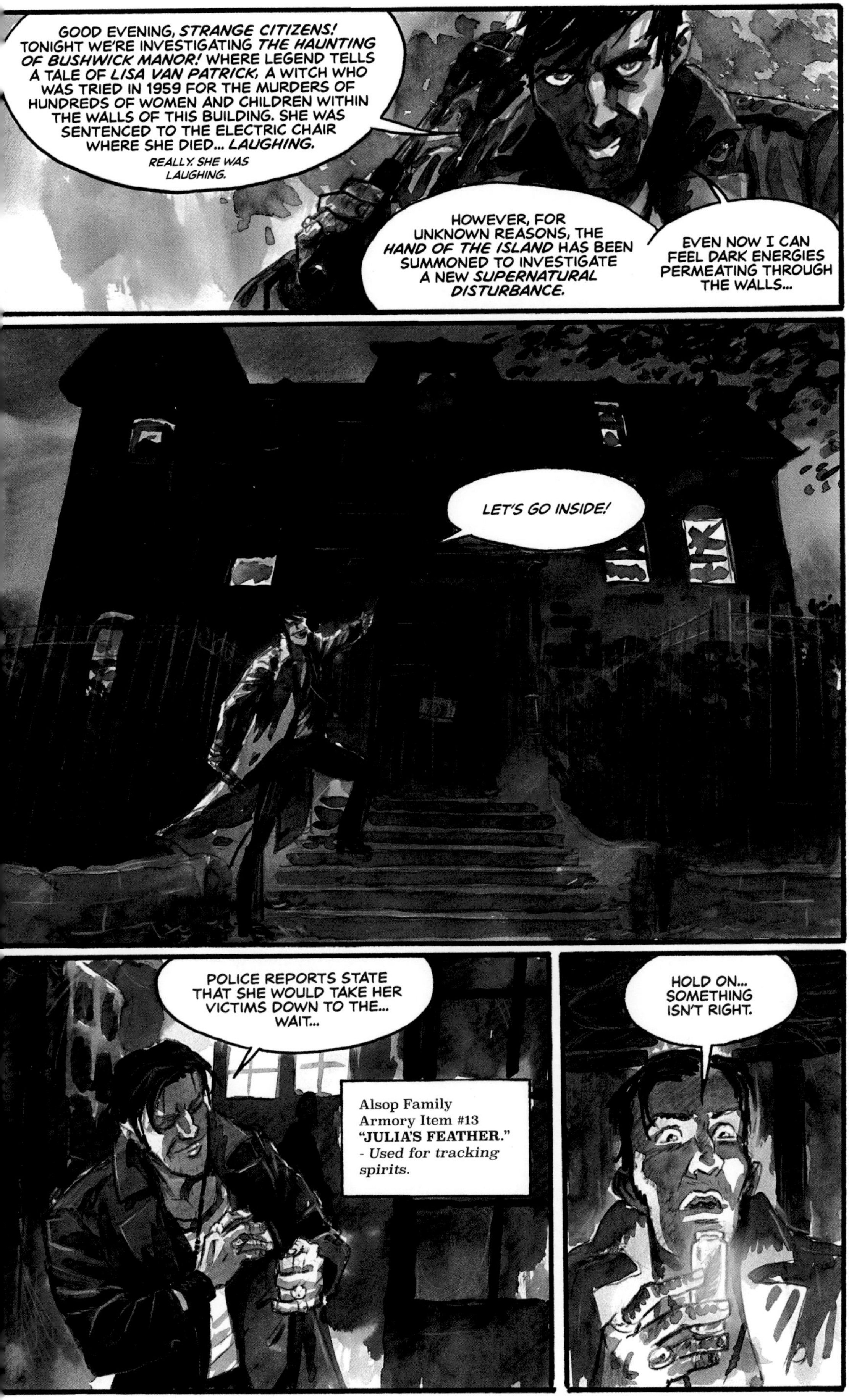
GOOD EVENING, STRANGE CITIZENS! TONIGHT WE'RE INVESTIGATING THE HAUNTING OF BUSHWICK MANOR! WHERE LEGEND TELLS A TALE OF LISA VAN PATRICK, A WITCH WHO WAS TRIED IN 1959 FOR THE MURDERS OF HUNDREDS OF WOMEN AND CHILDREN WITHIN THE WALLS OF THIS BUILDING. SHE WAS SENTENCED TO THE ELECTRIC CHAIR WHERE SHE DIED... LAUGHING.
REALLY. SHE WAS LAUGHING.
HOWEVER, FOR UNKNOWN REASONS, THE HAND OF THE ISLAND HAS BEEN SUMMONED TO INVESTIGATE A NEW SUPERNATURAL DISTURBANCE.
EVEN NOW I CAN FEEL DARK ENERGIES PERMEATING THROUGH THE WALLS...
LET'S GO INSIDE!
POLICE REPORTS STATE THAT SHE WOULD TAKE HER VICTIMS DOWN TO THE... WAIT...
Alsop Family Armory Item #13 "JULIA'S FEATHER." - Used for tracking spirits.
HOLD ON... SOMETHING ISN'T RIGHT.

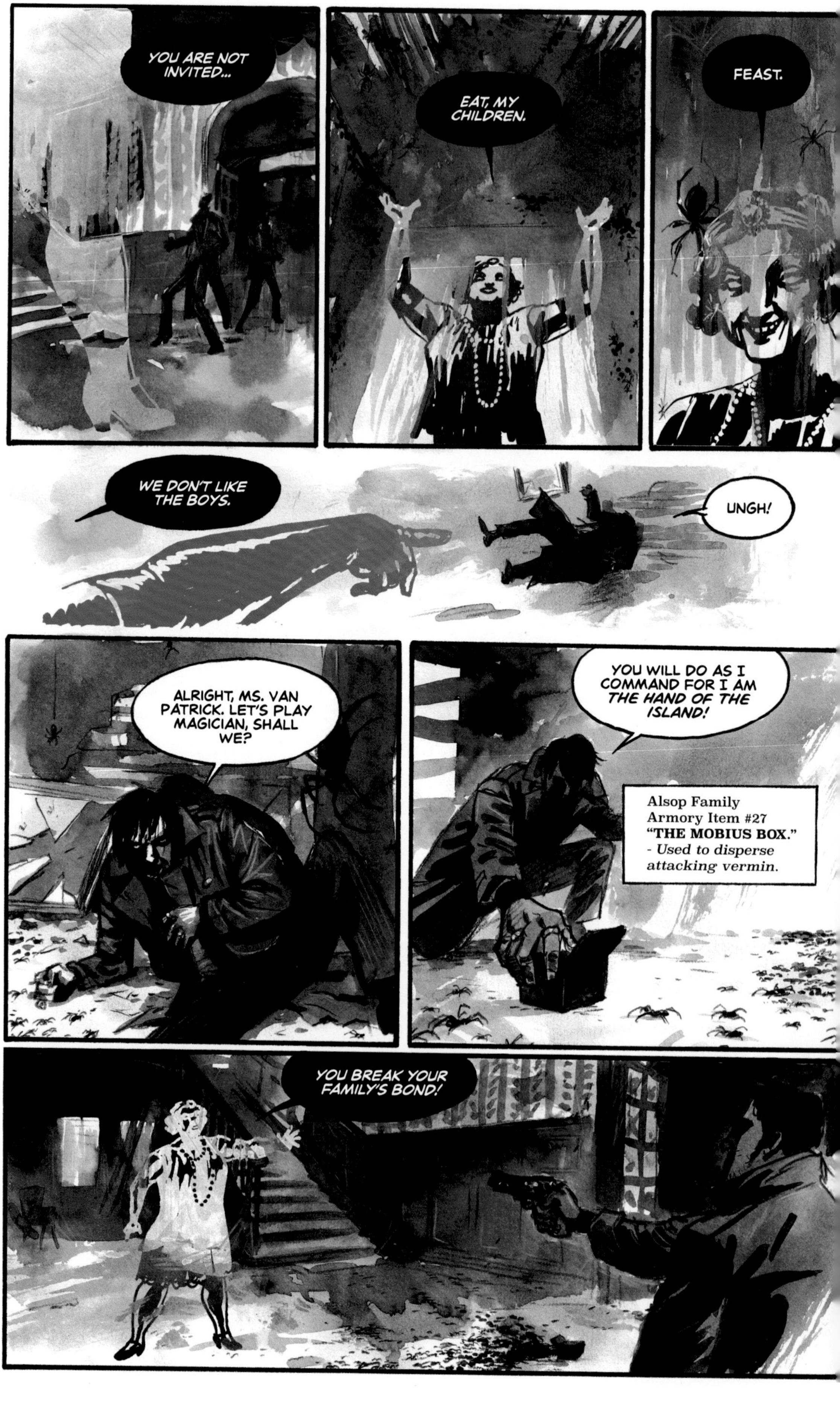
YOU ARE NOT INVITED...
EAT, MY CHILDREN.
FEAST.
WE DON'T LIKE THE BOYS.
UNGH!
ALRIGHT, MS. VAN PATRICK. LET'S PLAY MAGICIAN, SHALL WE?
YOU WILL DO AS I COMMAND FOR I AM THE HAND OF THE ISLAND!
Alsop Family Armory Item #27 "THE MOBIUS BOX." - Used to disperse attacking vermin.
YOU BREAK YOUR FAMILY'S BOND!

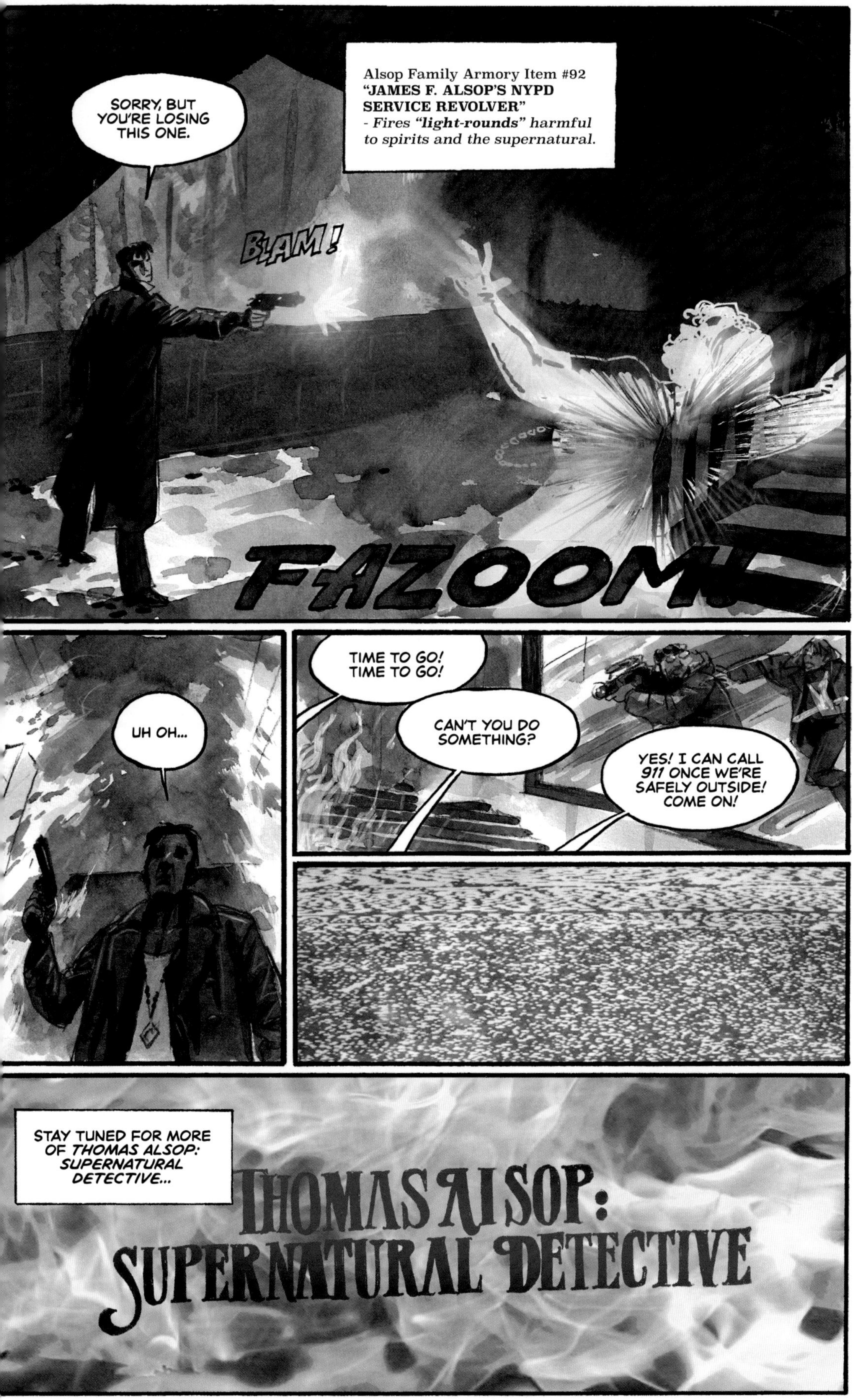
Alsop Family Armory Item #92
"JAMES F. ALSOP'S NYPD SERVICE REVOLVER"
- Fires "light-rounds" harmful to spirits and the supernatural.
SORRY, BUT YOU'RE LOSING THIS ONE.
BLAM!
FAZOOM!
UH OH...
TIME TO GO! TIME TO GO!
CAN'T YOU DO SOMETHING?
YES! I CAN CALL 911 ONCE WE'RE SAFELY OUTSIDE! COME ON!
STAY TUNED FOR MORE OF THOMAS ALSOP: SUPERNATURAL DETECTIVE...
THOMAS ALSOP: SUPERNATURAL DETECTIVE

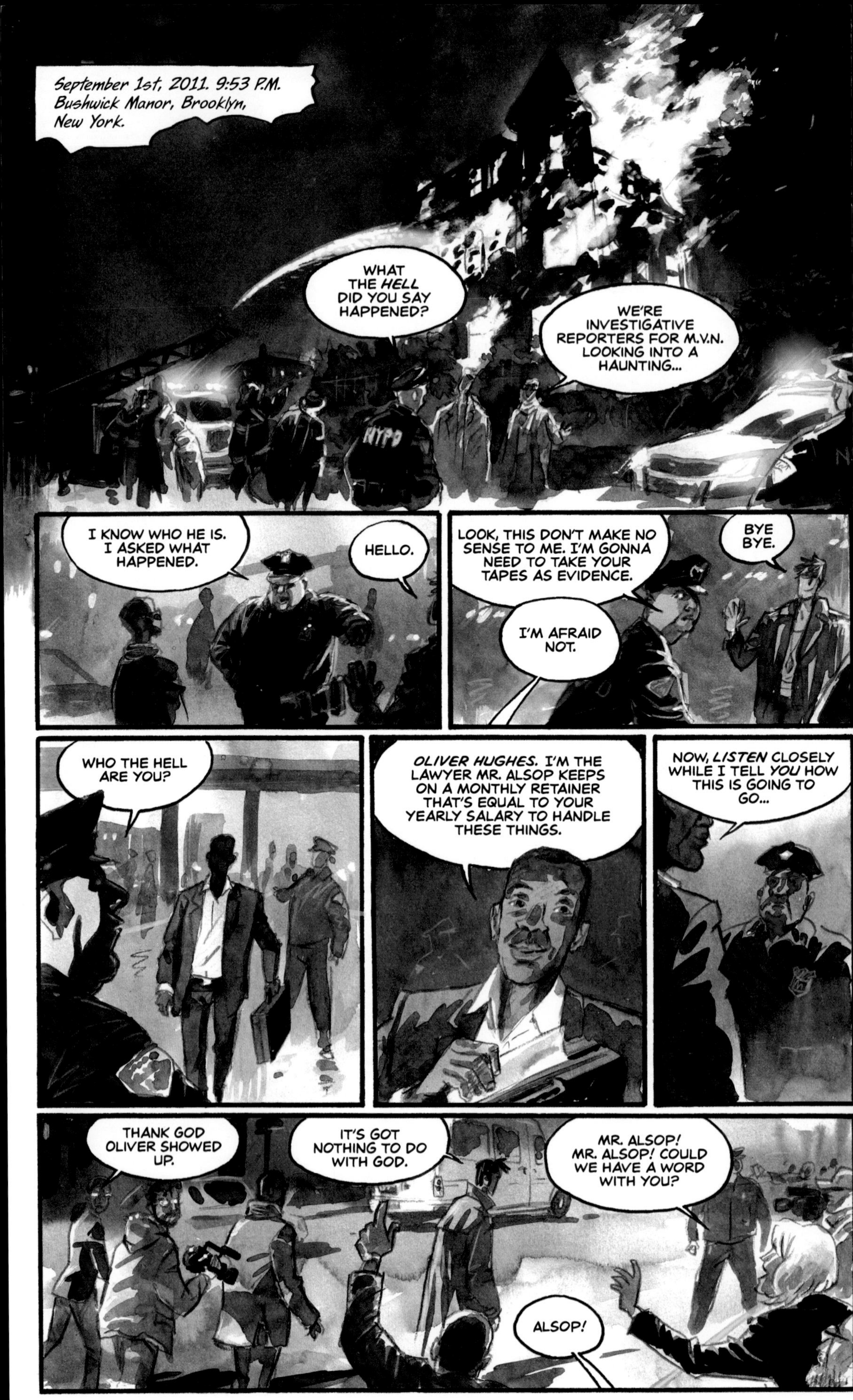
September 1st, 2011. 9:53 P.M. Bushwick Manor, Brooklyn, New York.
WHAT THE HELL DID YOU SAY HAPPENED?
WE'RE INVESTIGATIVE REPORTERS FOR M.V.N. LOOKING INTO A HAUNTING...
I KNOW WHO HE IS. I ASKED WHAT HAPPENED.
HELLO.
LOOK, THIS DON'T MAKE NO SENSE TO ME. I'M GONNA NEED TO TAKE YOUR TAPES AS EVIDENCE.
BYE BYE.
I'M AFRAID NOT.
WHO THE HELL ARE YOU?
OLIVER HUGHES. I'M THE LAWYER MR. ALSOP KEEPS ON A MONTHLY RETAINER THAT'S EQUAL TO YOUR YEARLY SALARY TO HANDLE THESE THINGS.
NOW, LISTEN CLOSELY WHILE I TELL YOU HOW THIS IS GOING TO GO...
THANK GOD OLIVER SHOWED UP.
IT'S GOT NOTHING TO DO WITH GOD.
MR. ALSOP! MR. ALSOP! COULD WE HAVE A WORD WITH YOU?
ALSOP!

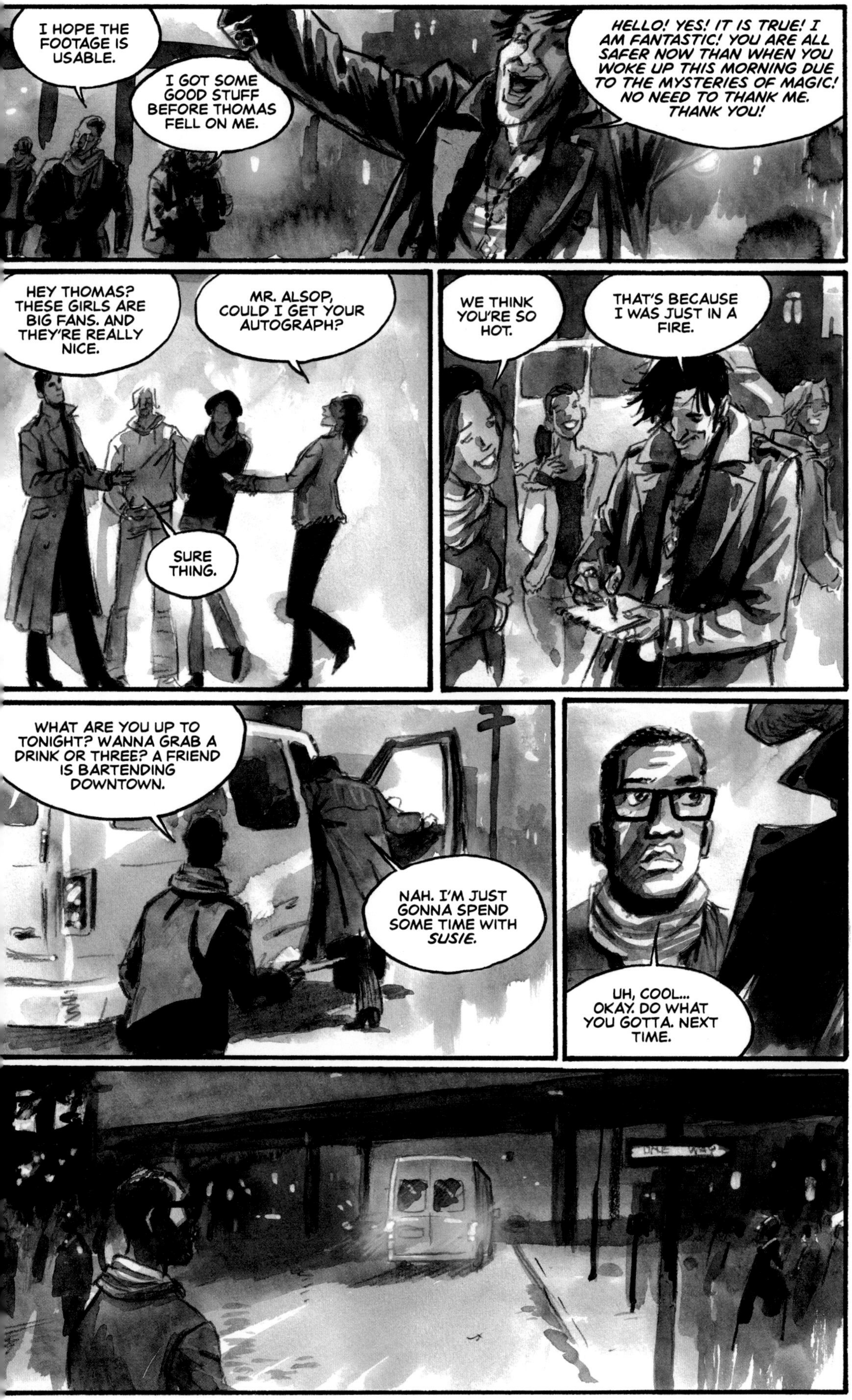
I HOPE THE FOOTAGE IS USABLE.
I GOT SOME GOOD STUFF BEFORE THOMAS FELL ON ME.
HELLO! YES! IT IS TRUE! I AM FANTASTIC! YOU ARE ALL SAFER NOW THAN WHEN YOU WOKE UP THIS MORNING DUE TO THE MYSTERIES OF MAGIC! NO NEED TO THANK ME. THANK YOU!
HEY THOMAS? THESE GIRLS ARE BIG FANS. AND THEY'RE REALLY NICE.
MR. ALSOP, COULD I GET YOUR AUTOGRAPH?
SURE THING.
WE THINK YOU'RE SO HOT.
THAT'S BECAUSE I WAS JUST IN A FIRE.
WHAT ARE YOU UP TO TONIGHT? WANNA GRAB A DRINK OR THREE? A FRIEND IS BARTENDING DOWNTOWN.
NAH. I'M JUST GONNA SPEND SOME TIME WITH *SUSIE*.
UH, COOL... OKAY. DO WHAT YOU GOTTA. NEXT TIME.

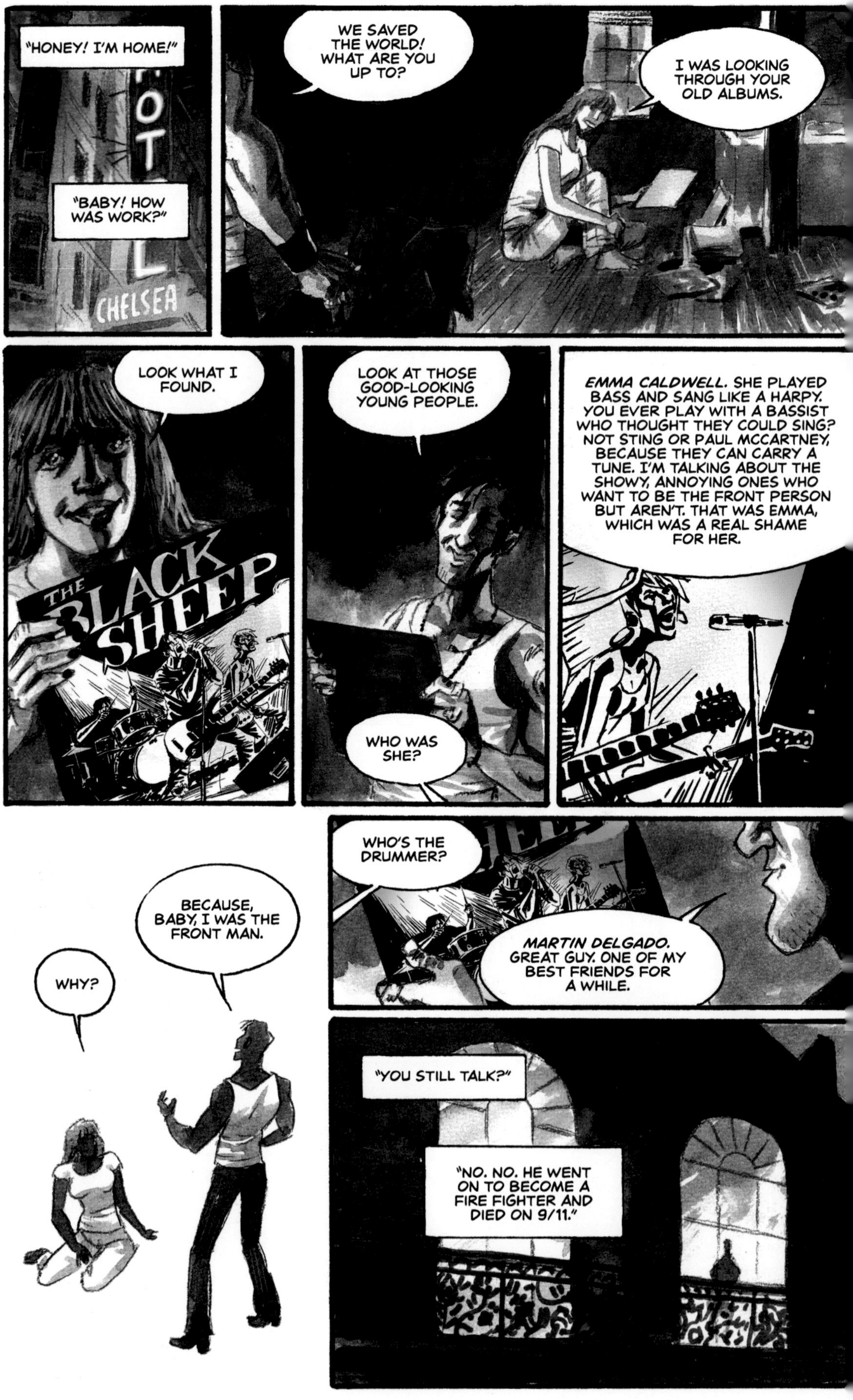
"HONEY! I'M HOME!"
"BABY! HOW WAS WORK?"
CHELSEA
WE SAVED THE WORLD! WHAT ARE YOU UP TO?
I WAS LOOKING THROUGH YOUR OLD ALBUMS.
LOOK WHAT I FOUND.
THE BLACK SHEEP
LOOK AT THOSE GOOD-LOOKING YOUNG PEOPLE.
WHO WAS SHE?
EMMA CALDWELL. SHE PLAYED BASS AND SANG LIKE A HARPY. YOU EVER PLAY WITH A BASSIST WHO THOUGHT THEY COULD SING? NOT STING OR PAUL MCCARTNEY, BECAUSE THEY CAN CARRY A TUNE. I'M TALKING ABOUT THE SHOWY, ANNOYING ONES WHO WANT TO BE THE FRONT PERSON BUT AREN'T. THAT WAS EMMA, WHICH WAS A REAL SHAME FOR HER.
WHY?
BECAUSE, BABY, I WAS THE FRONT MAN.
WHO'S THE DRUMMER?
MARTIN DELGADO. GREAT GUY. ONE OF MY BEST FRIENDS FOR A WHILE.
"YOU STILL TALK?"
"NO. NO. HE WENT ON TO BECOME A FIRE FIGHTER AND DIED ON 9/11."

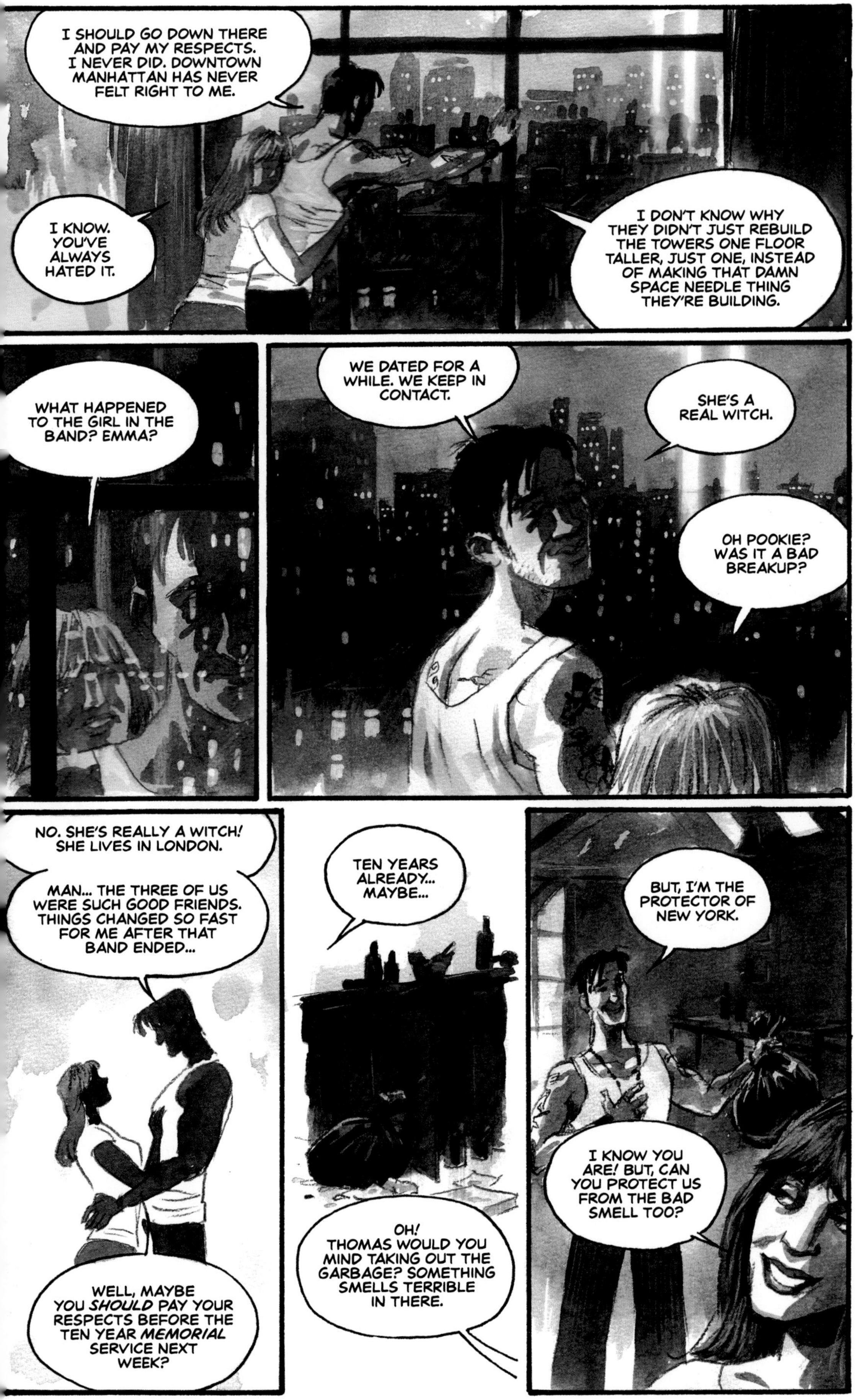

I SHOULD GO DOWN THERE AND PAY MY RESPECTS. I NEVER DID. DOWNTOWN MANHATTAN HAS NEVER FELT RIGHT TO ME.
I KNOW. YOU'VE ALWAYS HATED IT.
I DON'T KNOW WHY THEY DIDN'T JUST REBUILD THE TOWERS ONE FLOOR TALLER, JUST ONE, INSTEAD OF MAKING THAT DAMN SPACE NEEDLE THING THEY'RE BUILDING.
WHAT HAPPENED TO THE GIRL IN THE BAND? EMMA?
WE DATED FOR A WHILE. WE KEEP IN CONTACT.
SHE'S A REAL WITCH.
OH POOKIE? WAS IT A BAD BREAKUP?
NO. SHE'S REALLY A WITCH! SHE LIVES IN LONDON.
MAN... THE THREE OF US WERE SUCH GOOD FRIENDS. THINGS CHANGED SO FAST FOR ME AFTER THAT BAND ENDED...
WELL, MAYBE YOU *SHOULD* PAY YOUR RESPECTS BEFORE THE TEN YEAR *MEMORIAL* SERVICE NEXT WEEK?
TEN YEARS ALREADY... MAYBE...
OH! THOMAS WOULD YOU MIND TAKING OUT THE GARBAGE? SOMETHING SMELLS TERRIBLE IN THERE.
BUT, I'M THE PROTECTOR OF NEW YORK.
I KNOW YOU ARE! BUT, CAN YOU PROTECT US FROM THE BAD SMELL TOO?

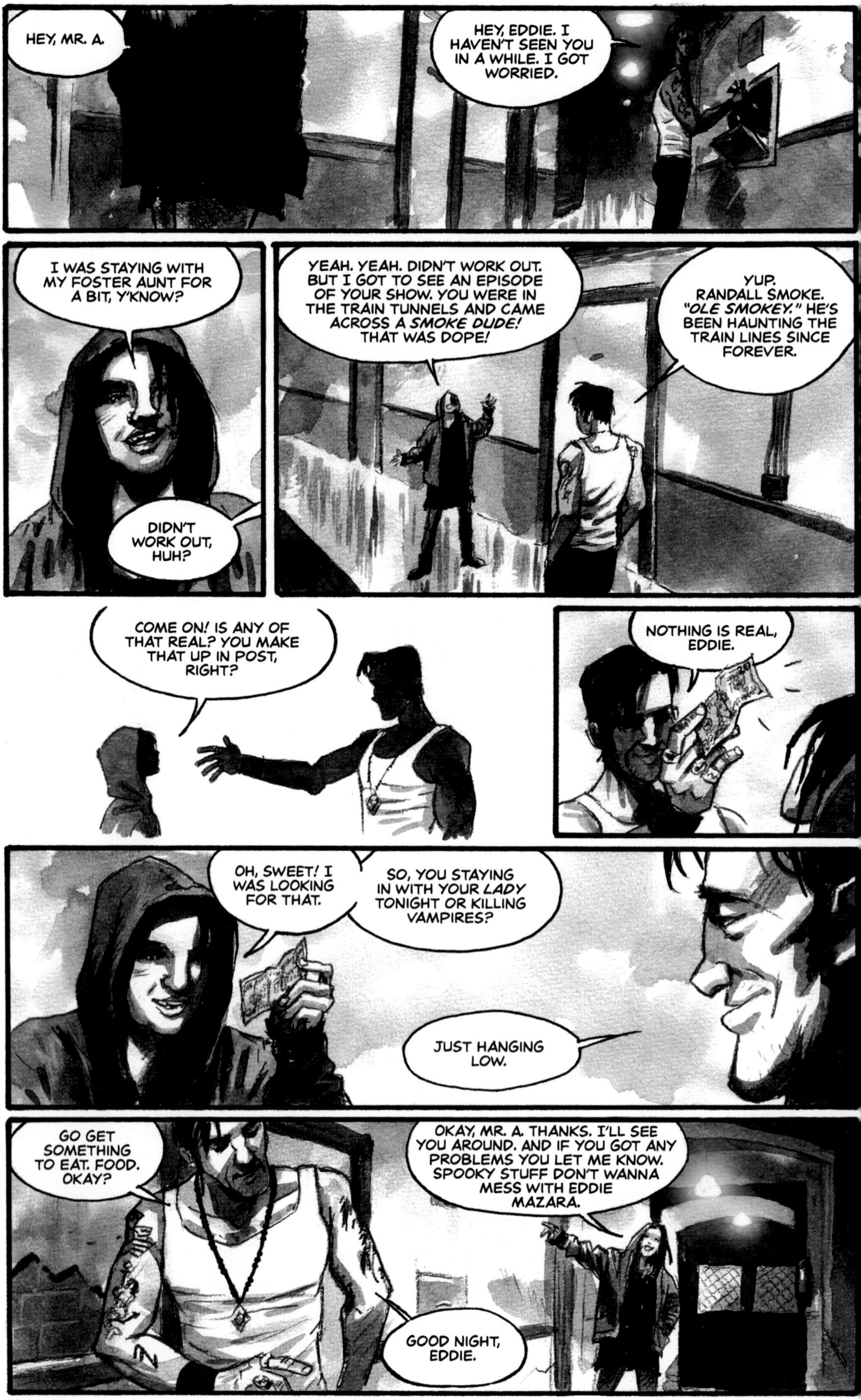
HEY, MR. A.
HEY, EDDIE. I HAVEN'T SEEN YOU IN A WHILE. I GOT WORRIED.
I WAS STAYING WITH MY FOSTER AUNT FOR A BIT, Y'KNOW?
DIDN'T WORK OUT, HUH?
YEAH. YEAH. DIDN'T WORK OUT. BUT I GOT TO SEE AN EPISODE OF YOUR SHOW. YOU WERE IN THE TRAIN TUNNELS AND CAME ACROSS A *SMOKE DUDE!* THAT WAS DOPE!
YUP. RANDALL SMOKE. *"OLE SMOKEY."* HE'S BEEN HAUNTING THE TRAIN LINES SINCE FOREVER.
COME ON! IS ANY OF THAT REAL? YOU MAKE THAT UP IN POST, RIGHT?
NOTHING IS REAL, EDDIE.
OH, SWEET! I WAS LOOKING FOR THAT.
SO, YOU STAYING IN WITH YOUR *LADY* TONIGHT OR KILLING VAMPIRES?
JUST HANGING LOW.
GO GET SOMETHING TO EAT. FOOD. OKAY?
OKAY, MR. A. THANKS. I'LL SEE YOU AROUND. AND IF YOU GOT ANY PROBLEMS YOU LET ME KNOW. SPOOKY STUFF DON'T WANNA MESS WITH EDDIE MAZARA.
GOOD NIGHT, EDDIE.

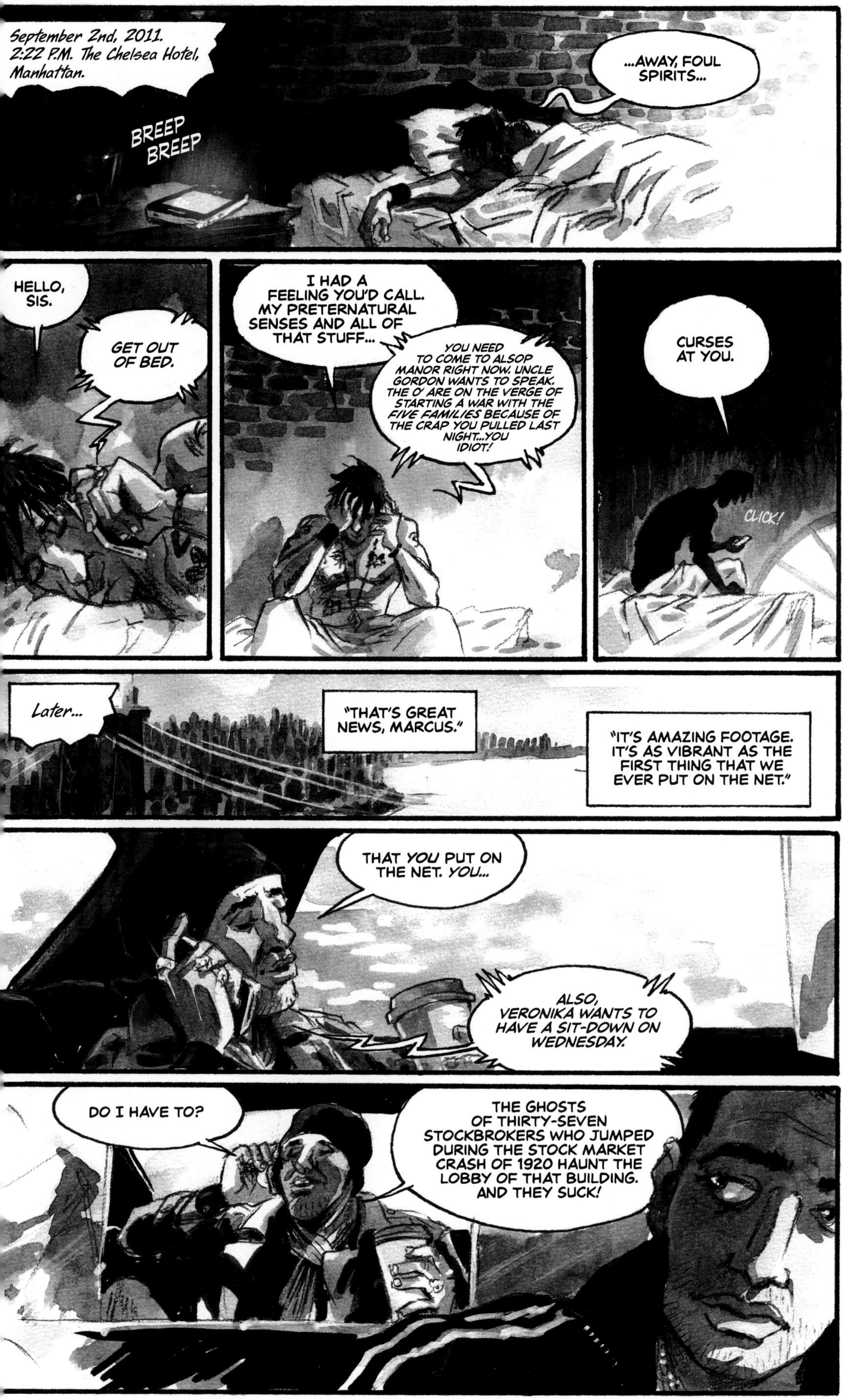
September 2nd, 2011. 2:22 P.M. The Chelsea Hotel, Manhattan.
BREEP BREEP
...AWAY, FOUL SPIRITS...
HELLO, SIS.
GET OUT OF BED.
I HAD A FEELING YOU'D CALL. MY PRETERNATURAL SENSES AND ALL OF THAT STUFF...
YOU NEED TO COME TO ALSOP MANOR RIGHT NOW. UNCLE GORDON WANTS TO SPEAK. THE O' ARE ON THE VERGE OF STARTING A WAR WITH THE FIVE FAMILIES BECAUSE OF THE CRAP YOU PULLED LAST NIGHT...YOU IDIOT!
CURSES AT YOU.
CLICK!
Later...
"THAT'S GREAT NEWS, MARCUS."
"IT'S AMAZING FOOTAGE. IT'S AS VIBRANT AS THE FIRST THING THAT WE EVER PUT ON THE NET."
THAT YOU PUT ON THE NET. YOU...
ALSO, VERONIKA WANTS TO HAVE A SIT-DOWN ON WEDNESDAY.
DO I HAVE TO?
THE GHOSTS OF THIRTY-SEVEN STOCKBROKERS WHO JUMPED DURING THE STOCK MARKET CRASH OF 1920 HAUNT THE LOBBY OF THAT BUILDING. AND THEY SUCK!

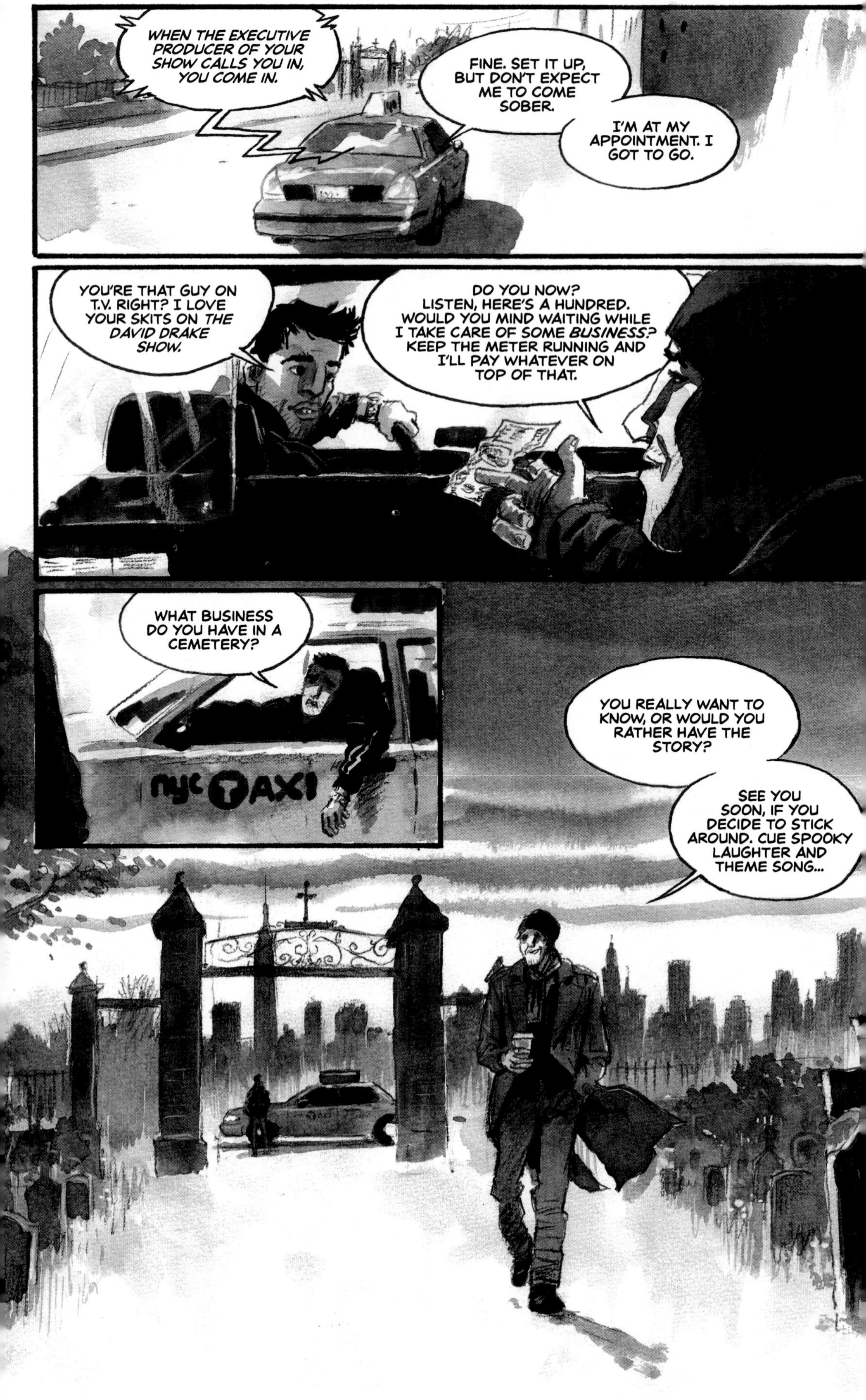
WHEN THE EXECUTIVE PRODUCER OF YOUR SHOW CALLS YOU IN, YOU COME IN.
FINE. SET IT UP, BUT DON'T EXPECT ME TO COME SOBER.
I'M AT MY APPOINTMENT. I GOT TO GO.
YOU'RE THAT GUY ON T.V. RIGHT? I LOVE YOUR SKITS ON THE DAVID DRAKE SHOW.
DO YOU NOW? LISTEN, HERE'S A HUNDRED. WOULD YOU MIND WAITING WHILE I TAKE CARE OF SOME BUSINESS? KEEP THE METER RUNNING AND I'LL PAY WHATEVER ON TOP OF THAT.
WHAT BUSINESS DO YOU HAVE IN A CEMETERY?
nyc TAXI
YOU REALLY WANT TO KNOW, OR WOULD YOU RATHER HAVE THE STORY?
SEE YOU SOON, IF YOU DECIDE TO STICK AROUND. CUE SPOOKY LAUGHTER AND THEME SONG...

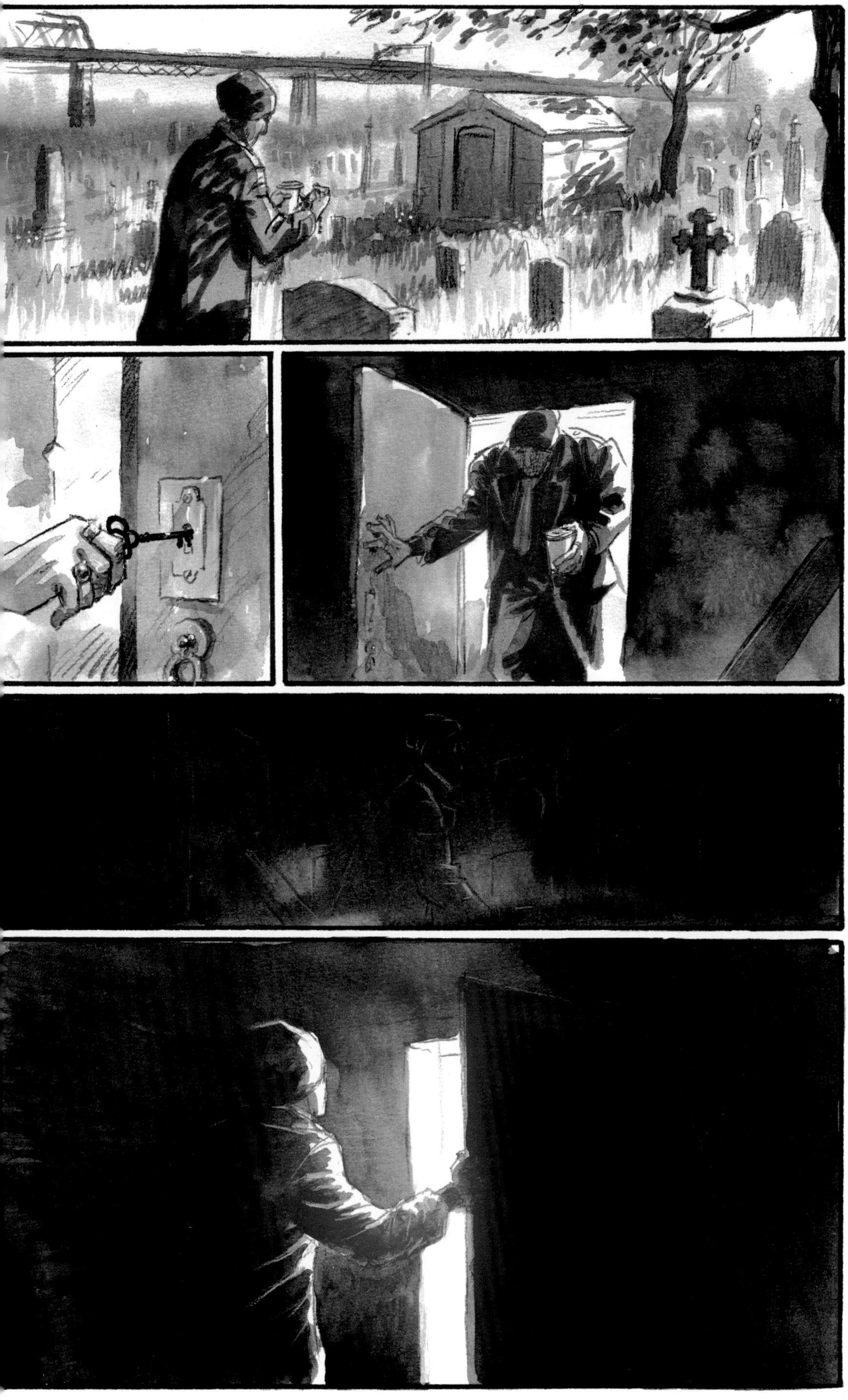

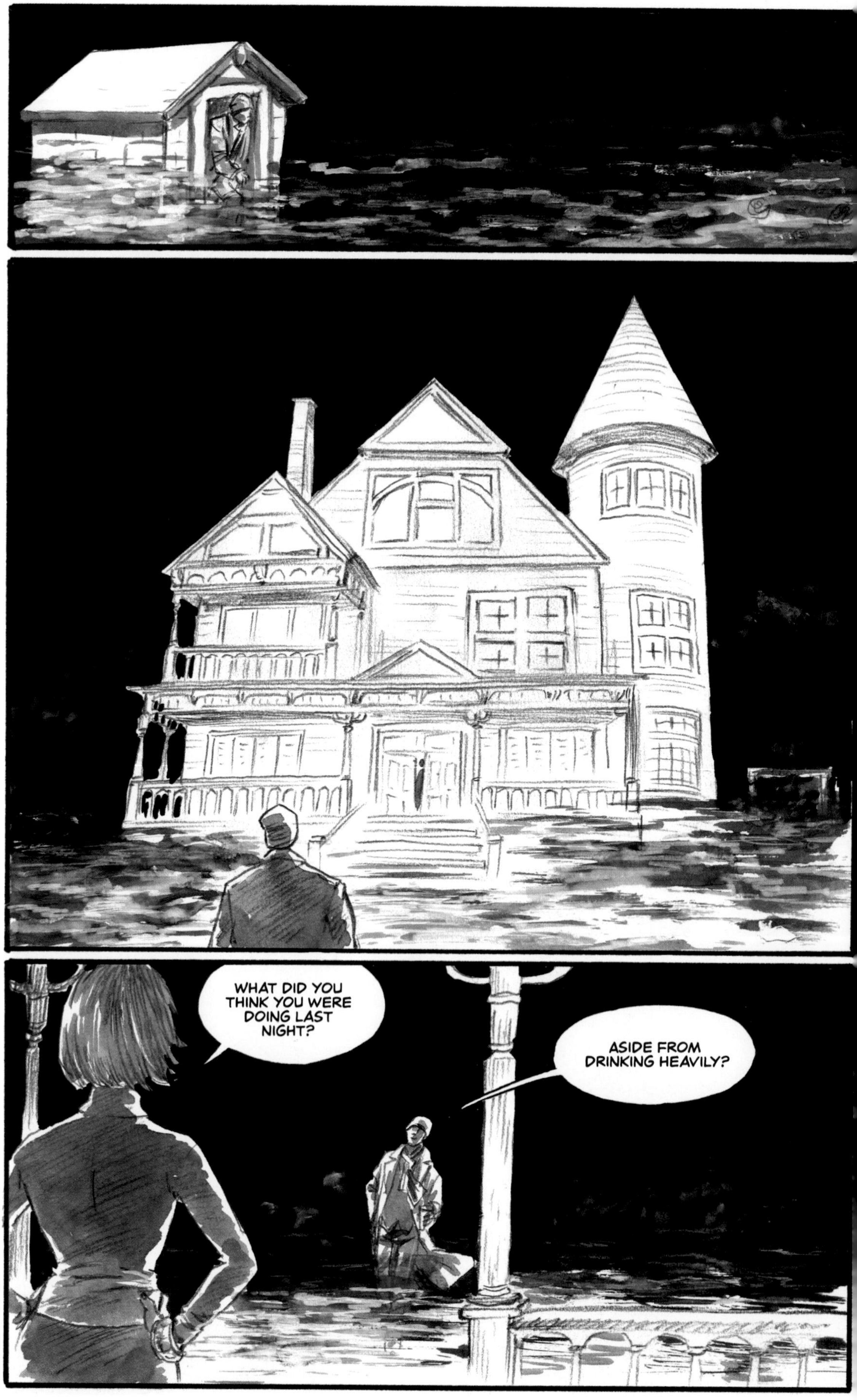
WHAT DID YOU THINK YOU WERE DOING LAST NIGHT?
ASIDE FROM DRINKING HEAVILY?

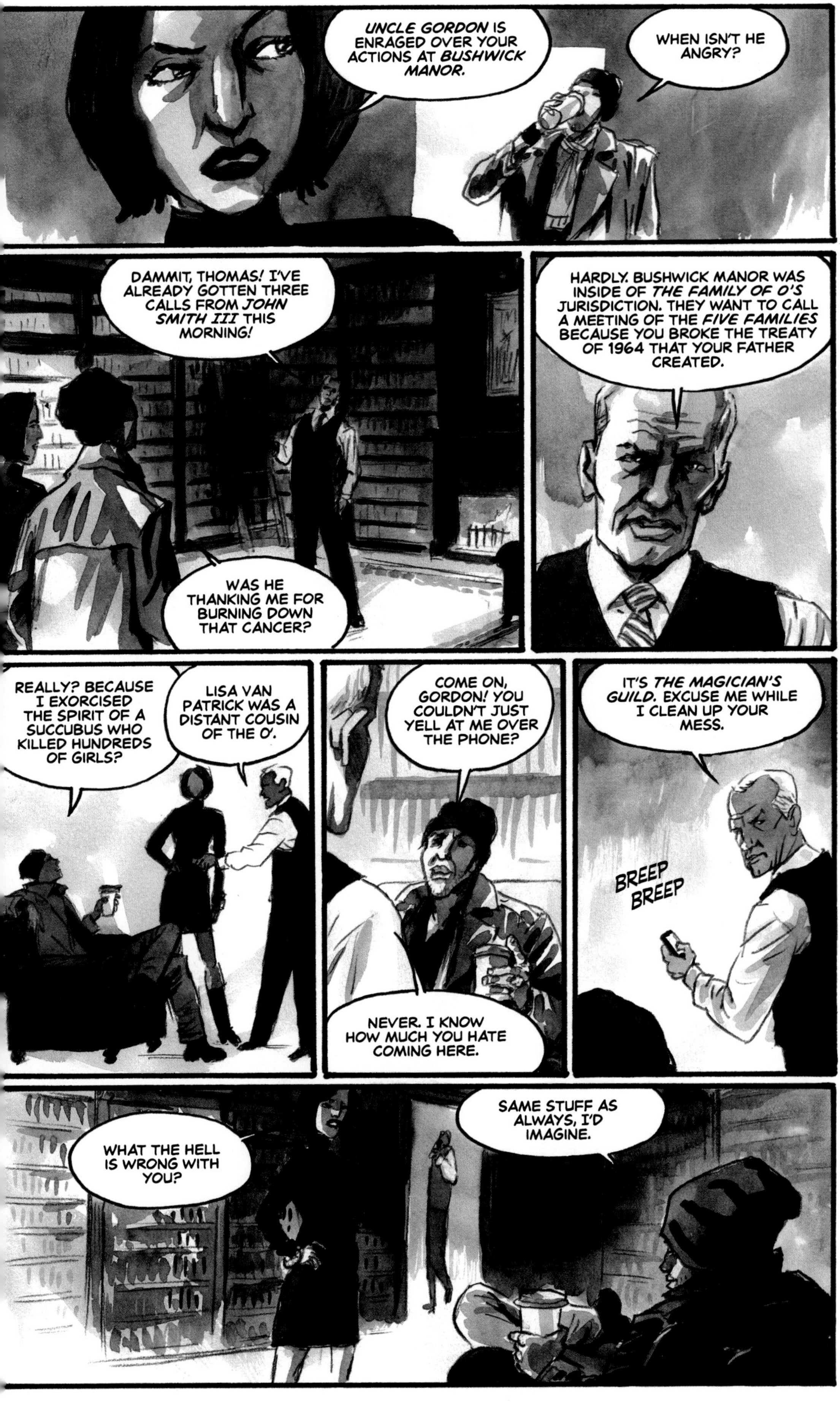
UNCLE GORDON IS ENRAGED OVER YOUR ACTIONS AT BUSHWICK MANOR.
WHEN ISN'T HE ANGRY?
DAMMIT, THOMAS! I'VE ALREADY GOTTEN THREE CALLS FROM JOHN SMITH III THIS MORNING!
WAS HE THANKING ME FOR BURNING DOWN THAT CANCER?
HARDLY. BUSHWICK MANOR WAS INSIDE OF THE FAMILY OF O'S JURISDICTION. THEY WANT TO CALL A MEETING OF THE FIVE FAMILIES BECAUSE YOU BROKE THE TREATY OF 1964 THAT YOUR FATHER CREATED.
REALLY? BECAUSE I EXORCISED THE SPIRIT OF A SUCCUBUS WHO KILLED HUNDREDS OF GIRLS?
LISA VAN PATRICK WAS A DISTANT COUSIN OF THE O'.
COME ON, GORDON! YOU COULDN'T JUST YELL AT ME OVER THE PHONE?
NEVER. I KNOW HOW MUCH YOU HATE COMING HERE.
BREEP
BREEP
IT'S THE MAGICIAN'S GUILD. EXCUSE ME WHILE I CLEAN UP YOUR MESS.
WHAT THE HELL IS WRONG WITH YOU?
SAME STUFF AS ALWAYS, I'D IMAGINE.

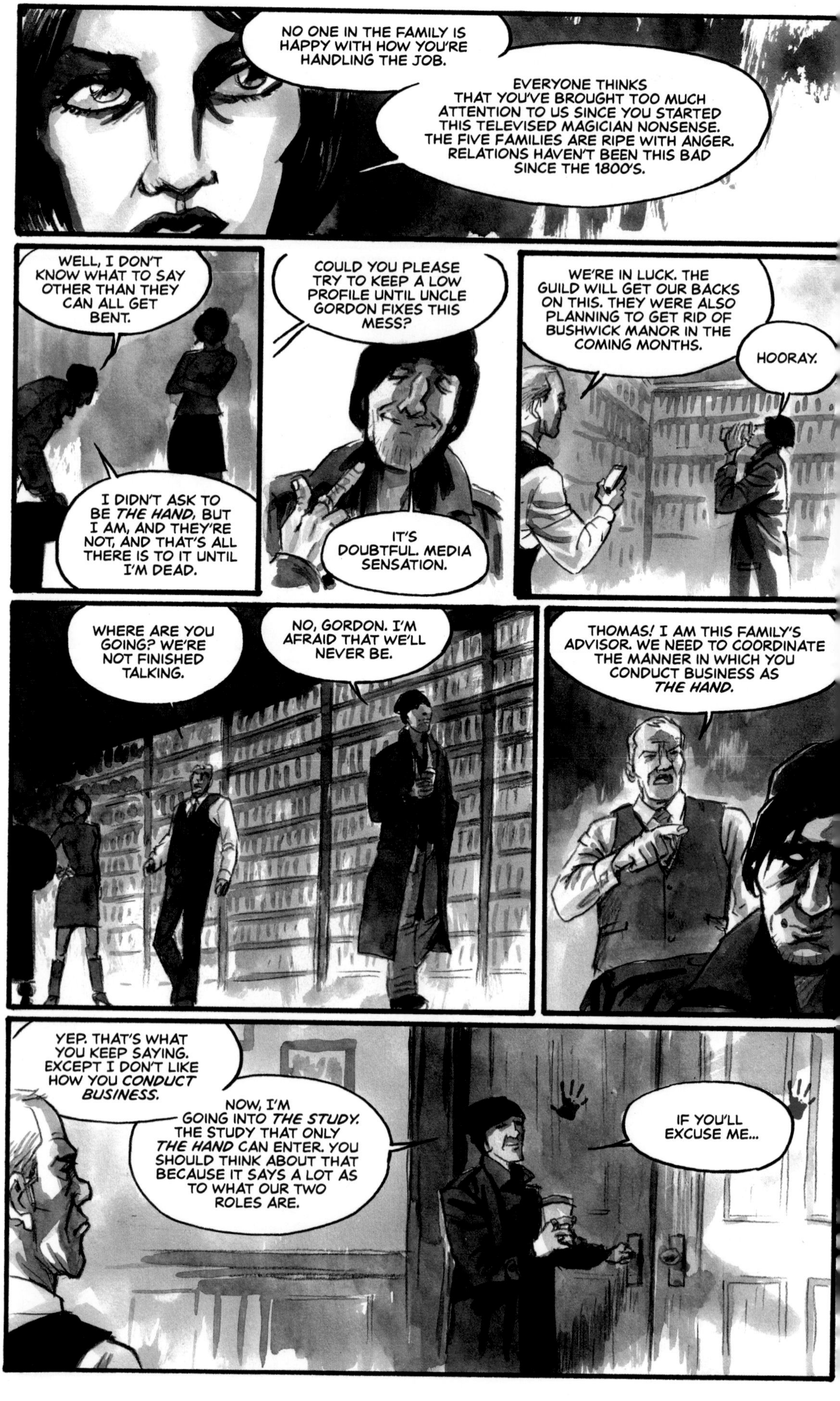

NO ONE IN THE FAMILY IS HAPPY WITH HOW YOU'RE HANDLING THE JOB.
EVERYONE THINKS THAT YOU'VE BROUGHT TOO MUCH ATTENTION TO US SINCE YOU STARTED THIS TELEVISED MAGICIAN NONSENSE. THE FIVE FAMILIES ARE RIPE WITH ANGER. RELATIONS HAVEN'T BEEN THIS BAD SINCE THE 1800'S.
WELL, I DON'T KNOW WHAT TO SAY OTHER THAN THEY CAN ALL GET BENT.
I DIDN'T ASK TO BE *THE HAND*, BUT I AM, AND THEY'RE NOT, AND THAT'S ALL THERE IS TO IT UNTIL I'M DEAD.
COULD YOU PLEASE TRY TO KEEP A LOW PROFILE UNTIL UNCLE GORDON FIXES THIS MESS?
IT'S DOUBTFUL. MEDIA SENSATION.
WE'RE IN LUCK. THE GUILD WILL GET OUR BACKS ON THIS. THEY WERE ALSO PLANNING TO GET RID OF BUSHWICK MANOR IN THE COMING MONTHS.
HOORAY.
WHERE ARE YOU GOING? WE'RE NOT FINISHED TALKING.
NO, GORDON. I'M AFRAID THAT WE'LL NEVER BE.
THOMAS! I AM THIS FAMILY'S ADVISOR. WE NEED TO COORDINATE THE MANNER IN WHICH YOU CONDUCT BUSINESS AS *THE HAND.*
YEP. THAT'S WHAT YOU KEEP SAYING. EXCEPT I DON'T LIKE HOW YOU *CONDUCT BUSINESS.*
NOW, I'M GOING INTO *THE STUDY.* THE STUDY THAT ONLY *THE HAND* CAN ENTER. YOU SHOULD THINK ABOUT THAT BECAUSE IT SAYS A LOT AS TO WHAT OUR TWO ROLES ARE.
IF YOU'LL EXCUSE ME...

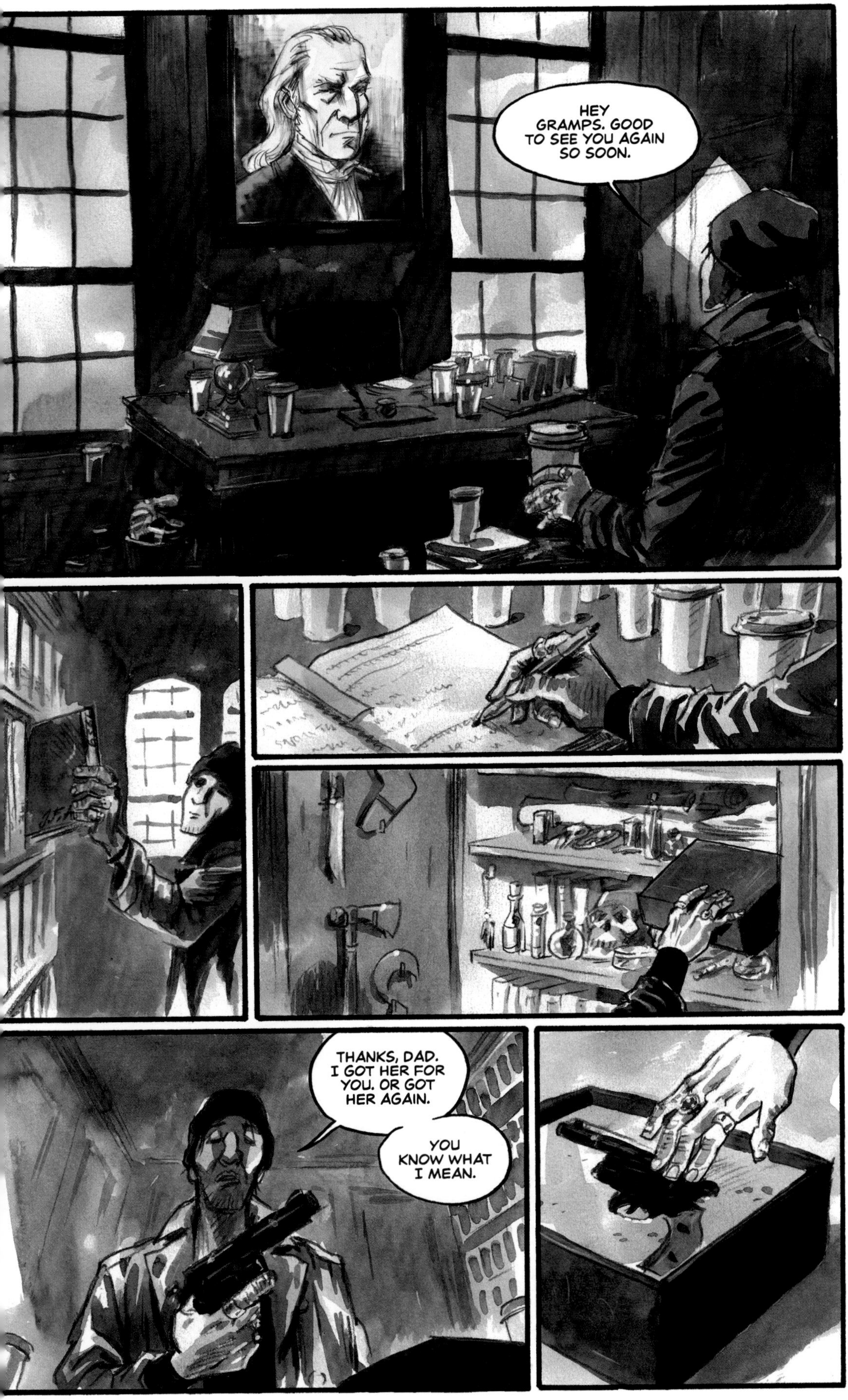
HEY GRAMPS. GOOD TO SEE YOU AGAIN SO SOON.
THANKS, DAD. I GOT HER FOR YOU. OR GOT HER AGAIN.
YOU KNOW WHAT I MEAN.

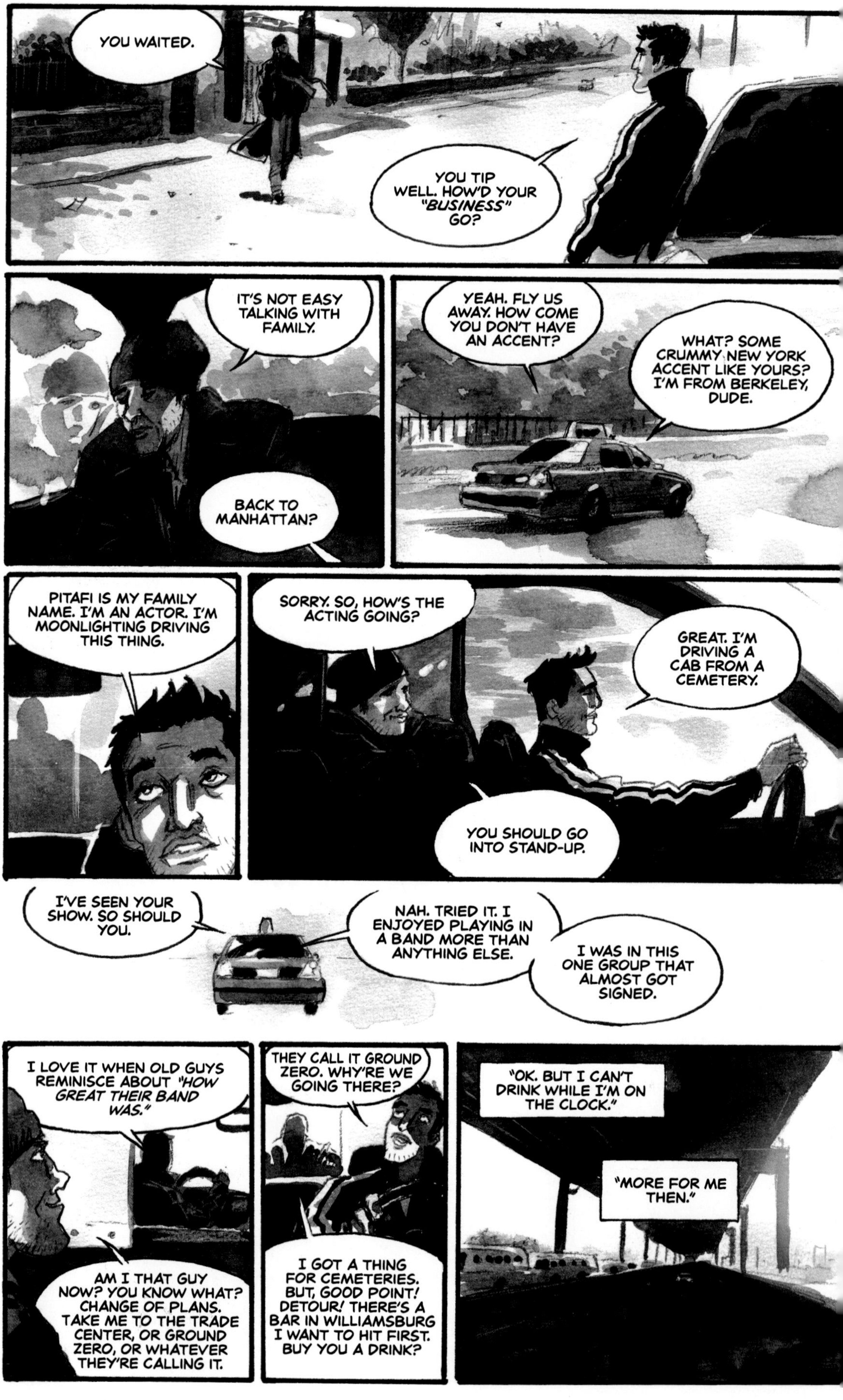
YOU WAITED.
YOU TIP WELL. HOW'D YOUR "BUSINESS" GO?
IT'S NOT EASY TALKING WITH FAMILY.
BACK TO MANHATTAN?
YEAH. FLY US AWAY. HOW COME YOU DON'T HAVE AN ACCENT?
WHAT? SOME CRUMMY NEW YORK ACCENT LIKE YOURS? I'M FROM BERKELEY, DUDE.
PITAFI IS MY FAMILY NAME. I'M AN ACTOR. I'M MOONLIGHTING DRIVING THIS THING.
SORRY. SO, HOW'S THE ACTING GOING?
GREAT. I'M DRIVING A CAB FROM A CEMETERY.
YOU SHOULD GO INTO STAND-UP.
I'VE SEEN YOUR SHOW. SO SHOULD YOU.
NAH. TRIED IT. I ENJOYED PLAYING IN A BAND MORE THAN ANYTHING ELSE.
I WAS IN THIS ONE GROUP THAT ALMOST GOT SIGNED.
I LOVE IT WHEN OLD GUYS REMINISCE ABOUT "HOW GREAT THEIR BAND WAS."
AM I THAT GUY NOW? YOU KNOW WHAT? CHANGE OF PLANS. TAKE ME TO THE TRADE CENTER, OR GROUND ZERO, OR WHATEVER THEY'RE CALLING IT.
THEY CALL IT GROUND ZERO. WHY'RE WE GOING THERE?
I GOT A THING FOR CEMETERIES. BUT, GOOD POINT! DETOUR! THERE'S A BAR IN WILLIAMSBURG I WANT TO HIT FIRST. BUY YOU A DRINK?
"OK. BUT I CAN'T DRINK WHILE I'M ON THE CLOCK."
"MORE FOR ME THEN."

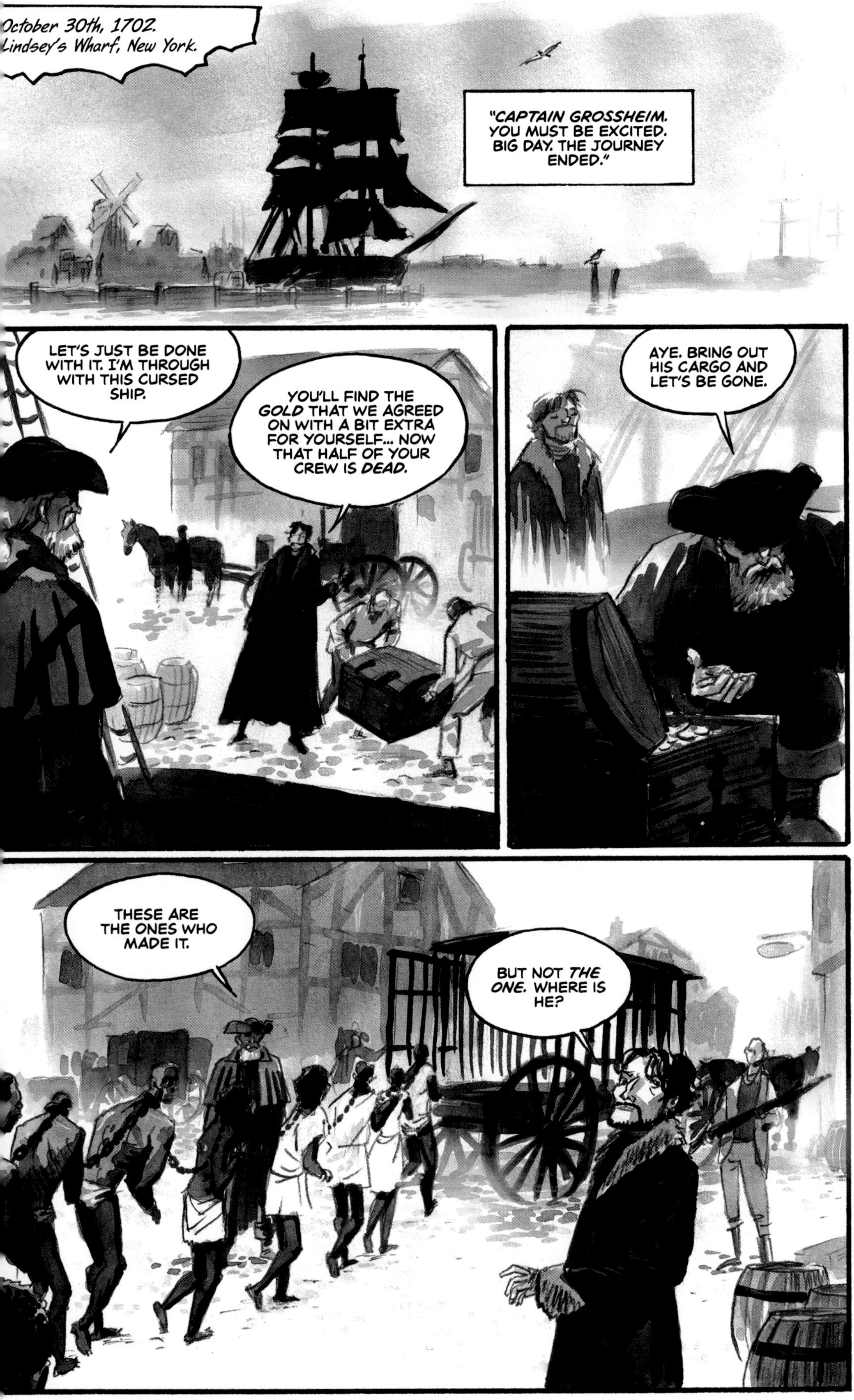
October 30th, 1702. Lindsey's Wharf, New York.
"CAPTAIN GROSSHEIM. YOU MUST BE EXCITED. BIG DAY. THE JOURNEY ENDED."
LET'S JUST BE DONE WITH IT. I'M THROUGH WITH THIS CURSED SHIP.
YOU'LL FIND THE GOLD THAT WE AGREED ON WITH A BIT EXTRA FOR YOURSELF... NOW THAT HALF OF YOUR CREW IS DEAD.
AYE. BRING OUT HIS CARGO AND LET'S BE GONE.
THESE ARE THE ONES WHO MADE IT.
BUT NOT THE ONE. WHERE IS HE?

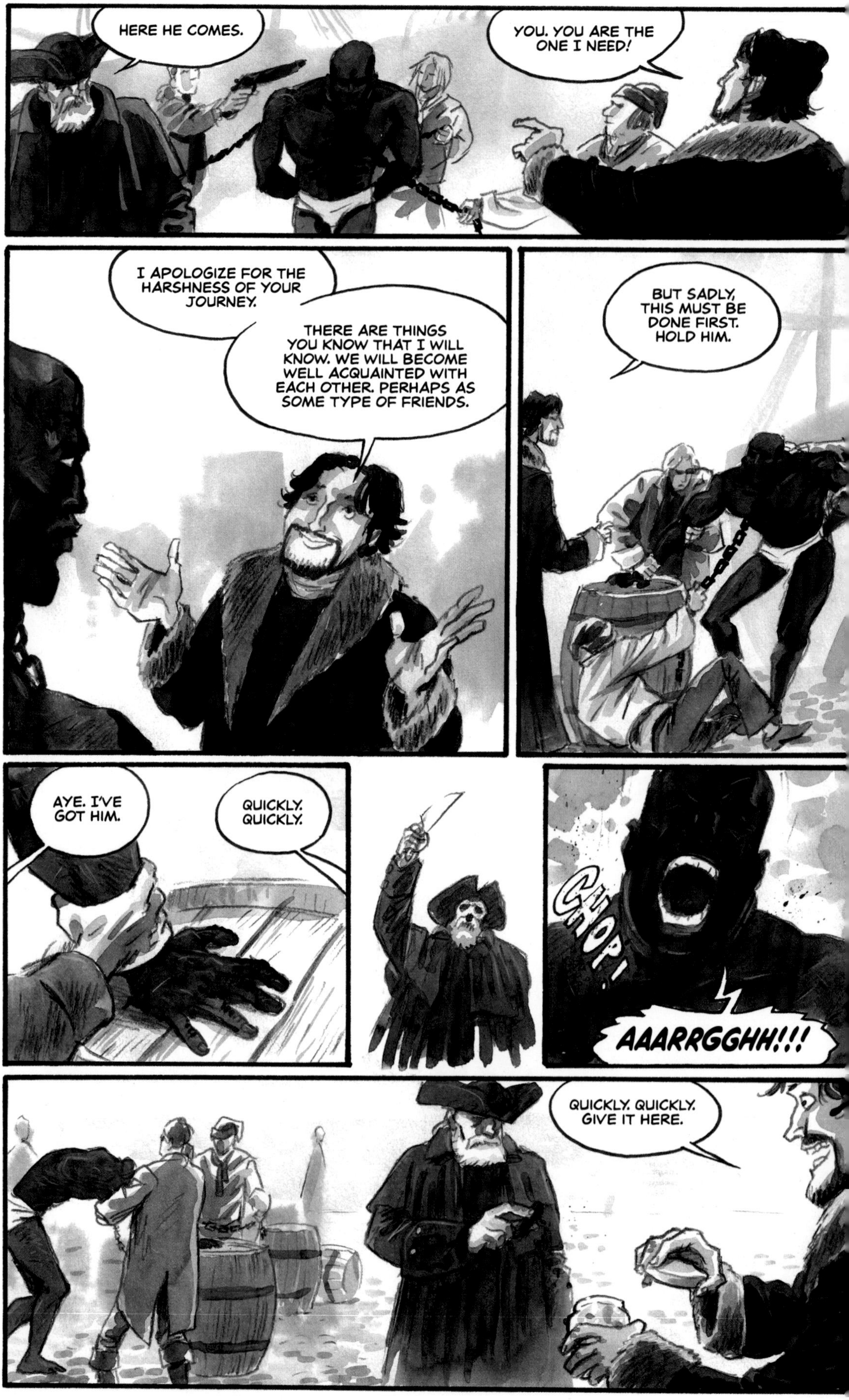
HERE HE COMES.
YOU. YOU ARE THE ONE I NEED!
I APOLOGIZE FOR THE HARSHNESS OF YOUR JOURNEY.
THERE ARE THINGS YOU KNOW THAT I WILL KNOW. WE WILL BECOME WELL ACQUAINTED WITH EACH OTHER. PERHAPS AS SOME TYPE OF FRIENDS.
BUT SADLY, THIS MUST BE DONE FIRST. HOLD HIM.
AYE. I'VE GOT HIM.
QUICKLY. QUICKLY.
CHOP!
AAARRGGHH!!!
QUICKLY. QUICKLY. GIVE IT HERE.

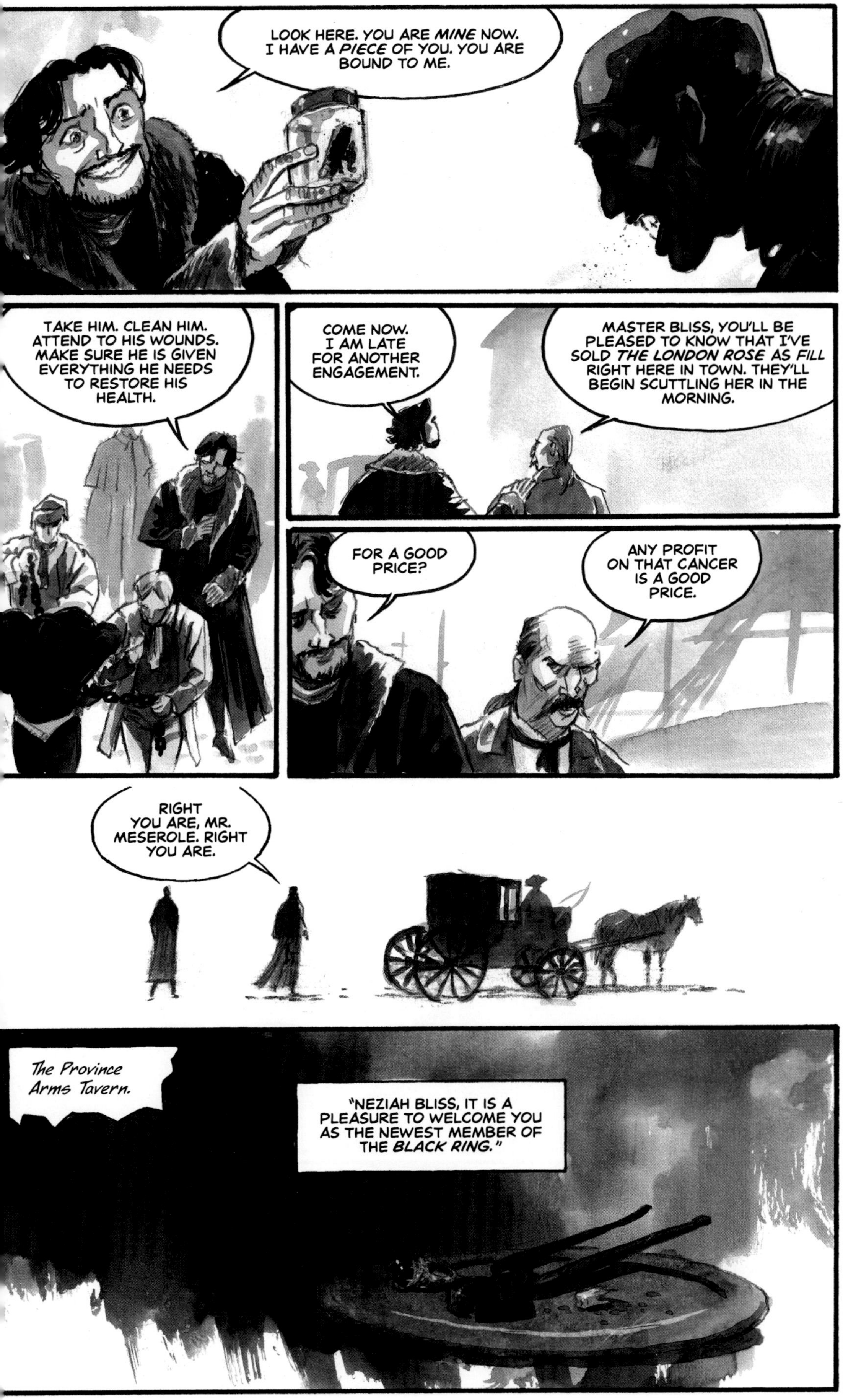
LOOK HERE. YOU ARE *MINE* NOW. I HAVE A *PIECE* OF YOU. YOU ARE BOUND TO ME.
TAKE HIM. CLEAN HIM. ATTEND TO HIS WOUNDS. MAKE SURE HE IS GIVEN EVERYTHING HE NEEDS TO RESTORE HIS HEALTH.
COME NOW. I AM LATE FOR ANOTHER ENGAGEMENT.
MASTER BLISS, YOU'LL BE PLEASED TO KNOW THAT I'VE SOLD *THE LONDON ROSE* AS *FILL* RIGHT HERE IN TOWN. THEY'LL BEGIN SCUTTLING HER IN THE MORNING.
FOR A GOOD PRICE?
ANY PROFIT ON THAT CANCER IS A GOOD PRICE.
RIGHT YOU ARE, MR. MESEROLE. RIGHT YOU ARE.
The Province Arms Tavern.
"NEZIAH BLISS, IT IS A PLEASURE TO WELCOME YOU AS THE NEWEST MEMBER OF THE *BLACK RING.*"

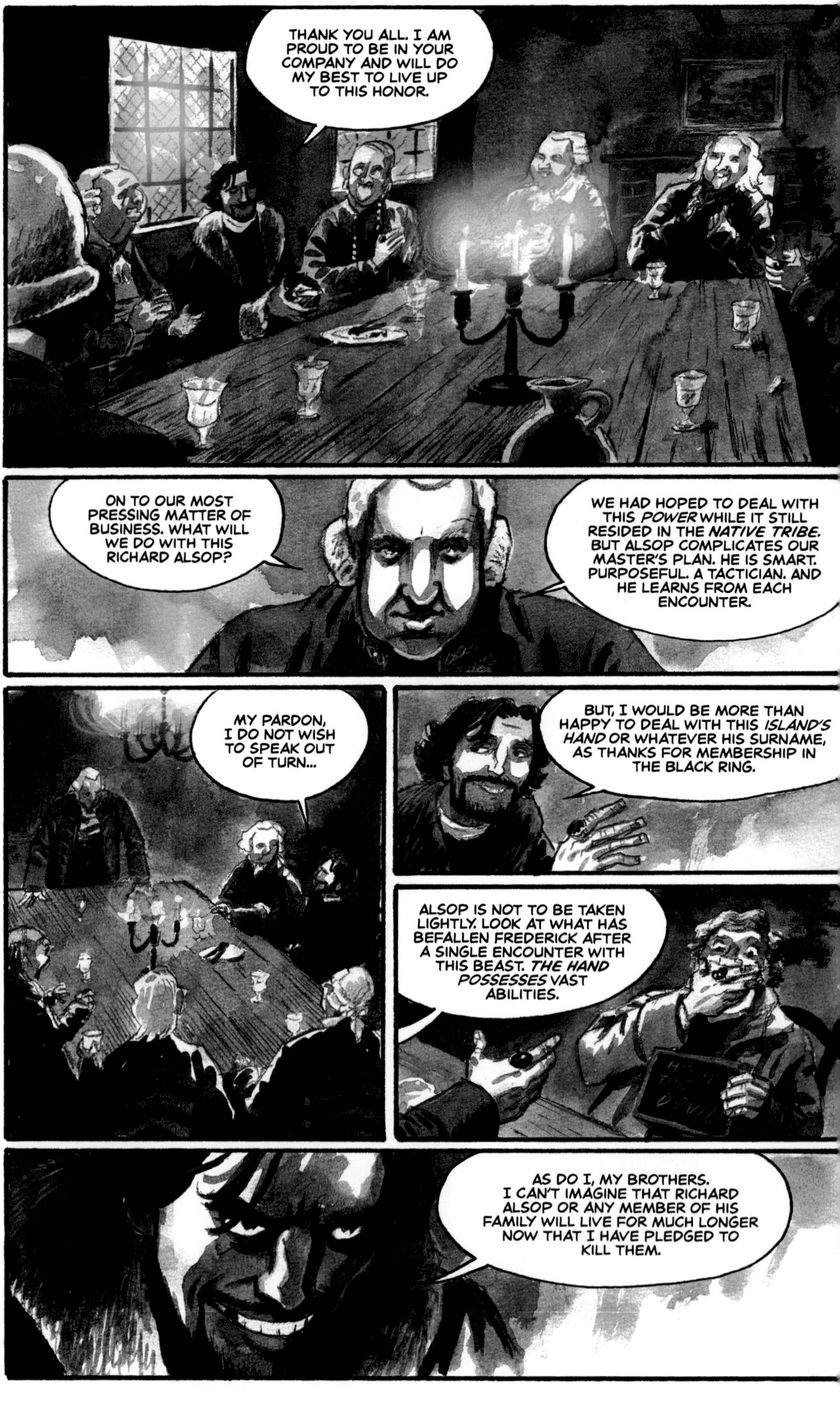
THANK YOU ALL. I AM PROUD TO BE IN YOUR COMPANY AND WILL DO MY BEST TO LIVE UP TO THIS HONOR.
ON TO OUR MOST PRESSING MATTER OF BUSINESS. WHAT WILL WE DO WITH THIS RICHARD ALSOP?
WE HAD HOPED TO DEAL WITH THIS *POWER* WHILE IT STILL RESIDED IN THE *NATIVE TRIBE.* BUT ALSOP COMPLICATES OUR MASTER'S PLAN. HE IS SMART. PURPOSEFUL. A TACTICIAN. AND HE LEARNS FROM EACH ENCOUNTER.
MY PARDON, I DO NOT WISH TO SPEAK OUT OF TURN...
BUT, I WOULD BE MORE THAN HAPPY TO DEAL WITH THIS *ISLAND'S HAND* OR WHATEVER HIS SURNAME, AS THANKS FOR MEMBERSHIP IN THE BLACK RING.
ALSOP IS NOT TO BE TAKEN LIGHTLY. LOOK AT WHAT HAS BEFALLEN FREDERICK AFTER A SINGLE ENCOUNTER WITH THIS BEAST. *THE HAND POSSESSES* VAST ABILITIES.
AS DO I, MY BROTHERS. I CAN'T IMAGINE THAT RICHARD ALSOP OR ANY MEMBER OF HIS FAMILY WILL LIVE FOR MUCH LONGER NOW THAT I HAVE PLEDGED TO KILL THEM.

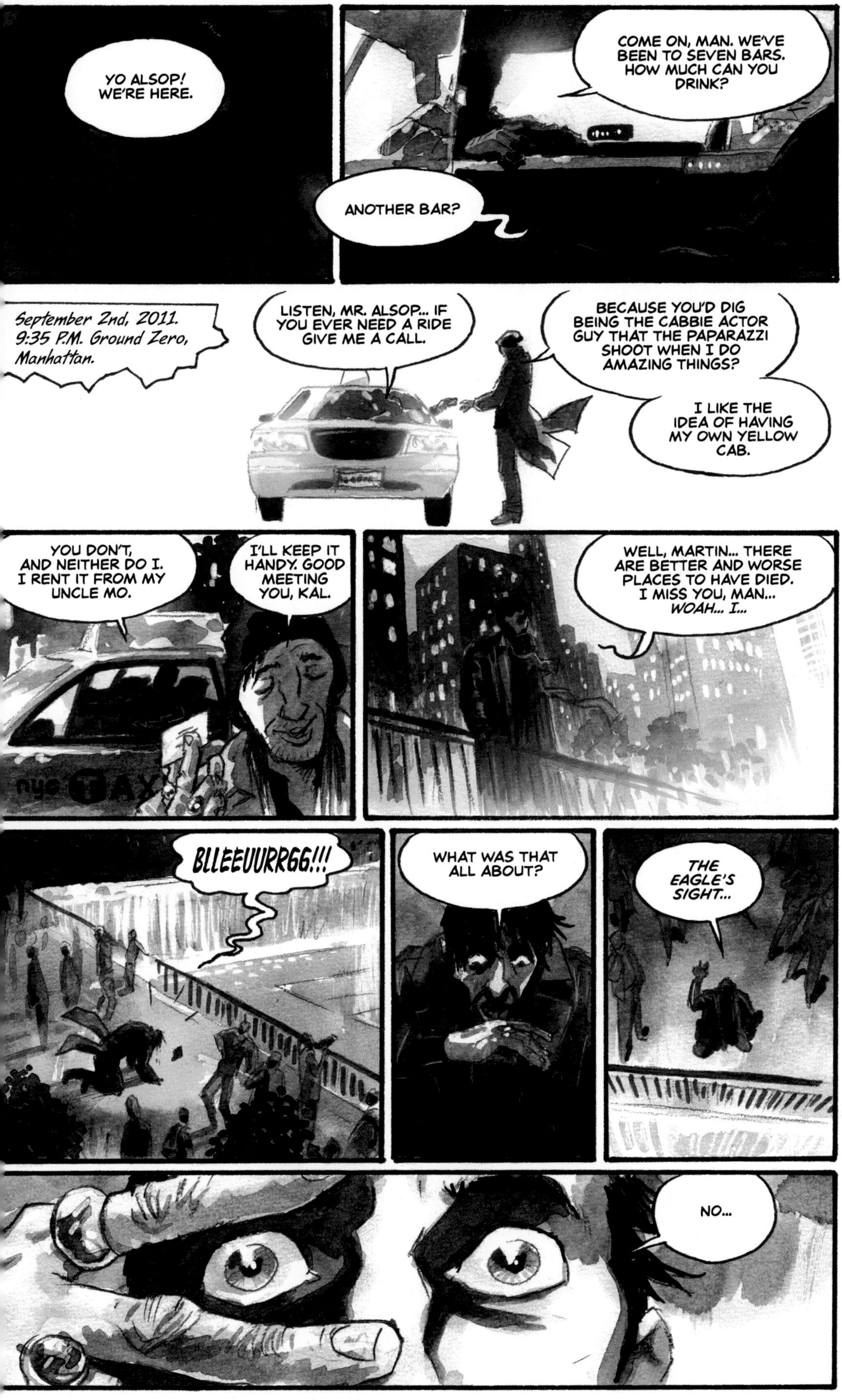
YO ALSOP! WE'RE HERE.
COME ON, MAN. WE'VE BEEN TO SEVEN BARS. HOW MUCH CAN YOU DRINK?
ANOTHER BAR?
September 2nd, 2011. 9:35 P.M. Ground Zero, Manhattan.
LISTEN, MR. ALSOP... IF YOU EVER NEED A RIDE GIVE ME A CALL.
BECAUSE YOU'D DIG BEING THE CABBIE ACTOR GUY THAT THE PAPARAZZI SHOOT WHEN I DO AMAZING THINGS?
I LIKE THE IDEA OF HAVING MY OWN YELLOW CAB.
YOU DON'T, AND NEITHER DO I. I RENT IT FROM MY UNCLE MO.
I'LL KEEP IT HANDY. GOOD MEETING YOU, KAL.
WELL, MARTIN... THERE ARE BETTER AND WORSE PLACES TO HAVE DIED. I MISS YOU, MAN... WOAH... I...
BLLEEUURRGG!!!
WHAT WAS THAT ALL ABOUT?
THE EAGLE'S SIGHT...
NO...

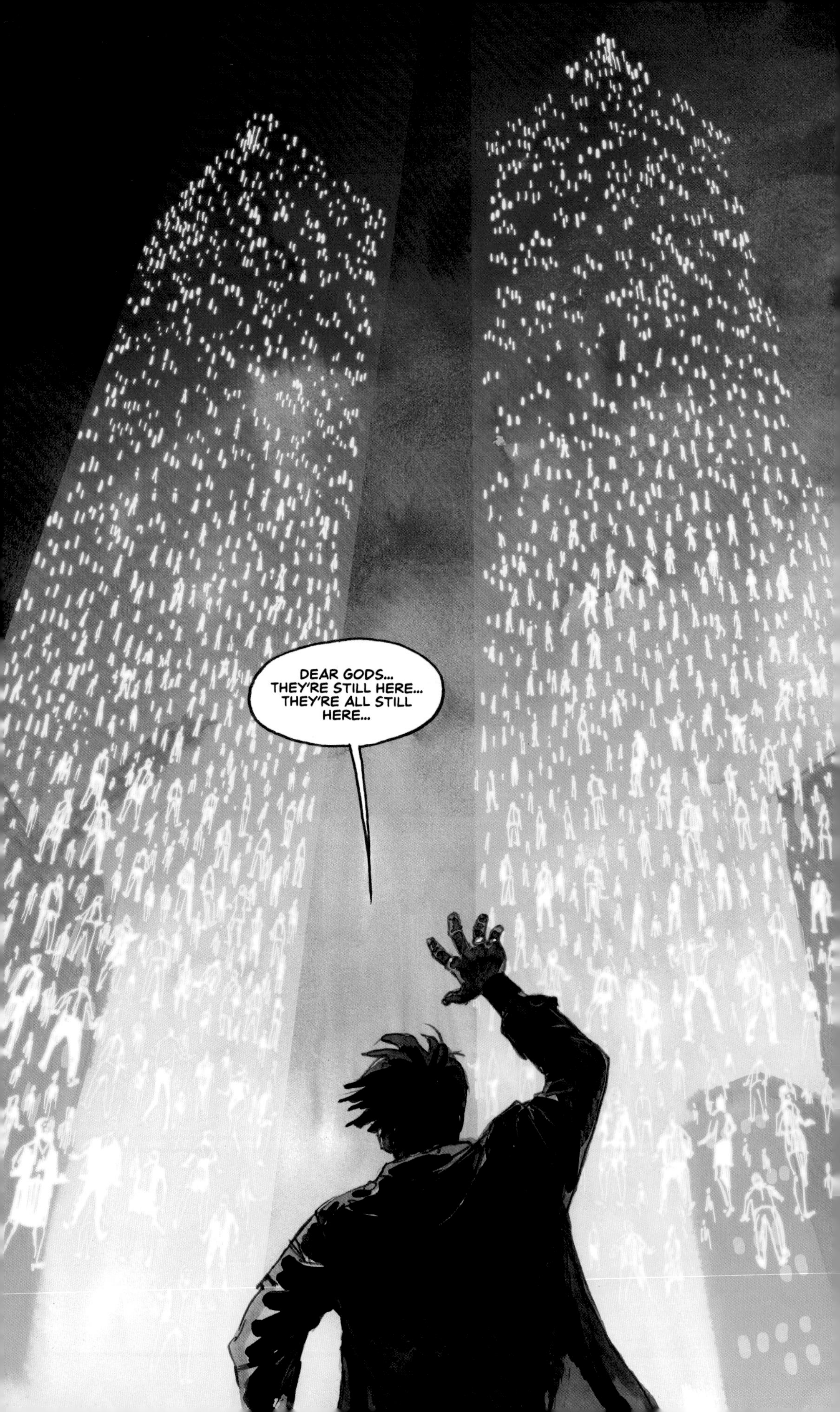
DEAR GODS... THEY'RE STILL HERE... THEY'RE ALL STILL HERE...

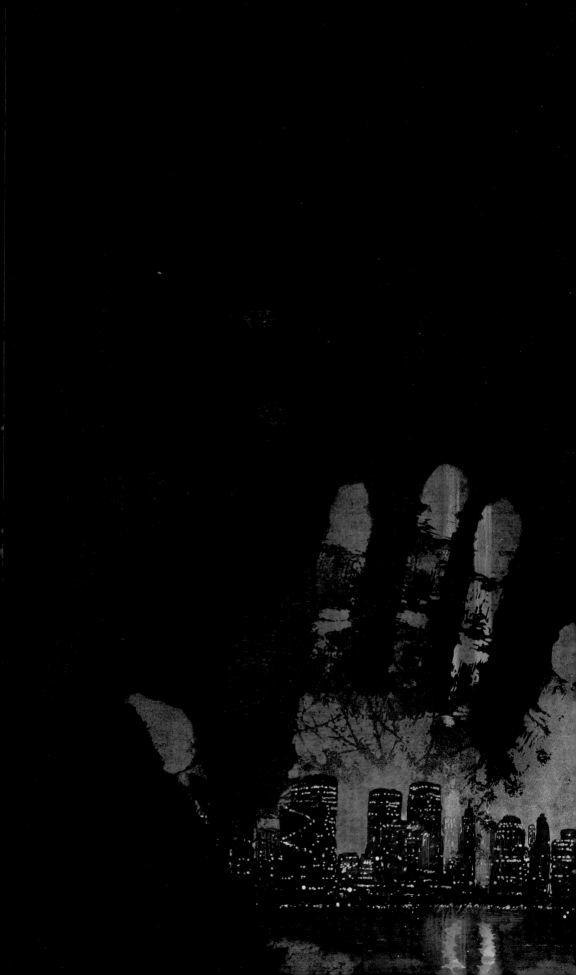

CHAPTER THREE

THE SEA OF SOULS

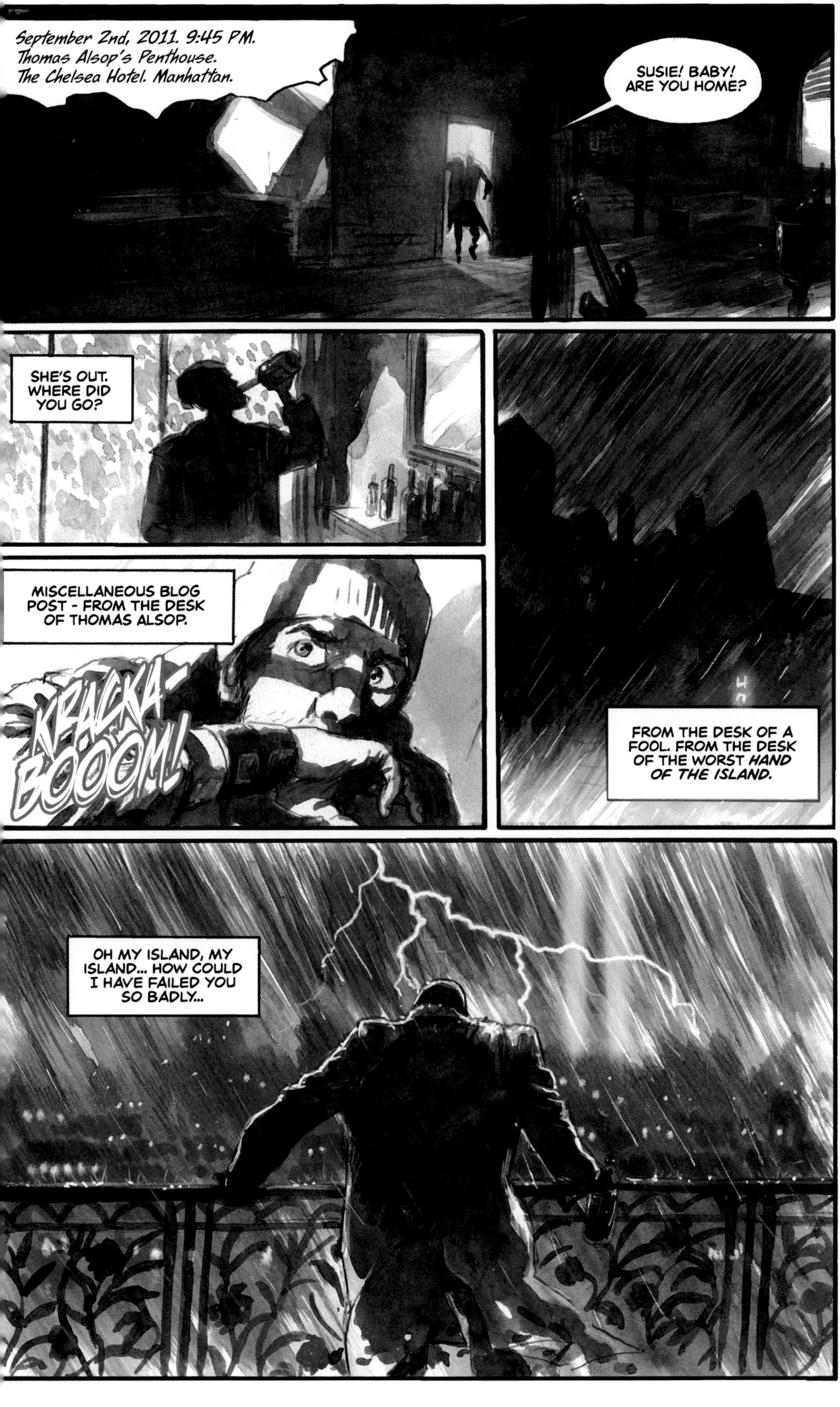
September 2nd, 2011. 9:45 PM.
Thomas Alsop's Penthouse.
The Chelsea Hotel. Manhattan.
SUSIE! BABY! ARE YOU HOME?
SHE'S OUT. WHERE DID YOU GO?
MISCELLANEOUS BLOG POST - FROM THE DESK OF THOMAS ALSOP.
KRACKA-BOOOM!
FROM THE DESK OF A FOOL. FROM THE DESK OF THE WORST HAND OF THE ISLAND.
OH MY ISLAND, MY ISLAND... HOW COULD I HAVE FAILED YOU SO BADLY...

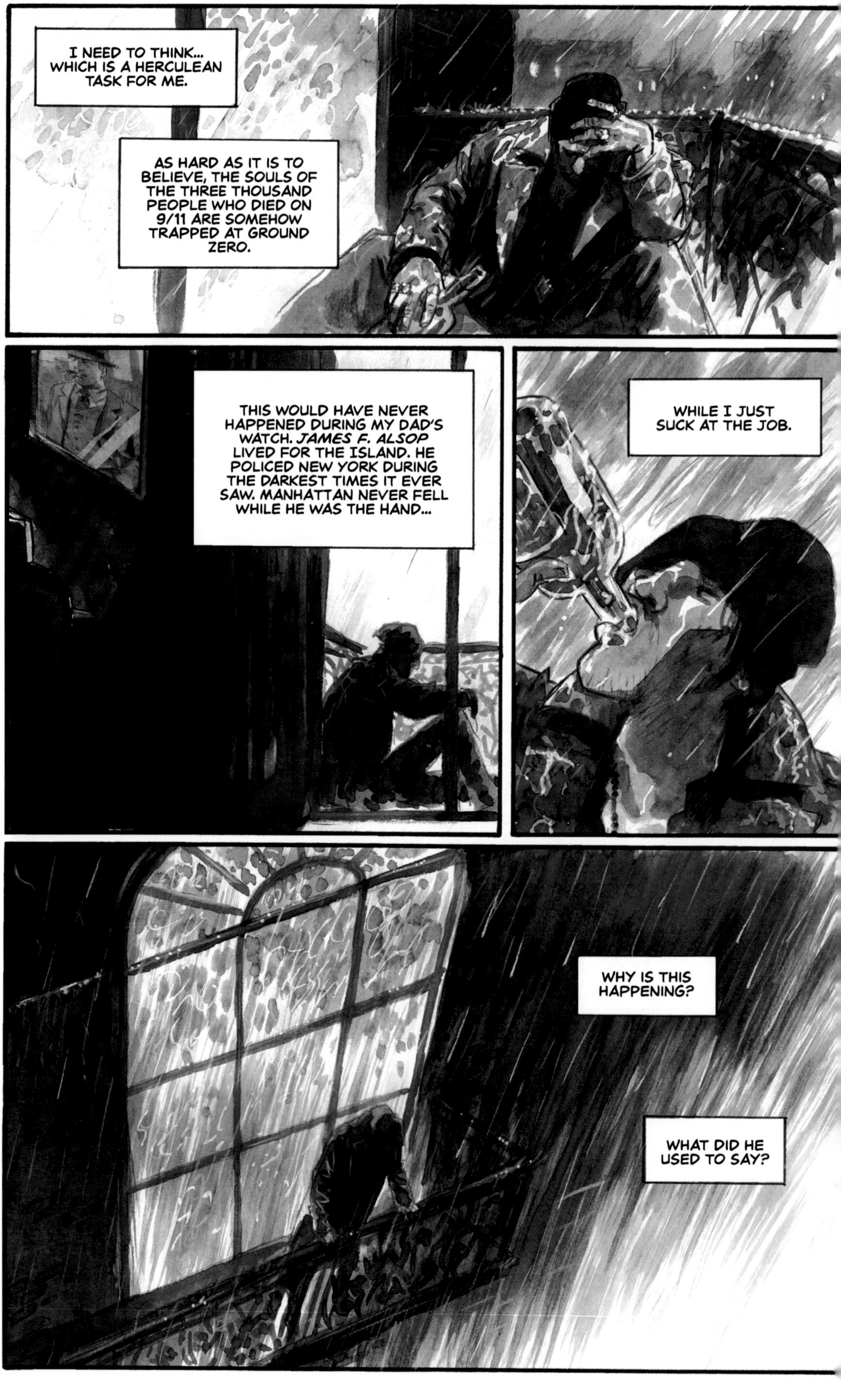
I NEED TO THINK... WHICH IS A HERCULEAN TASK FOR ME.
AS HARD AS IT IS TO BELIEVE, THE SOULS OF THE THREE THOUSAND PEOPLE WHO DIED ON 9/11 ARE SOMEHOW TRAPPED AT GROUND ZERO.
THIS WOULD HAVE NEVER HAPPENED DURING MY DAD'S WATCH. *JAMES F. ALSOP* LIVED FOR THE ISLAND. HE POLICED NEW YORK DURING THE DARKEST TIMES IT EVER SAW. MANHATTAN NEVER FELL WHILE HE WAS THE HAND...
WHILE I JUST SUCK AT THE JOB.
WHY IS THIS HAPPENING?
WHAT DID HE USED TO SAY?

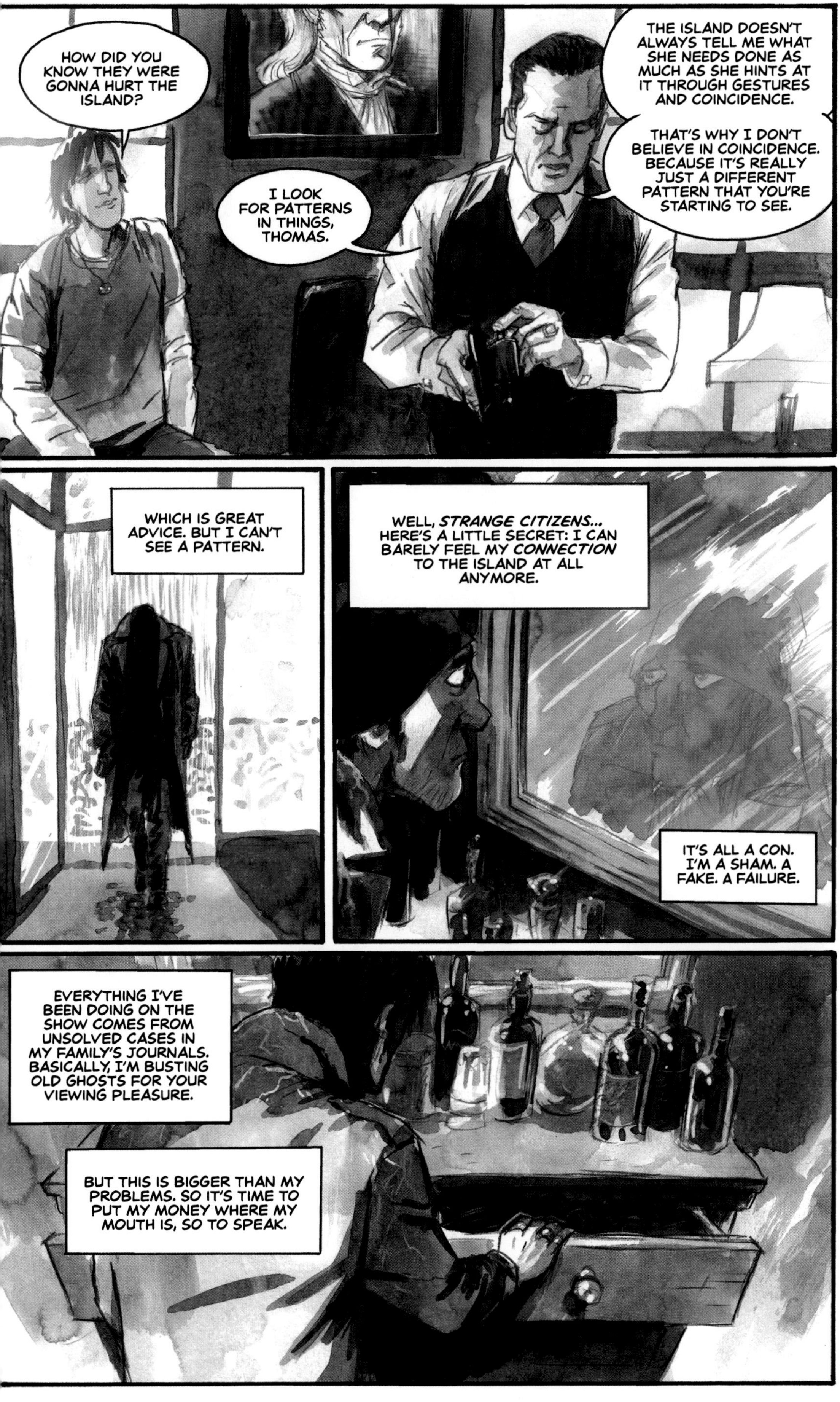
HOW DID YOU KNOW THEY WERE GONNA HURT THE ISLAND?
I LOOK FOR PATTERNS IN THINGS, THOMAS.
THE ISLAND DOESN'T ALWAYS TELL ME WHAT SHE NEEDS DONE AS MUCH AS SHE HINTS AT IT THROUGH GESTURES AND COINCIDENCE.
THAT'S WHY I DON'T BELIEVE IN COINCIDENCE. BECAUSE IT'S REALLY JUST A DIFFERENT PATTERN THAT YOU'RE STARTING TO SEE.
WHICH IS GREAT ADVICE. BUT I CAN'T SEE A PATTERN.
WELL, *STRANGE CITIZENS*... HERE'S A LITTLE SECRET: I CAN BARELY FEEL MY *CONNECTION* TO THE ISLAND AT ALL ANYMORE.
IT'S ALL A CON. I'M A SHAM. A FAKE. A FAILURE.
EVERYTHING I'VE BEEN DOING ON THE SHOW COMES FROM UNSOLVED CASES IN MY FAMILY'S JOURNALS. BASICALLY, I'M BUSTING OLD GHOSTS FOR YOUR VIEWING PLEASURE.
BUT THIS IS BIGGER THAN MY PROBLEMS. SO IT'S TIME TO PUT MY MONEY WHERE MY MOUTH IS, SO TO SPEAK.

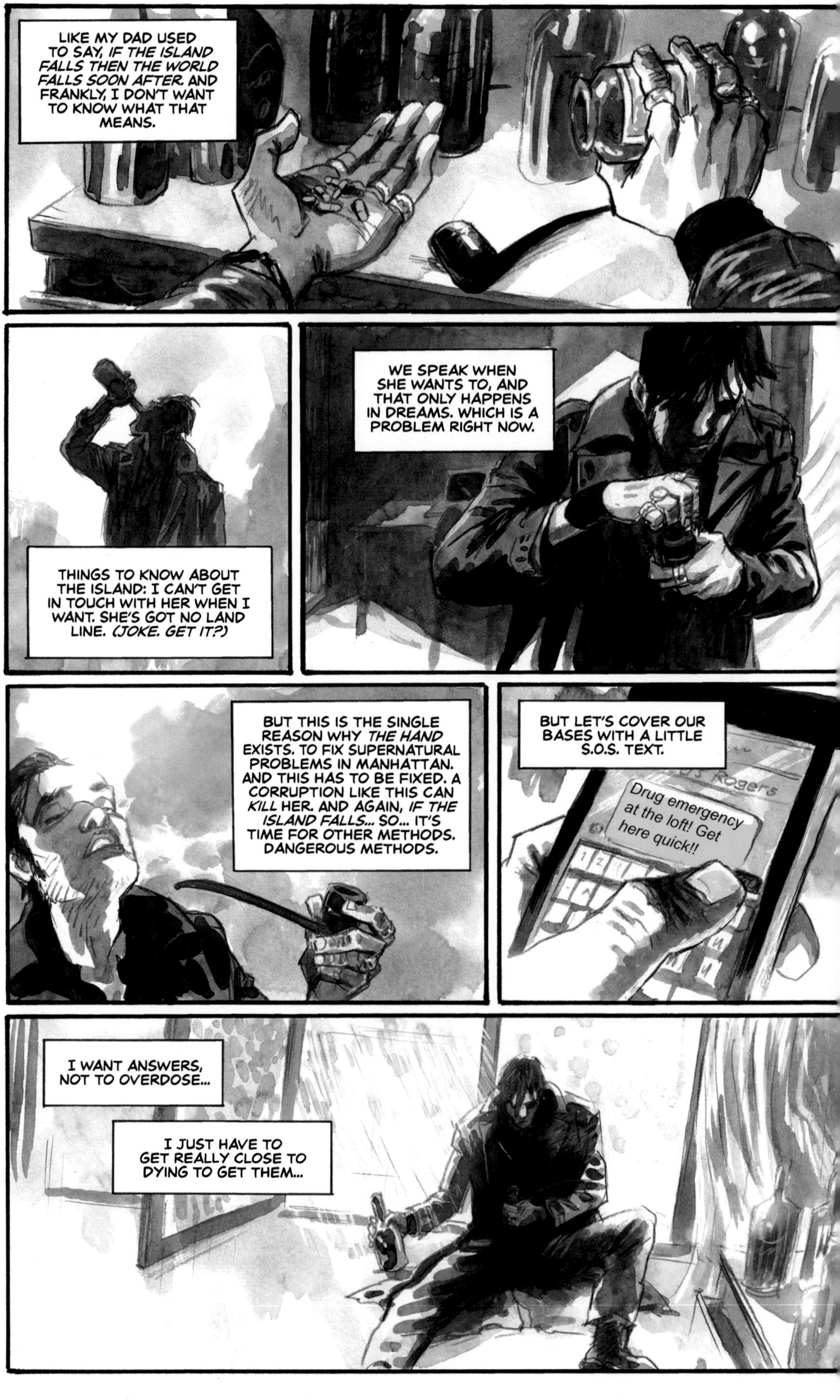
LIKE MY DAD USED TO SAY, *IF THE ISLAND FALLS THEN THE WORLD FALLS SOON AFTER.* AND FRANKLY, I DON'T WANT TO KNOW WHAT THAT MEANS.
THINGS TO KNOW ABOUT THE ISLAND: I CAN'T GET IN TOUCH WITH HER WHEN I WANT. SHE'S GOT NO LAND LINE. *(JOKE. GET IT?)*
WE SPEAK WHEN SHE WANTS TO, AND THAT ONLY HAPPENS IN DREAMS. WHICH IS A PROBLEM RIGHT NOW.
BUT THIS IS THE SINGLE REASON WHY *THE HAND* EXISTS. TO FIX SUPERNATURAL PROBLEMS IN MANHATTAN. AND THIS HAS TO BE FIXED. A CORRUPTION LIKE THIS CAN *KILL* HER. AND AGAIN, *IF THE ISLAND FALLS...* SO... IT'S TIME FOR OTHER METHODS. DANGEROUS METHODS.
BUT LET'S COVER OUR BASES WITH A LITTLE S.O.S. TEXT.
Drug emergency at the loft! Get here quick!!
I WANT ANSWERS, NOT TO OVERDOSE...
I JUST HAVE TO GET REALLY CLOSE TO DYING TO GET THEM...

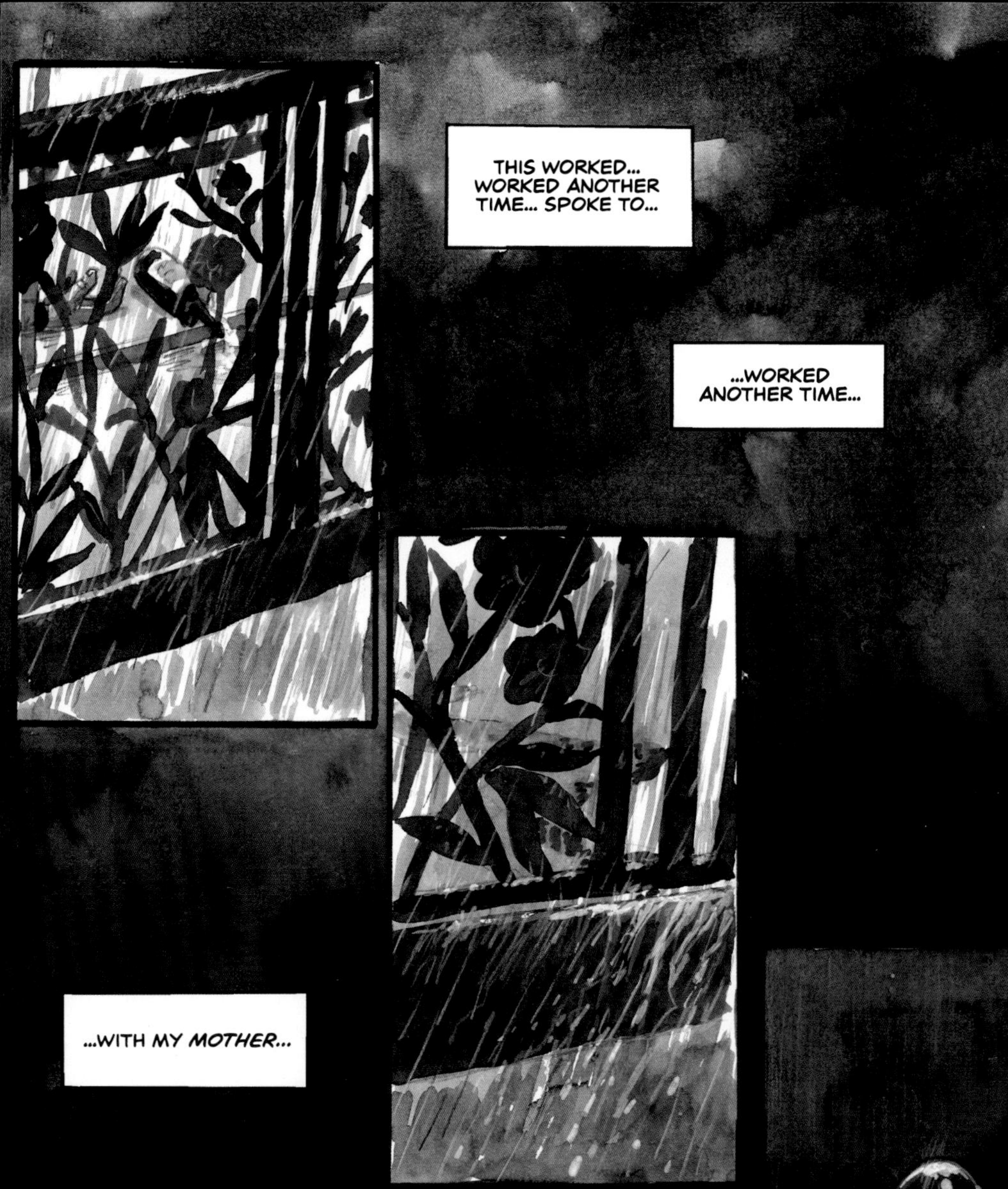
THIS WORKED... WORKED ANOTHER TIME... SPOKE TO...
...WORKED ANOTHER TIME...
...WITH MY *MOTHER*...

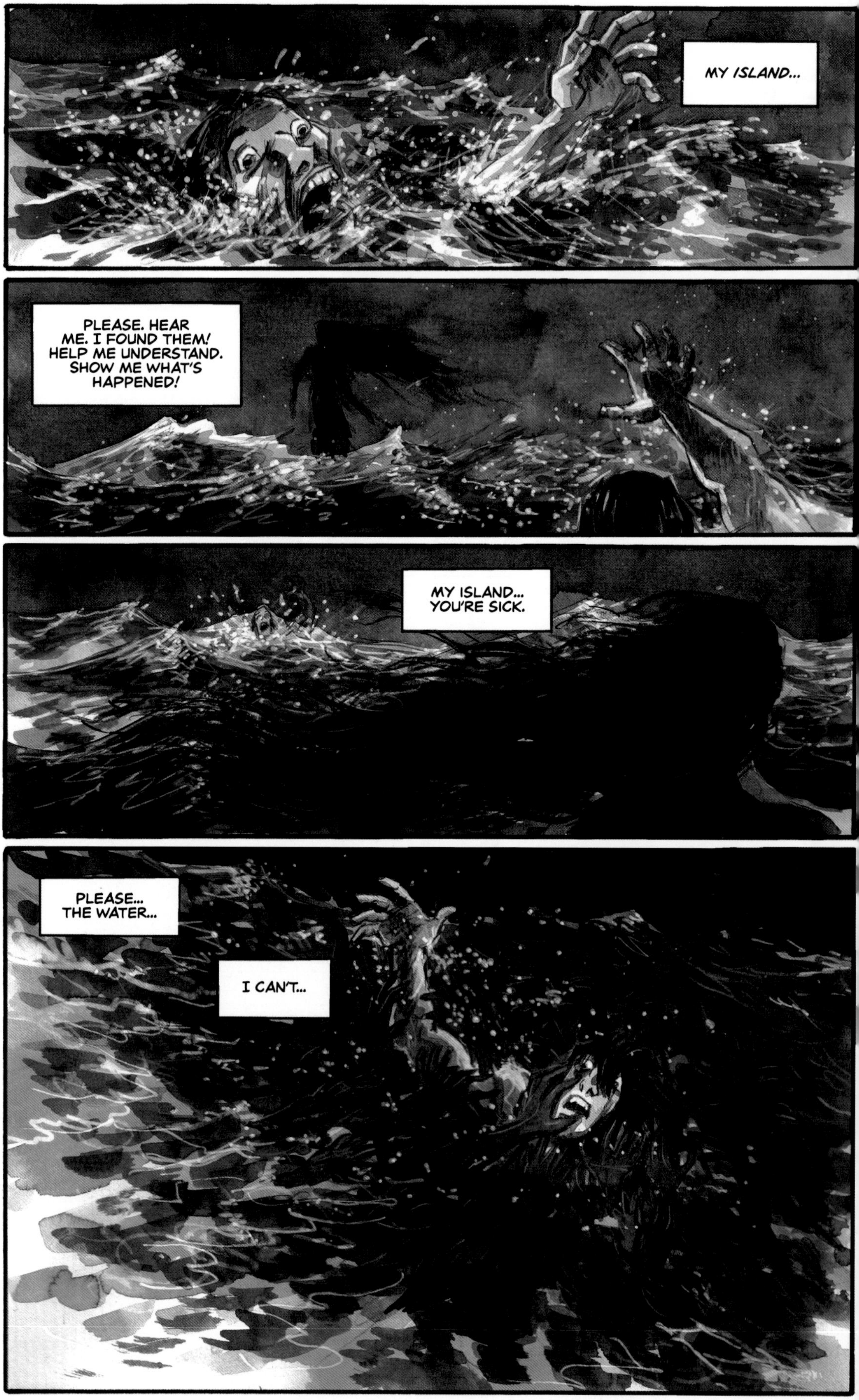
MY ISLAND...
PLEASE. HEAR ME. I FOUND THEM! HELP ME UNDERSTAND. SHOW ME WHAT'S HAPPENED!
MY ISLAND... YOU'RE SICK.
PLEASE... THE WATER...
I CAN'T...

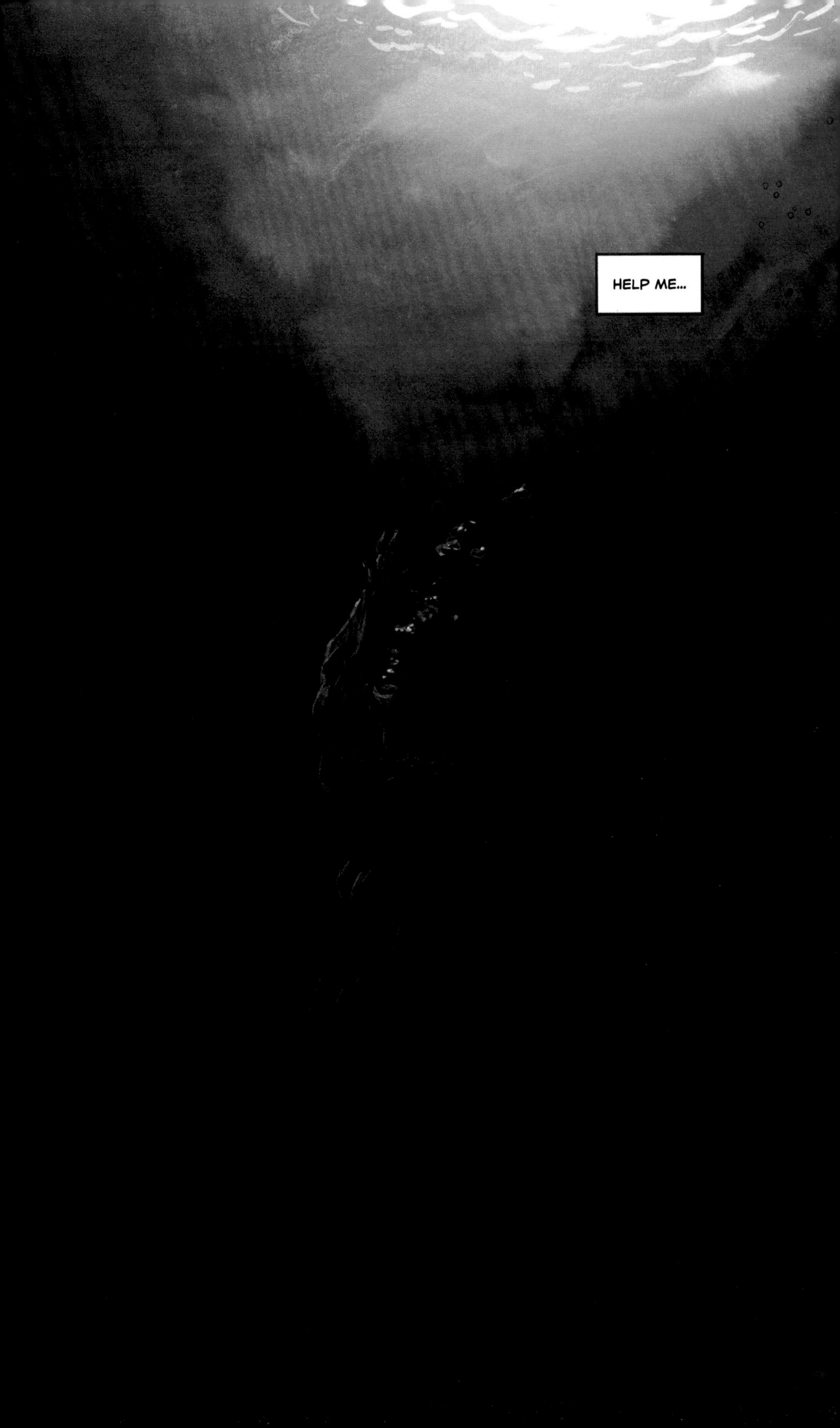

HELP ME...

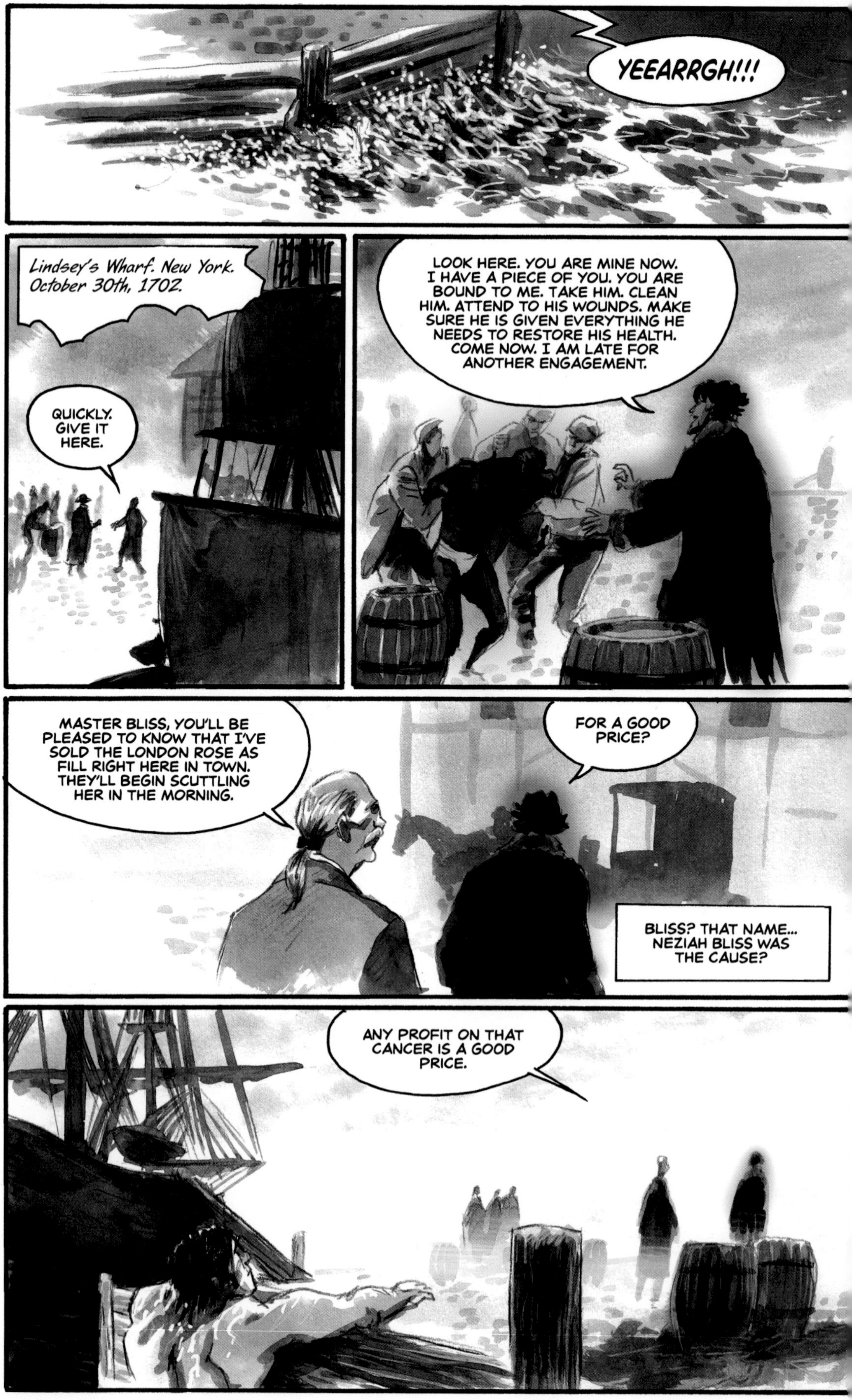

YEEARRGH!!!
Lindsey's Wharf. New York. October 30th, 1702.
QUICKLY. GIVE IT HERE.
LOOK HERE. YOU ARE MINE NOW. I HAVE A PIECE OF YOU. YOU ARE BOUND TO ME. TAKE HIM. CLEAN HIM. ATTEND TO HIS WOUNDS. MAKE SURE HE IS GIVEN EVERYTHING HE NEEDS TO RESTORE HIS HEALTH. COME NOW. I AM LATE FOR ANOTHER ENGAGEMENT.
MASTER BLISS, YOU'LL BE PLEASED TO KNOW THAT I'VE SOLD THE LONDON ROSE AS FILL RIGHT HERE IN TOWN. THEY'LL BEGIN SCUTTLING HER IN THE MORNING.
FOR A GOOD PRICE?
BLISS? THAT NAME... NEZIAH BLISS WAS THE CAUSE?
ANY PROFIT ON THAT CANCER IS A GOOD PRICE.

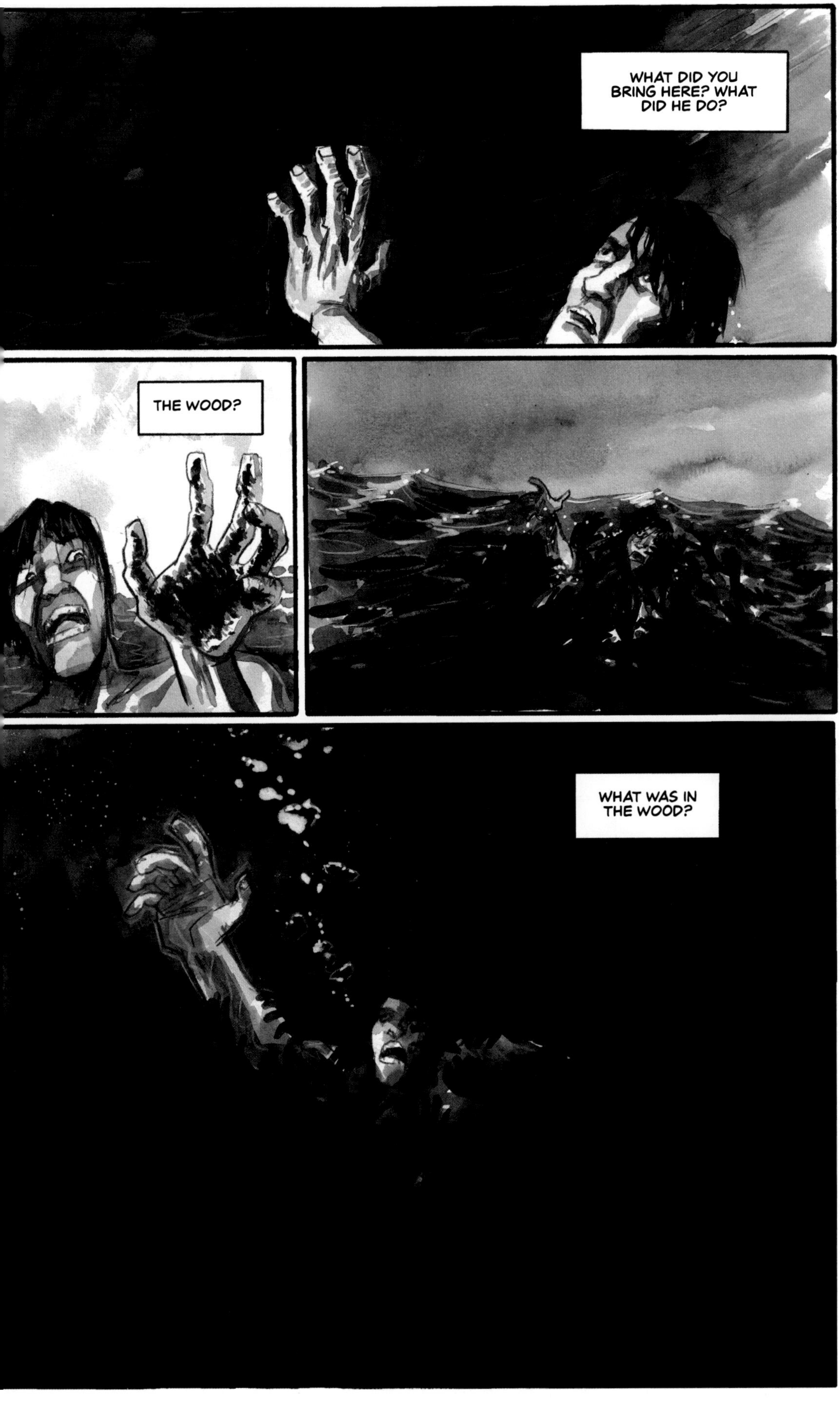
WHAT DID YOU BRING HERE? WHAT DID HE DO?
THE WOOD?
WHAT WAS IN THE WOOD?

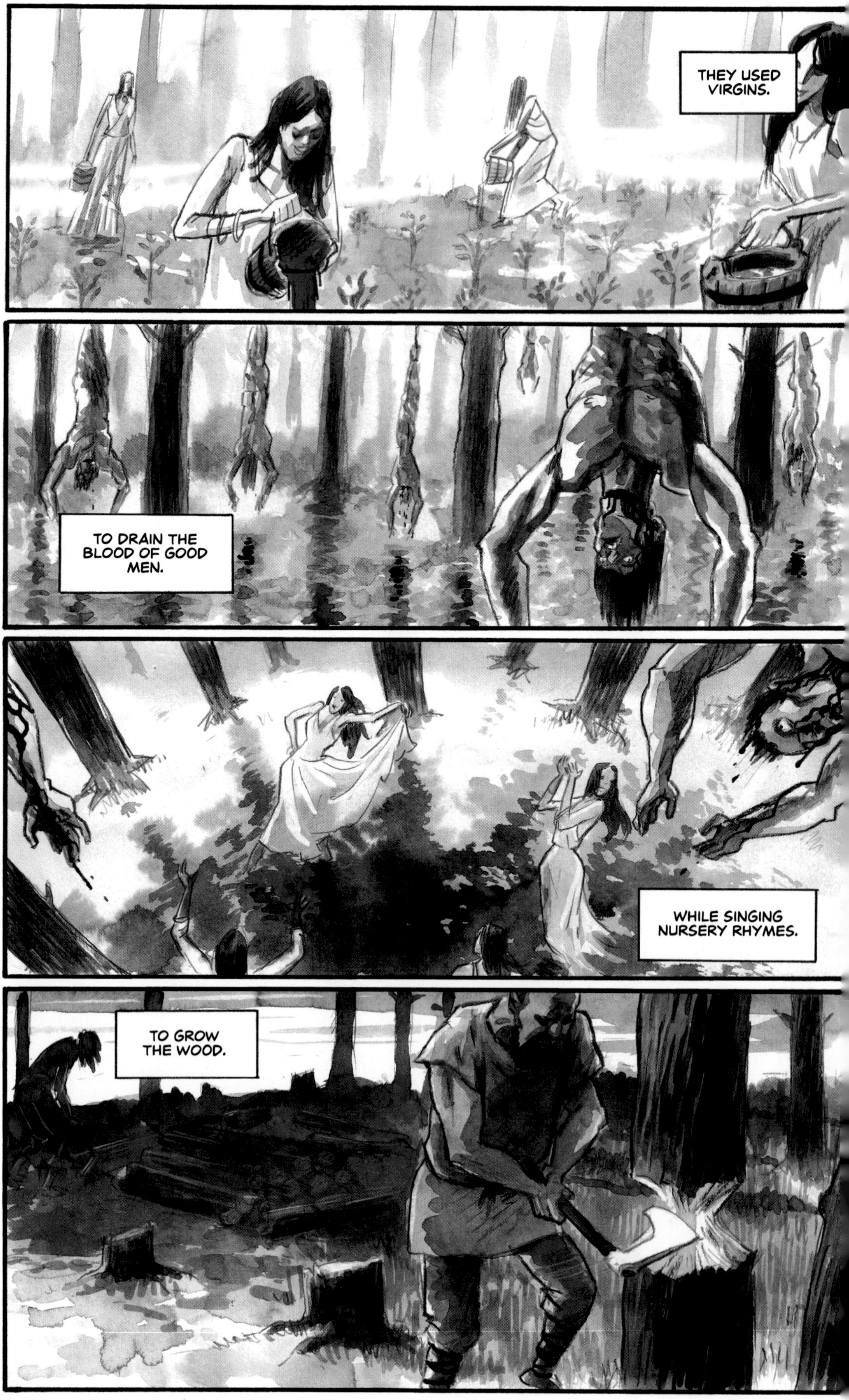
THEY USED VIRGINS.
TO DRAIN THE BLOOD OF GOOD MEN.
WHILE SINGING NURSERY RHYMES.
TO GROW THE WOOD.

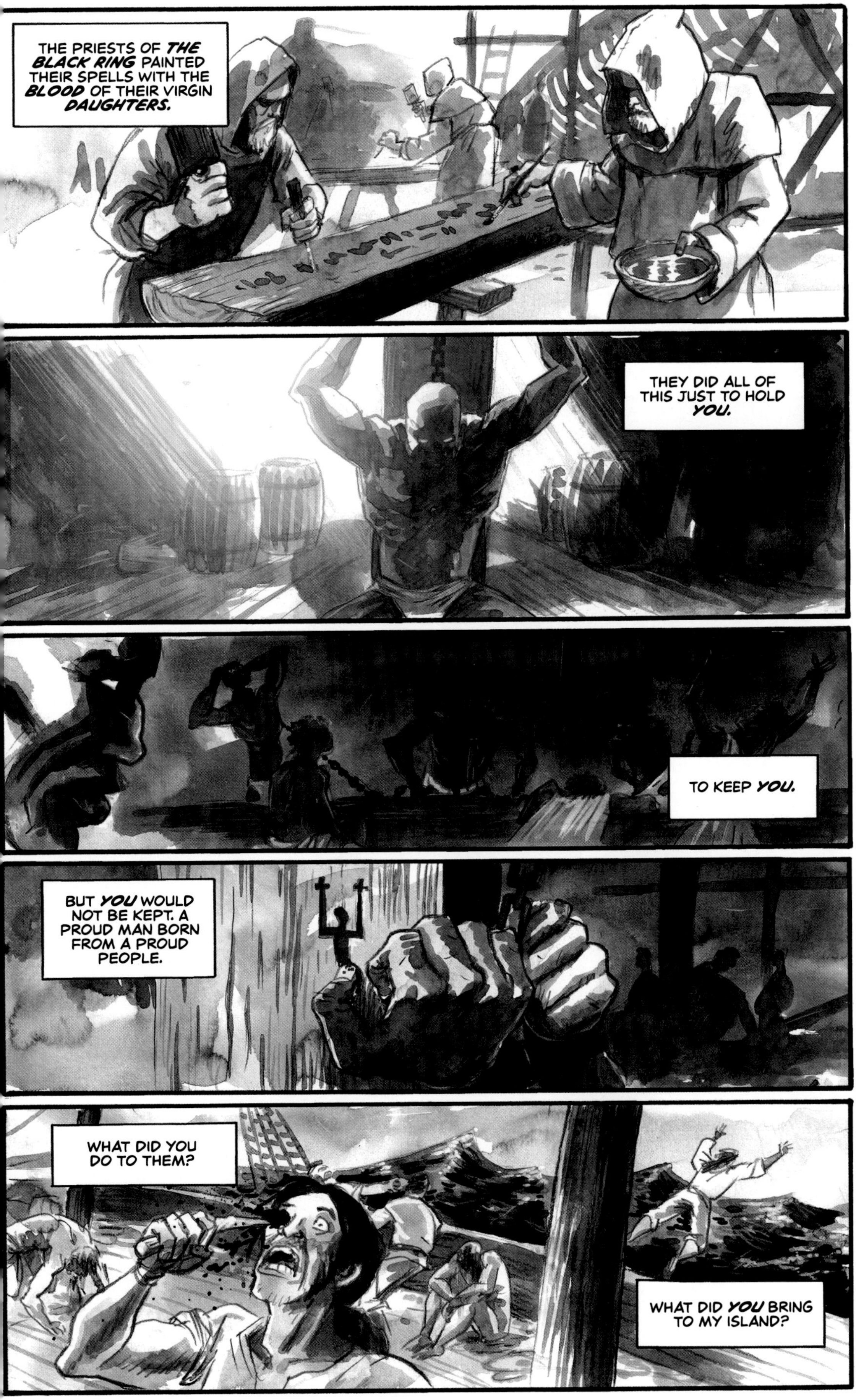
THE PRIESTS OF THE BLACK RING PAINTED THEIR SPELLS WITH THE BLOOD OF THEIR VIRGIN DAUGHTERS.
THEY DID ALL OF THIS JUST TO HOLD YOU.
TO KEEP YOU.
BUT YOU WOULD NOT BE KEPT. A PROUD MAN BORN FROM A PROUD PEOPLE.
WHAT DID YOU DO TO THEM?
WHAT DID YOU BRING TO MY ISLAND?

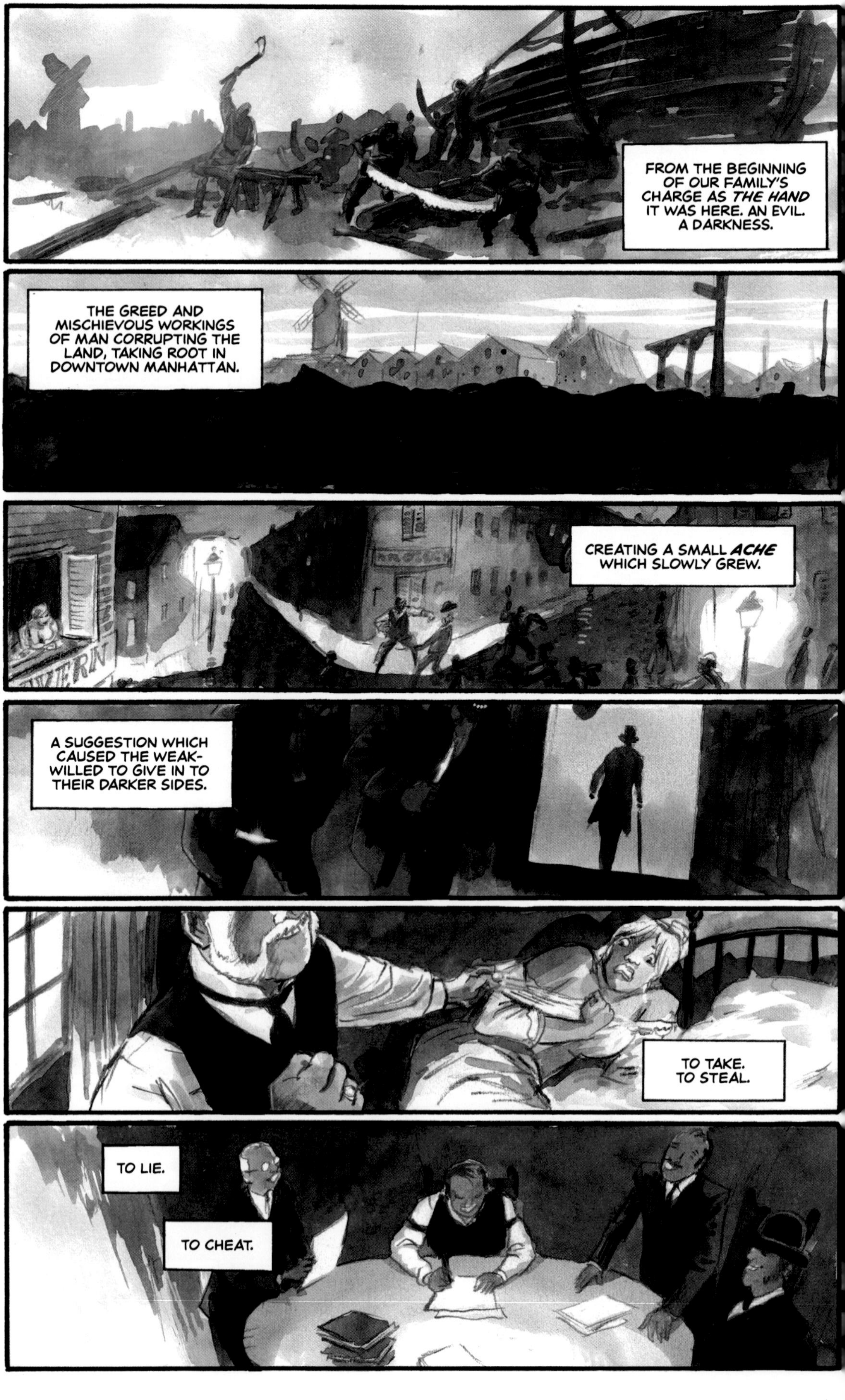

FROM THE BEGINNING OF OUR FAMILY'S CHARGE AS *THE HAND* IT WAS HERE. AN EVIL. A DARKNESS.
THE GREED AND MISCHIEVOUS WORKINGS OF MAN CORRUPTING THE LAND, TAKING ROOT IN DOWNTOWN MANHATTAN.
CREATING A SMALL ***ACHE*** WHICH SLOWLY GREW.
A SUGGESTION WHICH CAUSED THE WEAK-WILLED TO GIVE IN TO THEIR DARKER SIDES.
TO TAKE. TO STEAL.
TO LIE.
TO CHEAT.

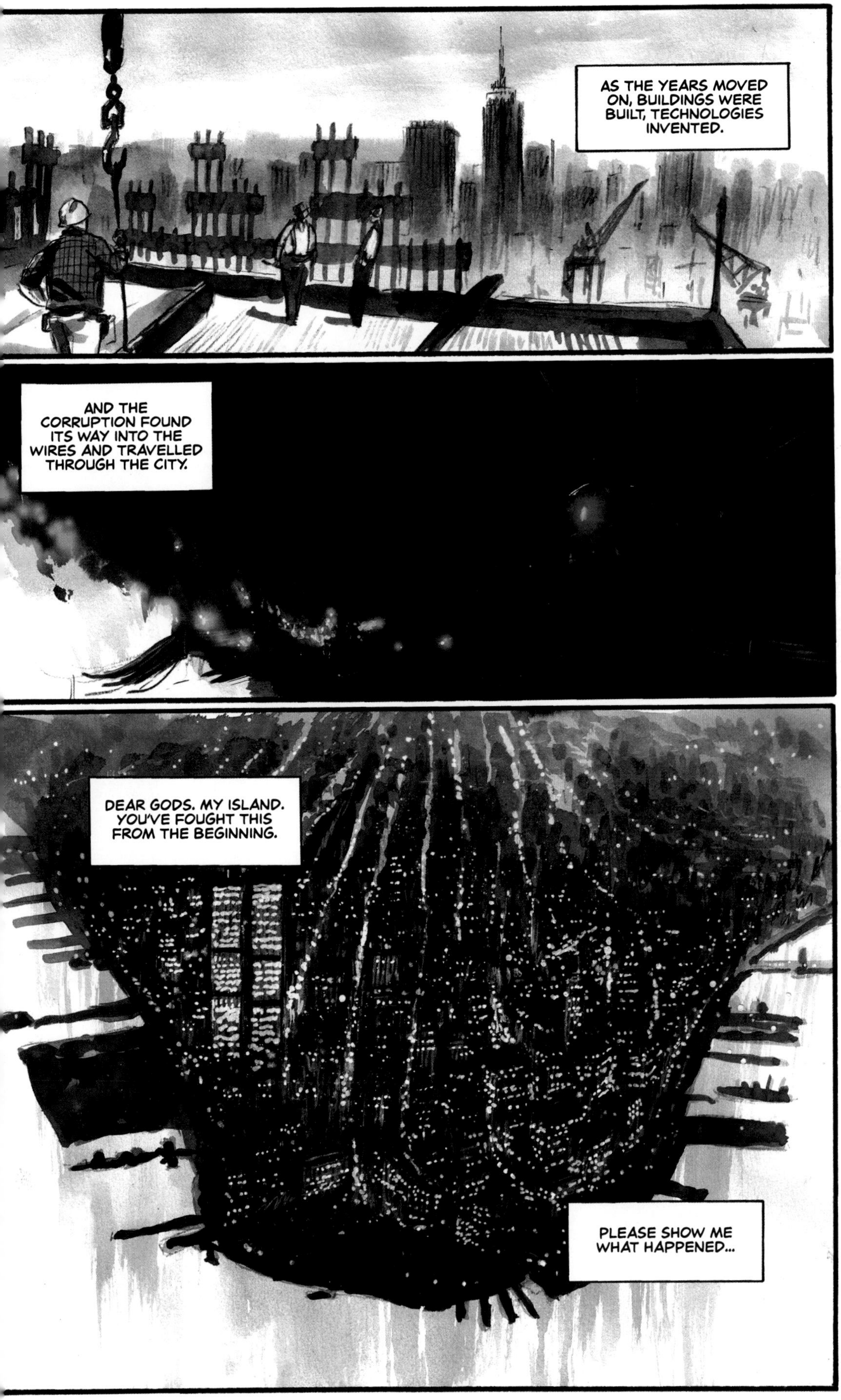
AS THE YEARS MOVED ON, BUILDINGS WERE BUILT, TECHNOLOGIES INVENTED.
AND THE CORRUPTION FOUND ITS WAY INTO THE WIRES AND TRAVELLED THROUGH THE CITY.
DEAR GODS. MY ISLAND. YOU'VE FOUGHT THIS FROM THE BEGINNING.
PLEASE SHOW ME WHAT HAPPENED...

October 15th, 1992.
8:15 P.M. CBGB Basement,
Manhattan.

Armory Item #26
"THE BOX OF LOST THINGS."
- Used to keep items safe in
a space in between.

NOW SAY THE WORDS TO YOURSELF.

HOLD ON. HOLD ON. THIS SPELL IS SUPPOSED TO KEEP US SAFE?

MORE THAN THAT. IT'LL GET US NOTICED. BUT YES, IF YOU EVER FIND YOURSELF IN A BAD SPOT THE PROTECTION PART OF THIS SPELL WILL HELP YOU.

SO, IF I'M GONNA GET MESSED UP, I MUMBLE YOUR MUMBO-JUMBO AND I WON'T GET MESSED UP?

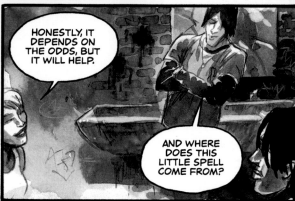

HONESTLY, IT DEPENDS ON THE ODDS, BUT IT WILL HELP.

AND WHERE DOES THIS LITTLE SPELL COME FROM?

BLOODY HELL, TOMMY. A GIRL DOESN'T GIVE AWAY HER SECRETS. AND YOU REALLY DON'T WANT TO KNOW ANYWAY, LUV.

AND YOU'RE GONNA PUT THE MAGIC BOX BEHIND THE TOILET?

NO. I'M GOING TO PUT THE SPELL INSIDE ONE OF TOMMY'S GRANDFATHER'S MAGIC BOXES. THEN PUT THAT IN A SOFT SPOT THAT OPENS BEHIND THE FILTHY TOILET.

Y'ALL ARE CRAZY.

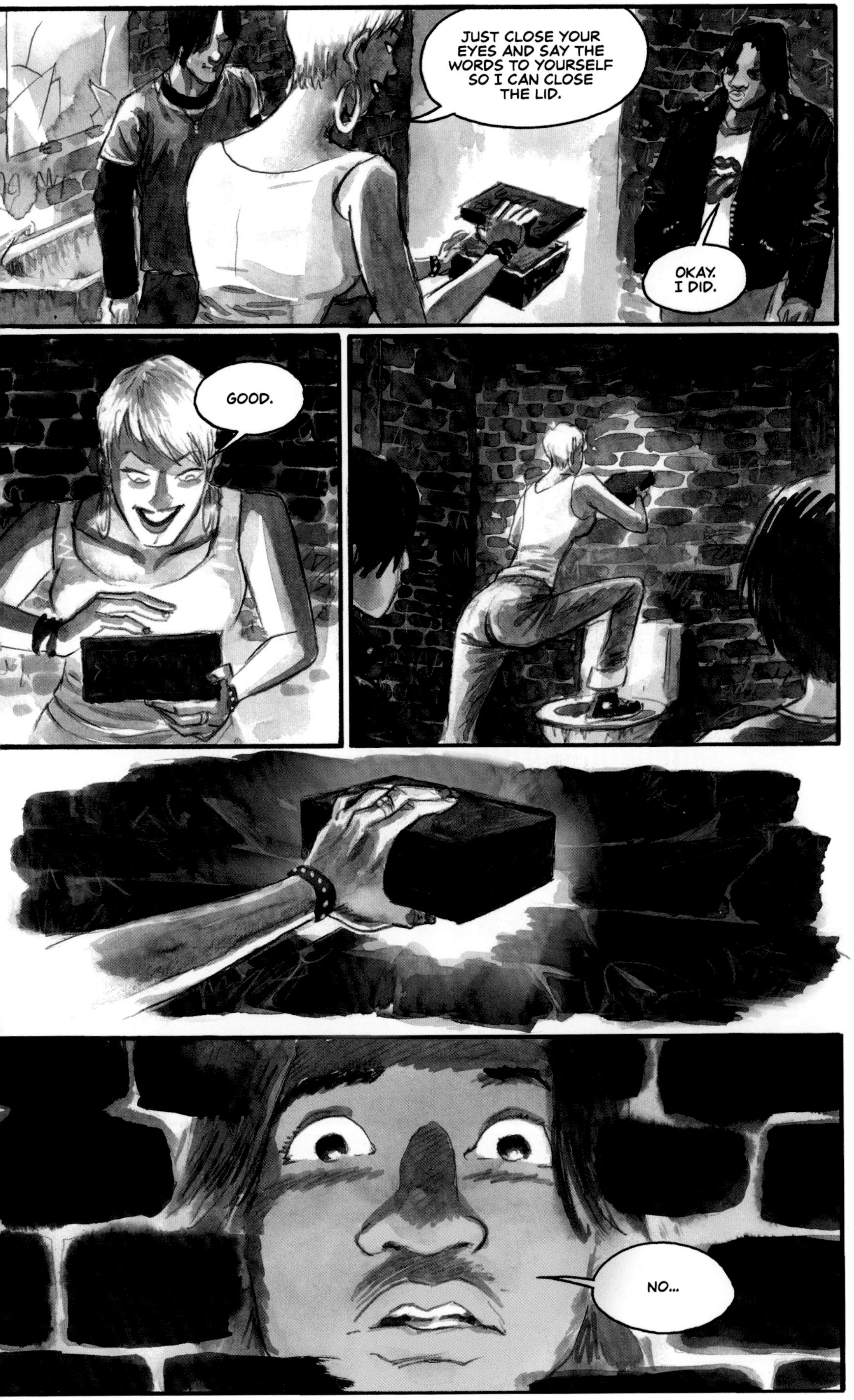
JUST CLOSE YOUR EYES AND SAY THE WORDS TO YOURSELF SO I CAN CLOSE THE LID.
OKAY. I DID.
GOOD.
NO...

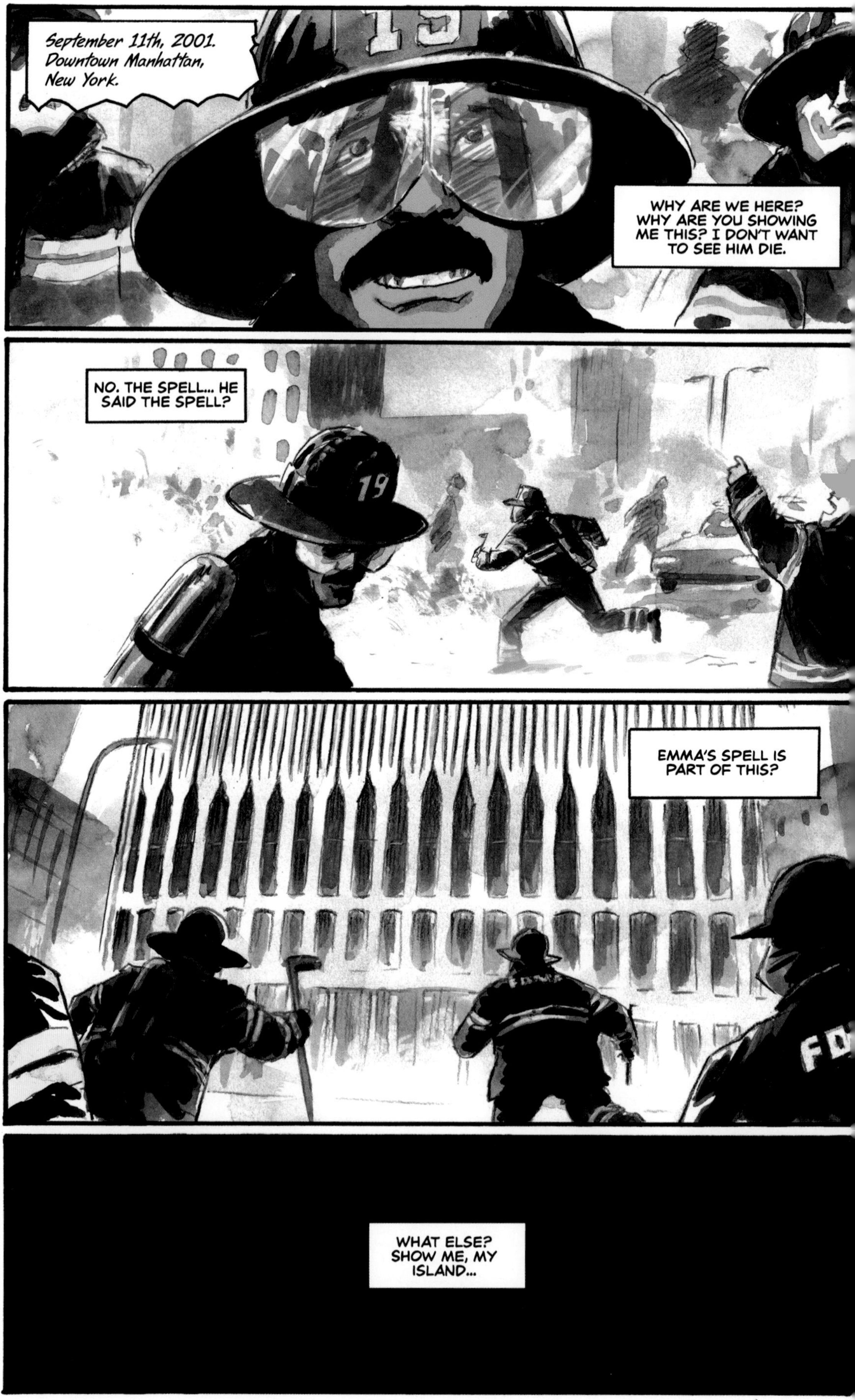
September 11th, 2001. Downtown Manhattan, New York.
WHY ARE WE HERE? WHY ARE YOU SHOWING ME THIS? I DON'T WANT TO SEE HIM DIE.
NO. THE SPELL... HE SAID THE SPELL?
EMMA'S SPELL IS PART OF THIS?
WHAT ELSE? SHOW ME, MY ISLAND...

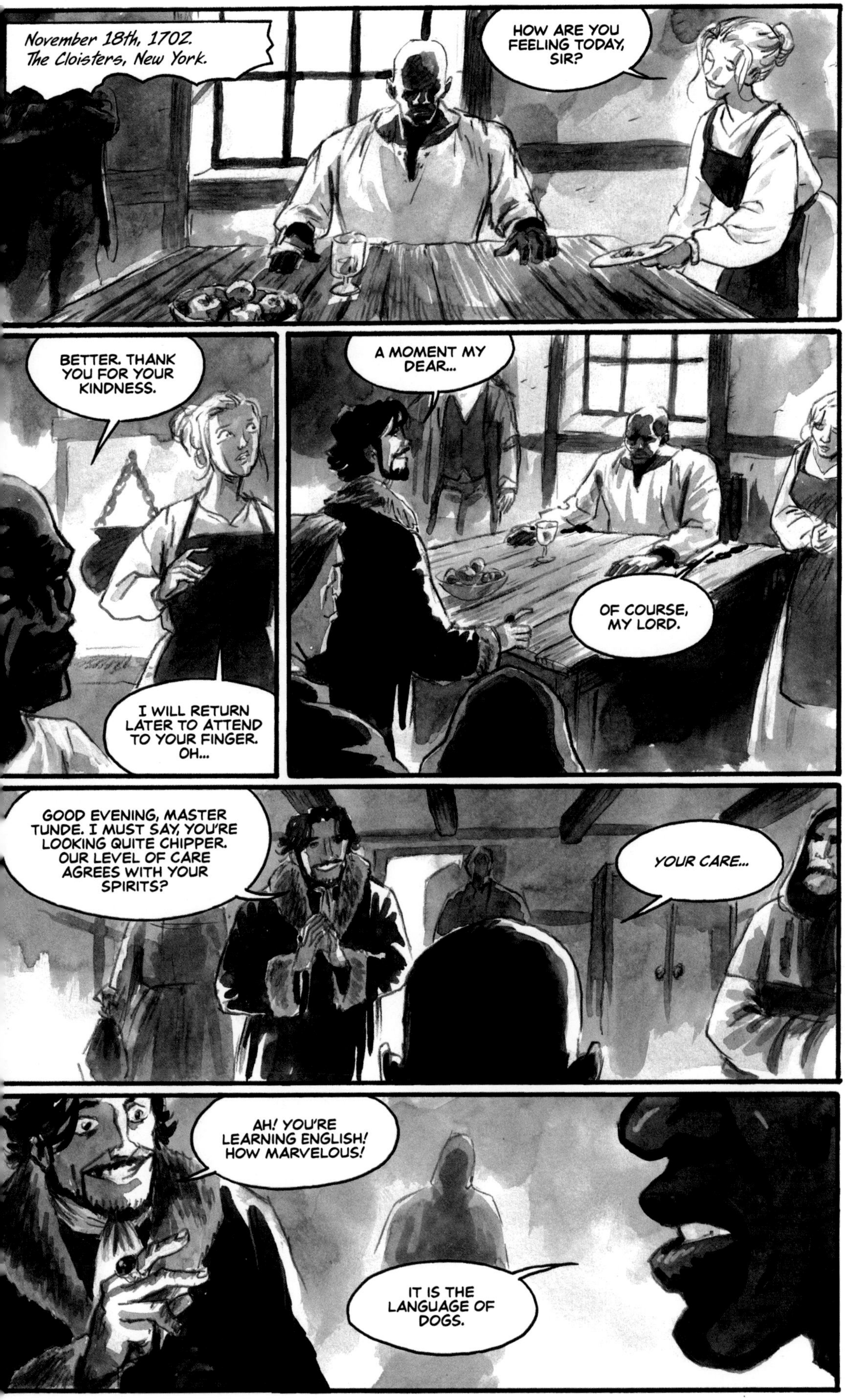
November 18th, 1702. The Cloisters, New York.
HOW ARE YOU FEELING TODAY, SIR?
BETTER. THANK YOU FOR YOUR KINDNESS.
I WILL RETURN LATER TO ATTEND TO YOUR FINGER. OH...
A MOMENT MY DEAR...
OF COURSE, MY LORD.
GOOD EVENING, MASTER TUNDE. I MUST SAY, YOU'RE LOOKING QUITE CHIPPER. OUR LEVEL OF CARE AGREES WITH YOUR SPIRITS?
YOUR CARE...
AH! YOU'RE LEARNING ENGLISH! HOW MARVELOUS!
IT IS THE LANGUAGE OF DOGS.

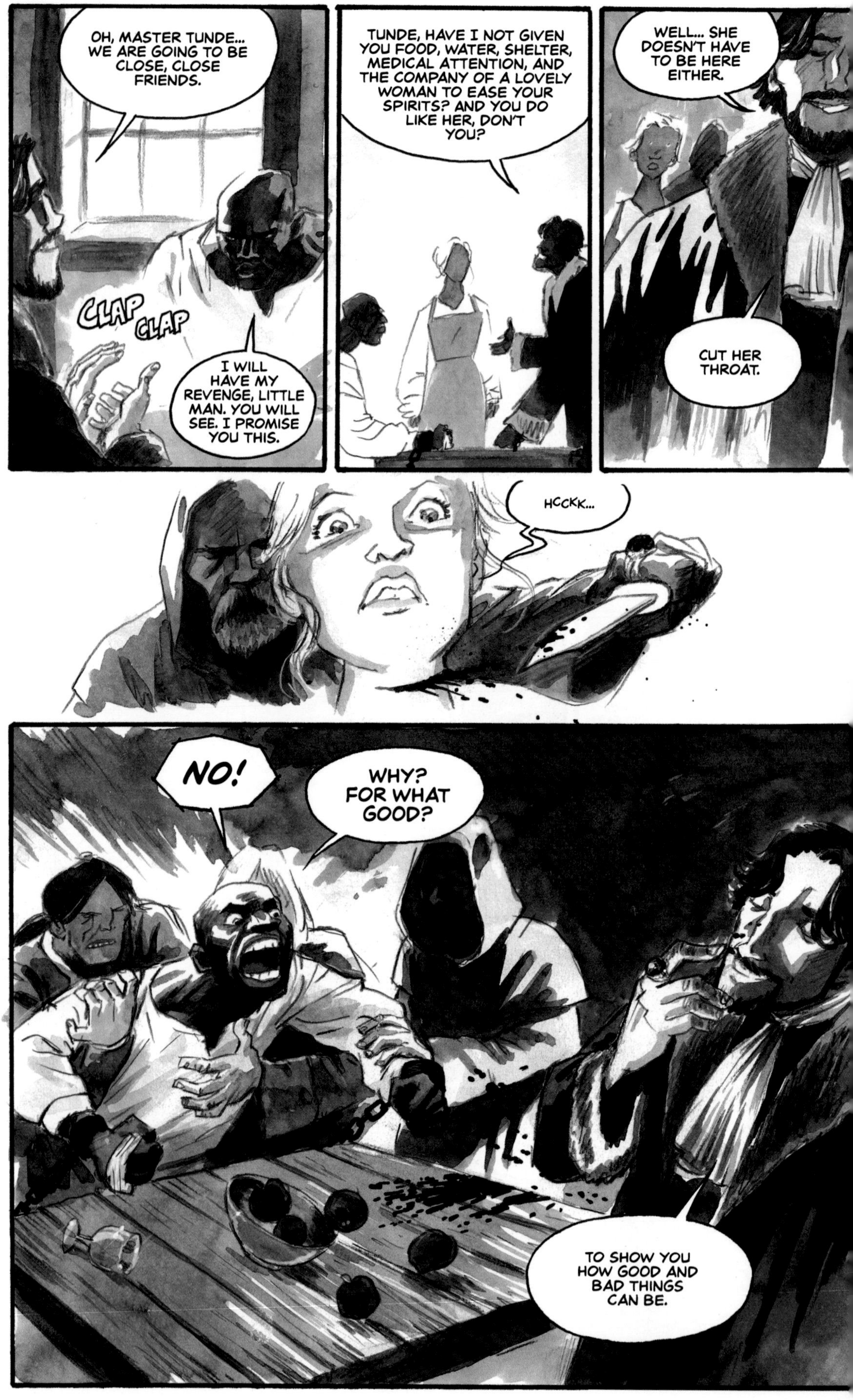
OH, MASTER TUNDE... WE ARE GOING TO BE CLOSE, CLOSE FRIENDS.
CLAP CLAP
I WILL HAVE MY REVENGE, LITTLE MAN. YOU WILL SEE. I PROMISE YOU THIS.
TUNDE, HAVE I NOT GIVEN YOU FOOD, WATER, SHELTER, MEDICAL ATTENTION, AND THE COMPANY OF A LOVELY WOMAN TO EASE YOUR SPIRITS? AND YOU DO LIKE HER, DON'T YOU?
WELL... SHE DOESN'T HAVE TO BE HERE EITHER.
CUT HER THROAT.
HCCKK...
NO!
WHY? FOR WHAT GOOD?
TO SHOW YOU HOW GOOD AND BAD THINGS CAN BE.

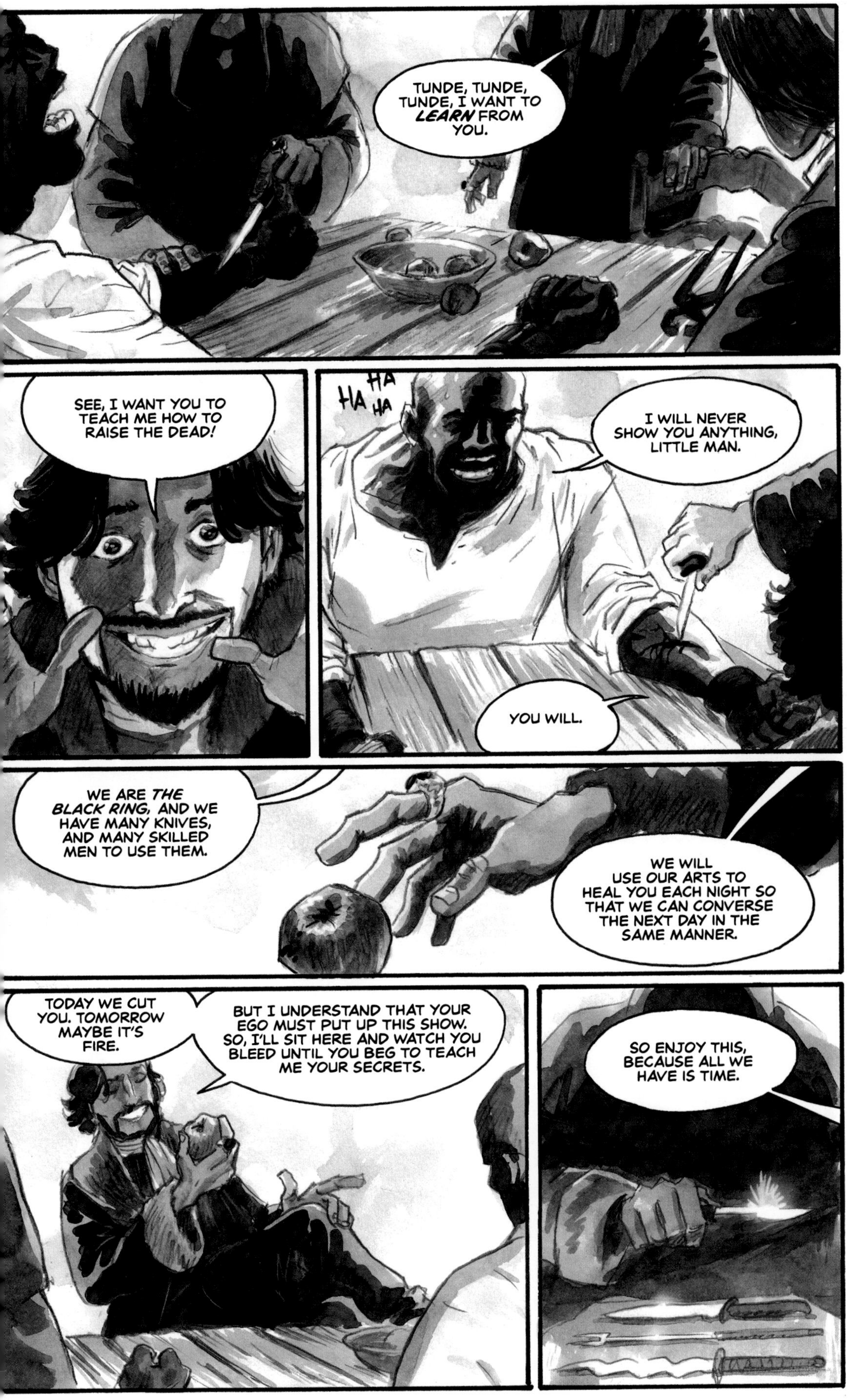
TUNDE, TUNDE, TUNDE, I WANT TO *LEARN* FROM YOU.
SEE, I WANT YOU TO TEACH ME HOW TO RAISE THE DEAD!
HA HA HA
I WILL NEVER SHOW YOU ANYTHING, LITTLE MAN.
YOU WILL.
WE ARE *THE BLACK RING,* AND WE HAVE MANY KNIVES, AND MANY SKILLED MEN TO USE THEM.
WE WILL USE OUR ARTS TO HEAL YOU EACH NIGHT SO THAT WE CAN CONVERSE THE NEXT DAY IN THE SAME MANNER.
TODAY WE CUT YOU. TOMORROW MAYBE IT'S FIRE.
BUT I UNDERSTAND THAT YOUR EGO MUST PUT UP THIS SHOW. SO, I'LL SIT HERE AND WATCH YOU BLEED UNTIL YOU BEG TO TEACH ME YOUR SECRETS.
SO ENJOY THIS, BECAUSE ALL WE HAVE IS TIME.

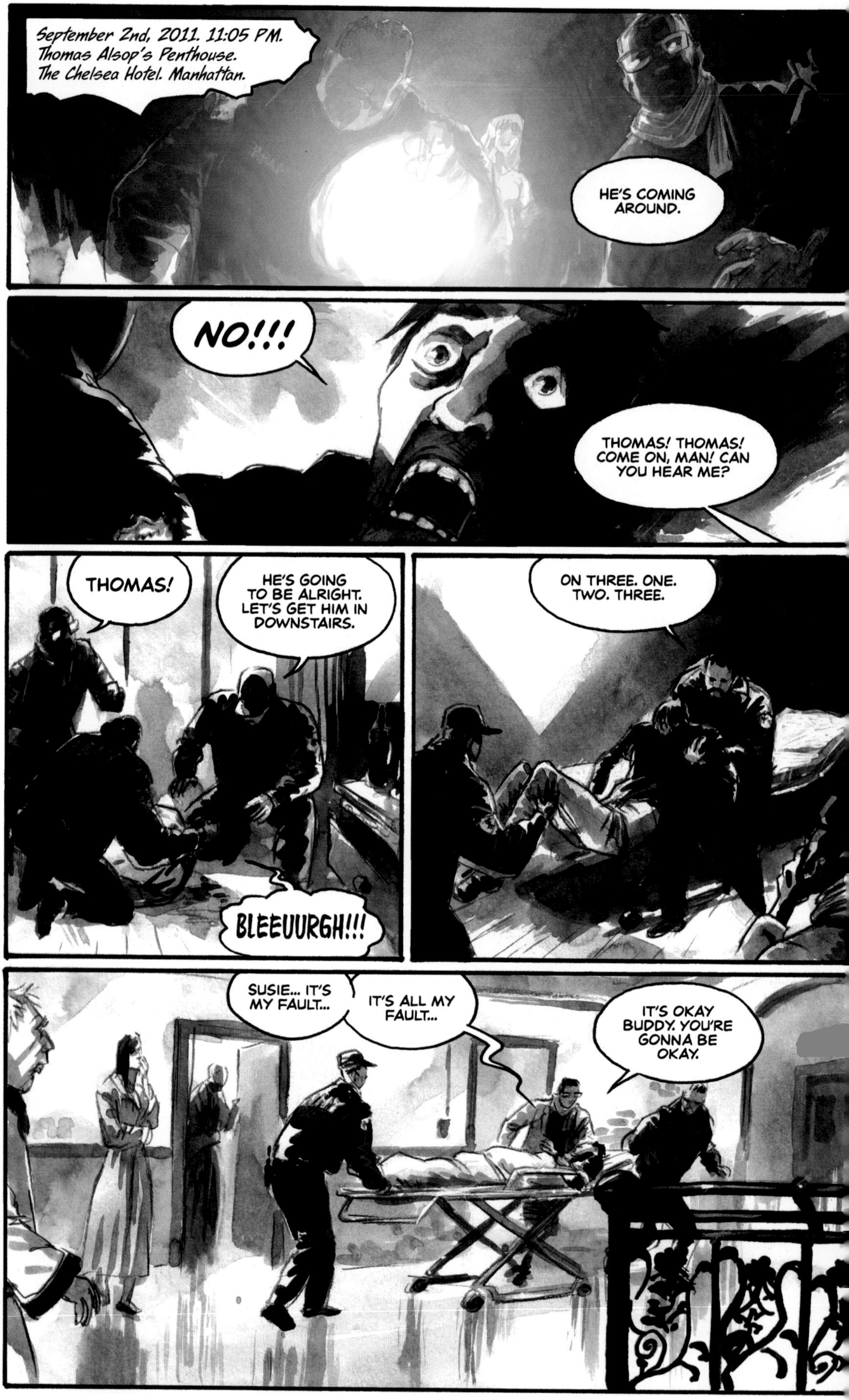
September 2nd, 2011. 11:05 PM. Thomas Alsop's Penthouse. The Chelsea Hotel. Manhattan.
HE'S COMING AROUND.
NO!!!
THOMAS! THOMAS! COME ON, MAN! CAN YOU HEAR ME?
THOMAS!
HE'S GOING TO BE ALRIGHT. LET'S GET HIM IN DOWNSTAIRS.
BLEEUURGH!!!
ON THREE. ONE. TWO. THREE.
SUSIE... IT'S MY FAULT...
IT'S ALL MY FAULT...
IT'S OKAY BUDDY. YOU'RE GONNA BE OKAY.

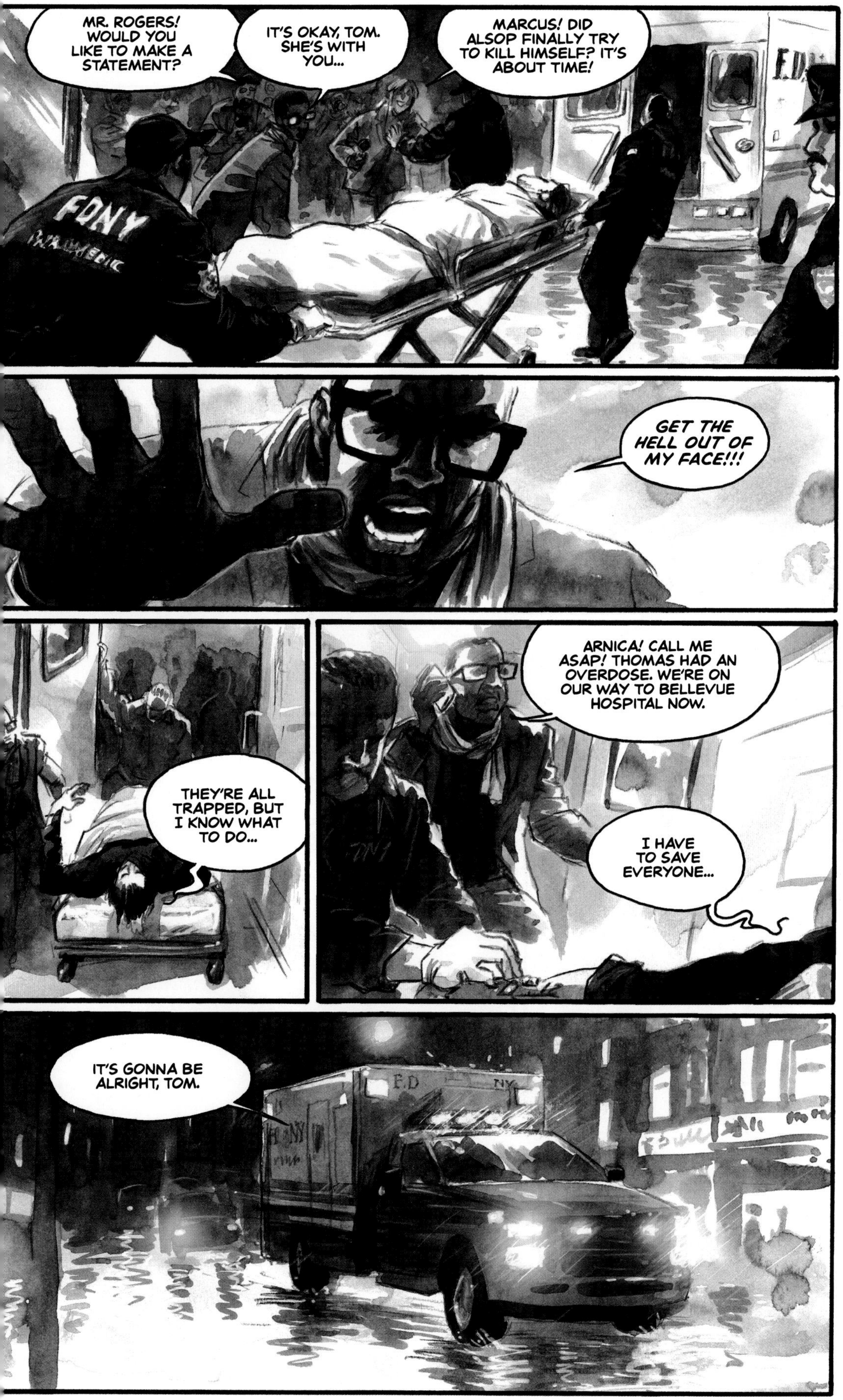
MR. ROGERS! WOULD YOU LIKE TO MAKE A STATEMENT?
IT'S OKAY, TOM. SHE'S WITH YOU...
MARCUS! DID ALSOP FINALLY TRY TO KILL HIMSELF? IT'S ABOUT TIME!
FDNY
GET THE HELL OUT OF MY FACE!!!
THEY'RE ALL TRAPPED, BUT I KNOW WHAT TO DO...
ARNICA! CALL ME ASAP! THOMAS HAD AN OVERDOSE. WE'RE ON OUR WAY TO BELLEVUE HOSPITAL NOW.
I HAVE TO SAVE EVERYONE...
IT'S GONNA BE ALRIGHT, TOM.

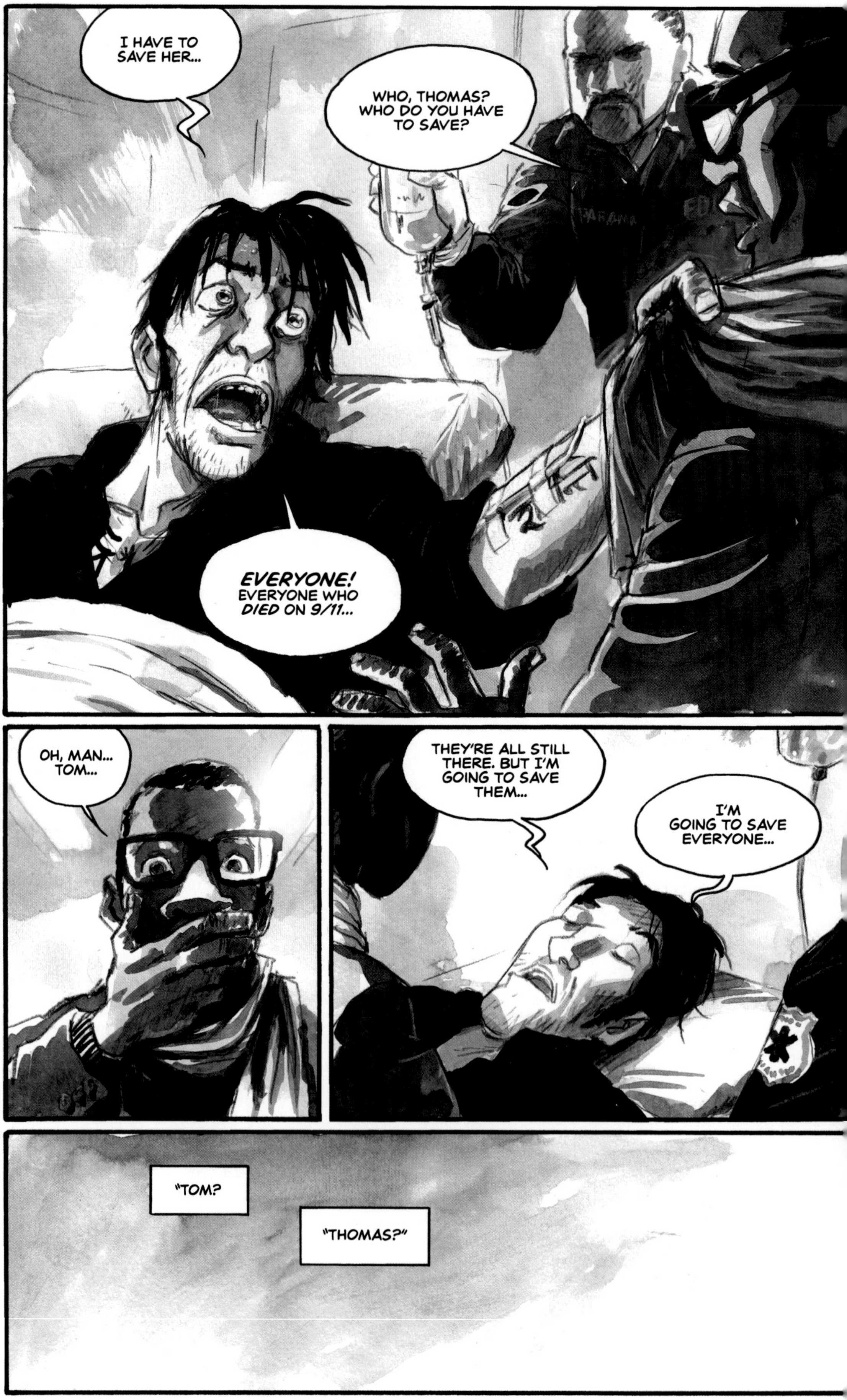

I HAVE TO SAVE HER...
WHO, THOMAS? WHO DO YOU HAVE TO SAVE?
EVERYONE! EVERYONE WHO DIED ON 9/11...
OH, MAN... TOM...
THEY'RE ALL STILL THERE. BUT I'M GOING TO SAVE THEM...
I'M GOING TO SAVE EVERYONE...
"TOM?
"THOMAS?"

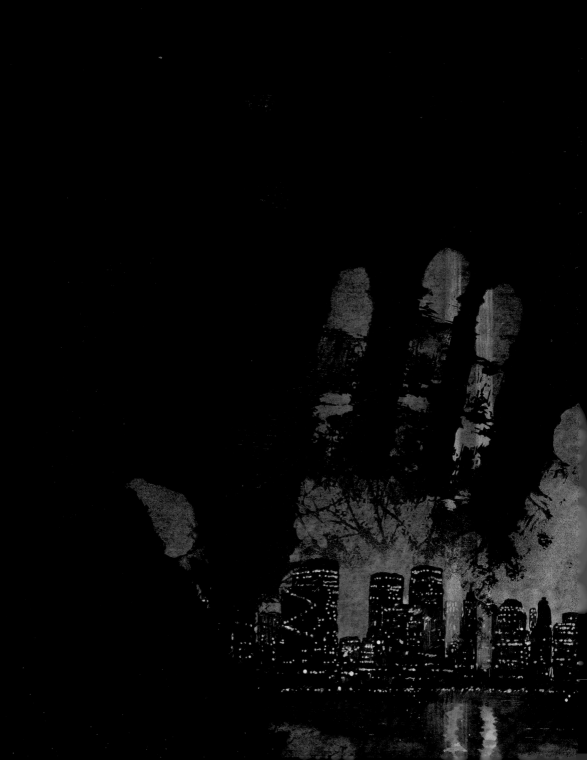

CHAPTER FOUR
ROCK AND ROLL MAGIC

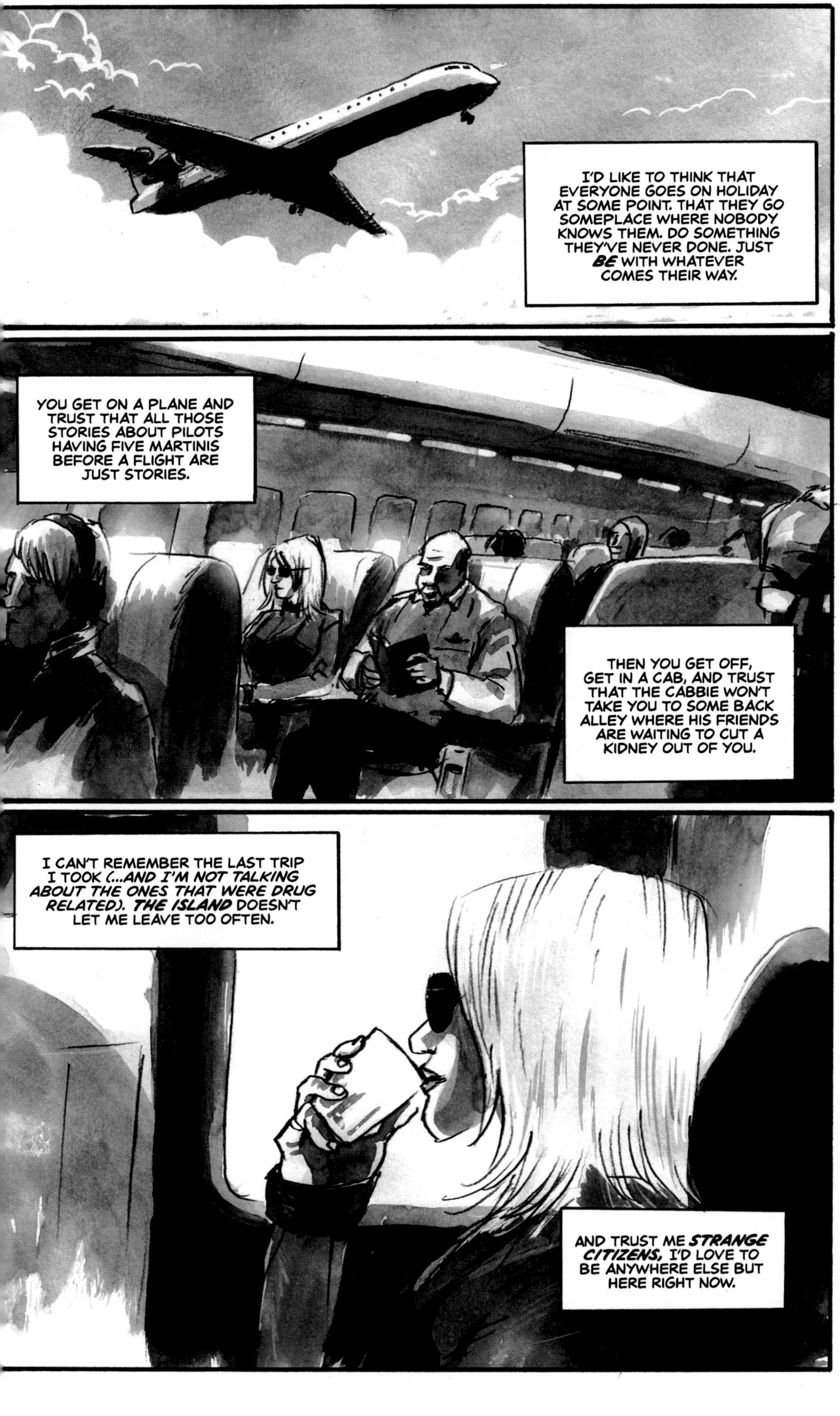
I'D LIKE TO THINK THAT EVERYONE GOES ON HOLIDAY AT SOME POINT. THAT THEY GO SOMEPLACE WHERE NOBODY KNOWS THEM. DO SOMETHING THEY'VE NEVER DONE. JUST ***BE*** WITH WHATEVER COMES THEIR WAY.
YOU GET ON A PLANE AND TRUST THAT ALL THOSE STORIES ABOUT PILOTS HAVING FIVE MARTINIS BEFORE A FLIGHT ARE JUST STORIES.
THEN YOU GET OFF, GET IN A CAB, AND TRUST THAT THE CABBIE WON'T TAKE YOU TO SOME BACK ALLEY WHERE HIS FRIENDS ARE WAITING TO CUT A KIDNEY OUT OF YOU.
I CAN'T REMEMBER THE LAST TRIP I TOOK *(...AND I'M NOT TALKING ABOUT THE ONES THAT WERE DRUG RELATED)*. ***THE ISLAND*** DOESN'T LET ME LEAVE TOO OFTEN.
AND TRUST ME ***STRANGE CITIZENS,*** I'D LOVE TO BE ANYWHERE ELSE BUT HERE RIGHT NOW.

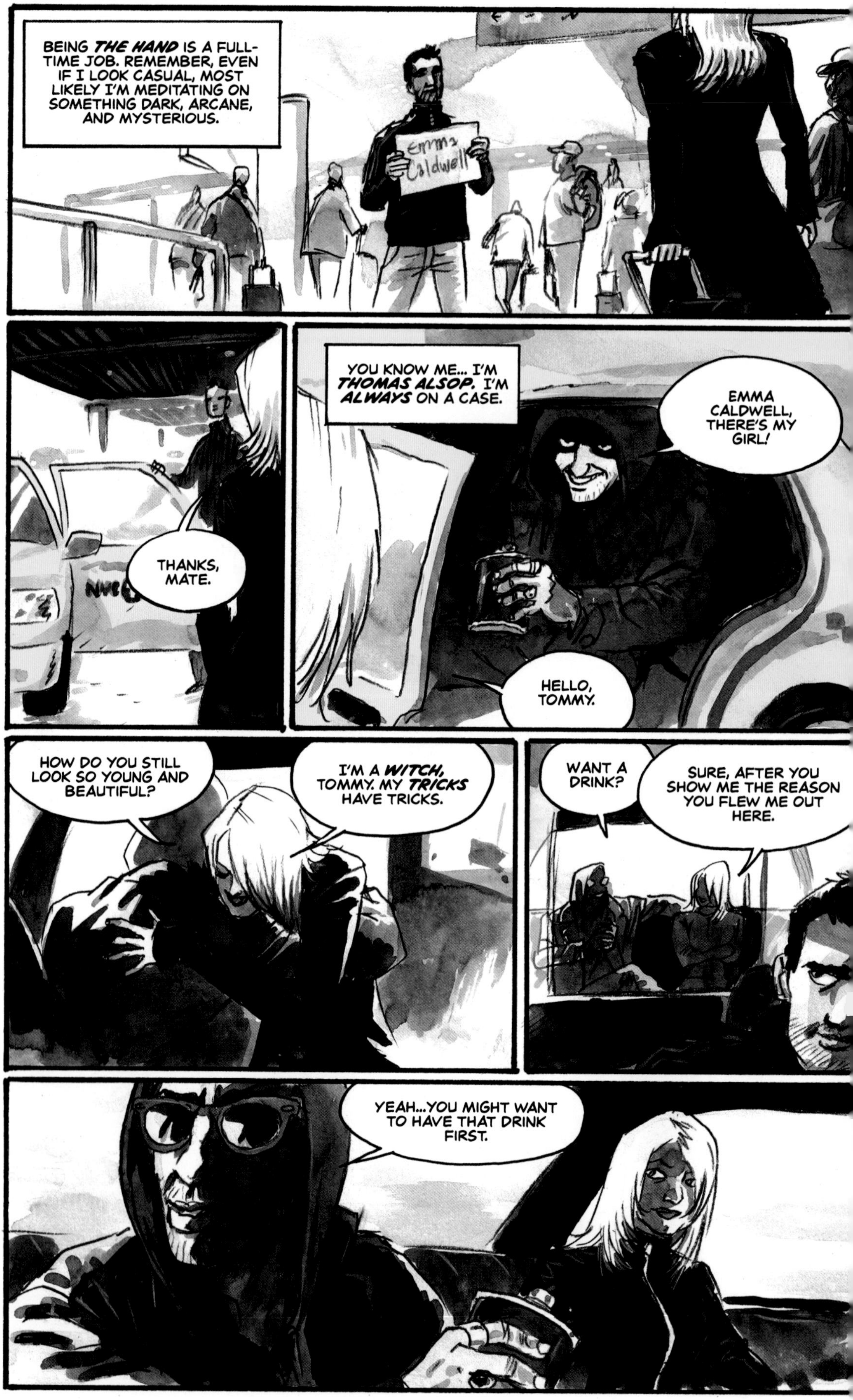
BEING THE HAND IS A FULL-TIME JOB. REMEMBER, EVEN IF I LOOK CASUAL, MOST LIKELY I'M MEDITATING ON SOMETHING DARK, ARCANE, AND MYSTERIOUS.
Emma Caldwell
THANKS, MATE.
YOU KNOW ME... I'M THOMAS ALSOP. I'M ALWAYS ON A CASE.
EMMA CALDWELL, THERE'S MY GIRL!
HELLO, TOMMY.
HOW DO YOU STILL LOOK SO YOUNG AND BEAUTIFUL?
I'M A WITCH, TOMMY. MY TRICKS HAVE TRICKS.
WANT A DRINK?
SURE, AFTER YOU SHOW ME THE REASON YOU FLEW ME OUT HERE.
YEAH...YOU MIGHT WANT TO HAVE THAT DRINK FIRST.

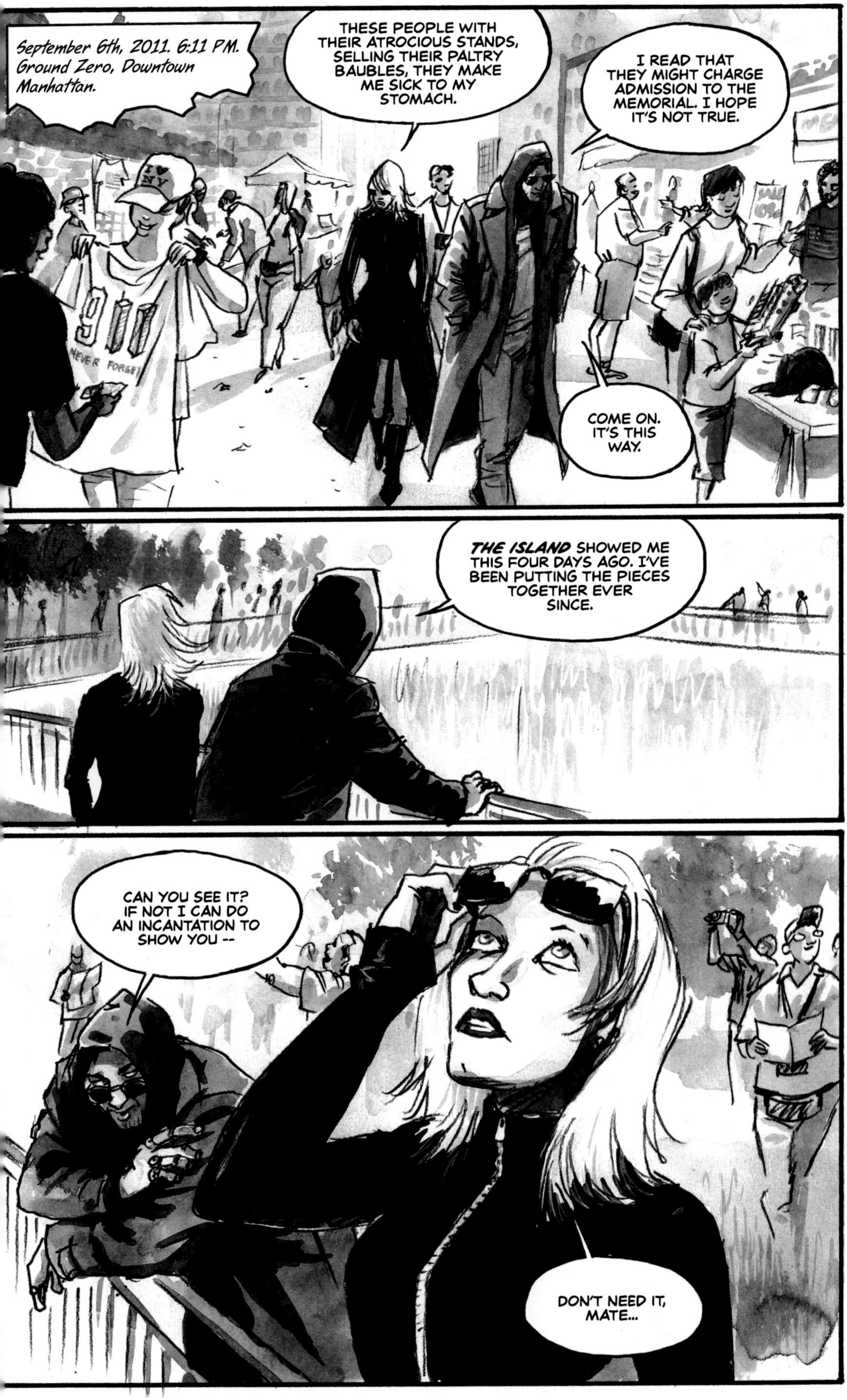
September 6th, 2011. 6:11 PM. Ground Zero, Downtown Manhattan.
THESE PEOPLE WITH THEIR ATROCIOUS STANDS, SELLING THEIR PALTRY BAUBLES, THEY MAKE ME SICK TO MY STOMACH.
I READ THAT THEY MIGHT CHARGE ADMISSION TO THE MEMORIAL. I HOPE IT'S NOT TRUE.
COME ON. IT'S THIS WAY.
I ♥ NY
911
NEVER FORGET
THE ISLAND SHOWED ME THIS FOUR DAYS AGO. I'VE BEEN PUTTING THE PIECES TOGETHER EVER SINCE.
CAN YOU SEE IT? IF NOT I CAN DO AN INCANTATION TO SHOW YOU --
DON'T NEED IT, MATE...

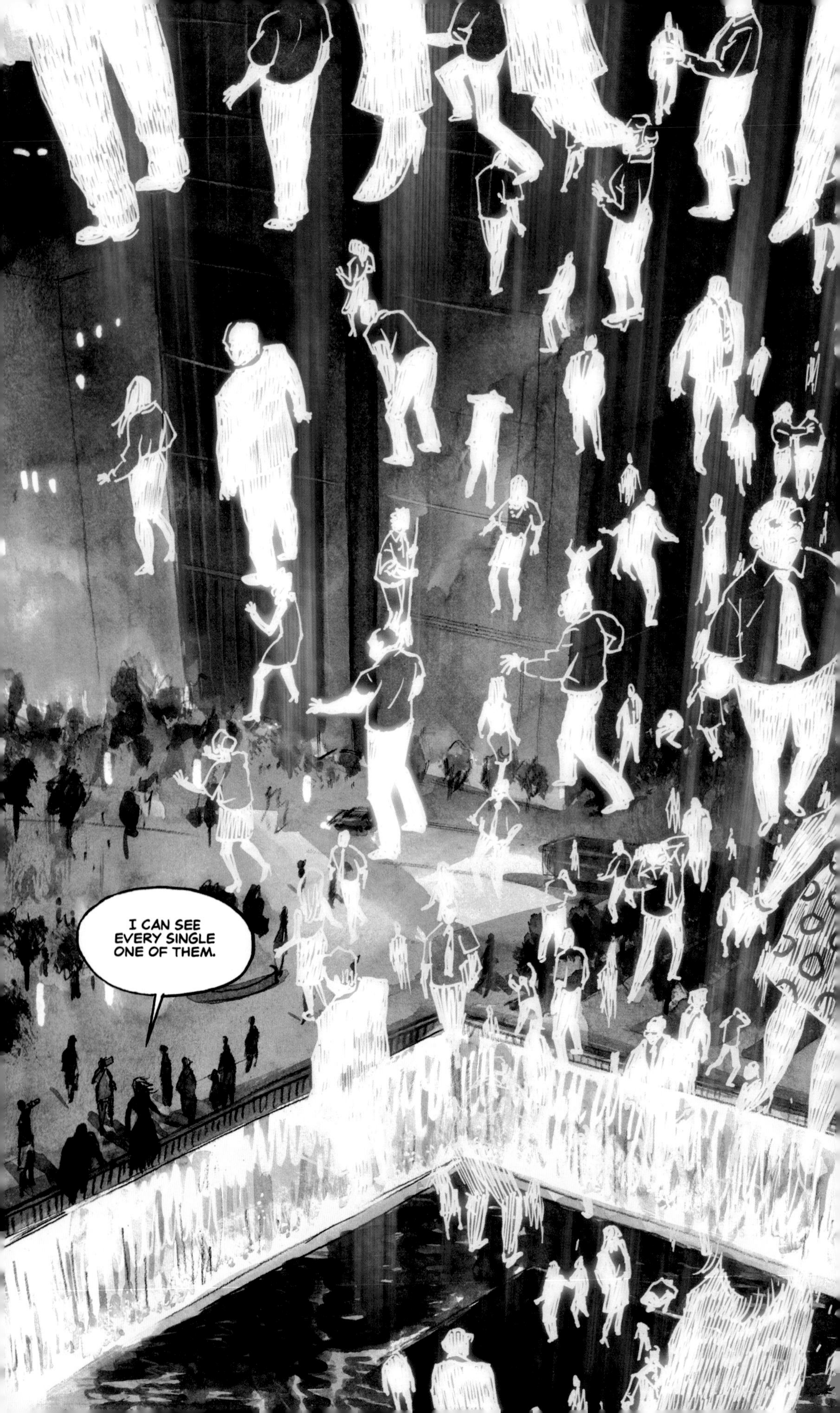
I CAN SEE EVERY SINGLE ONE OF THEM.

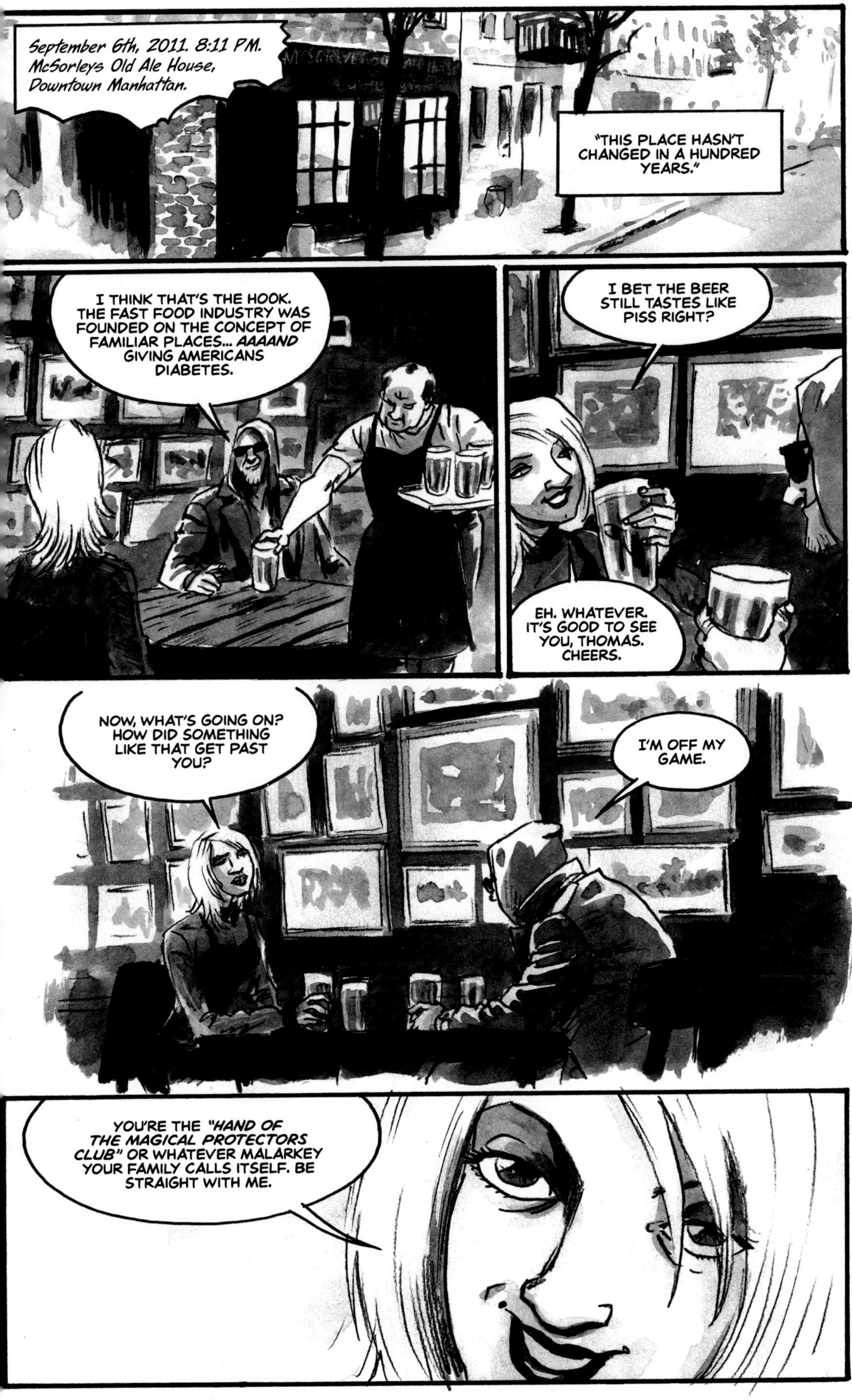
September 6th, 2011. 8:11 PM. McSorleys Old Ale House, Downtown Manhattan.
"THIS PLACE HASN'T CHANGED IN A HUNDRED YEARS."
I THINK THAT'S THE HOOK. THE FAST FOOD INDUSTRY WAS FOUNDED ON THE CONCEPT OF FAMILIAR PLACES... *AAAAND* GIVING AMERICANS DIABETES.
I BET THE BEER STILL TASTES LIKE PISS RIGHT?
EH. WHATEVER. IT'S GOOD TO SEE YOU, THOMAS. CHEERS.
NOW, WHAT'S GOING ON? HOW DID SOMETHING LIKE THAT GET PAST YOU?
I'M OFF MY GAME.
YOU'RE THE *"HAND OF THE MAGICAL PROTECTORS CLUB"* OR WHATEVER MALARKEY YOUR FAMILY CALLS ITSELF. BE STRAIGHT WITH ME.

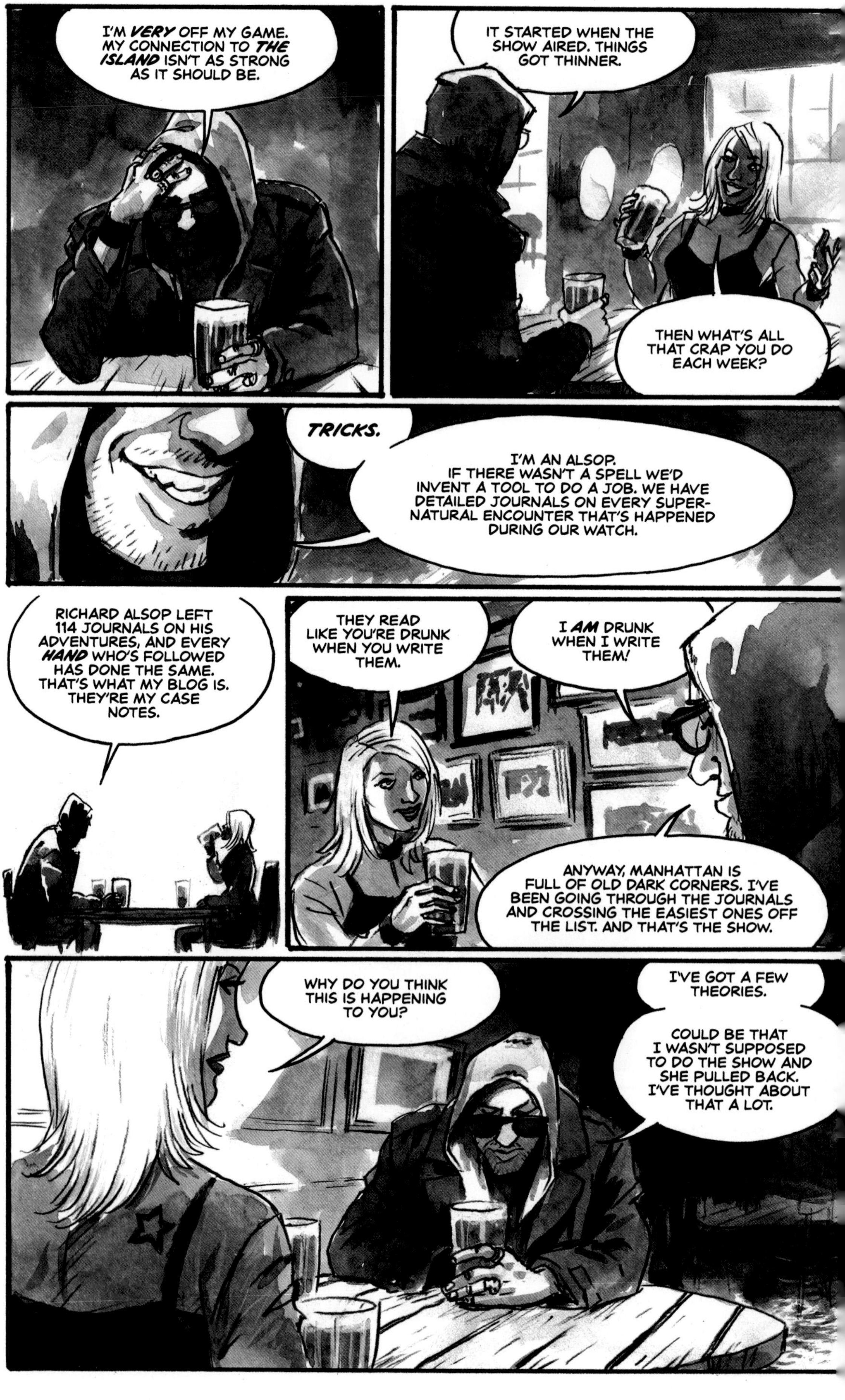
I'M VERY OFF MY GAME. MY CONNECTION TO THE ISLAND ISN'T AS STRONG AS IT SHOULD BE.
IT STARTED WHEN THE SHOW AIRED. THINGS GOT THINNER.
THEN WHAT'S ALL THAT CRAP YOU DO EACH WEEK?
TRICKS.
I'M AN ALSOP. IF THERE WASN'T A SPELL WE'D INVENT A TOOL TO DO A JOB. WE HAVE DETAILED JOURNALS ON EVERY SUPER-NATURAL ENCOUNTER THAT'S HAPPENED DURING OUR WATCH.
RICHARD ALSOP LEFT 114 JOURNALS ON HIS ADVENTURES, AND EVERY HAND WHO'S FOLLOWED HAS DONE THE SAME. THAT'S WHAT MY BLOG IS. THEY'RE MY CASE NOTES.
THEY READ LIKE YOU'RE DRUNK WHEN YOU WRITE THEM.
I AM DRUNK WHEN I WRITE THEM!
ANYWAY, MANHATTAN IS FULL OF OLD DARK CORNERS. I'VE BEEN GOING THROUGH THE JOURNALS AND CROSSING THE EASIEST ONES OFF THE LIST. AND THAT'S THE SHOW.
WHY DO YOU THINK THIS IS HAPPENING TO YOU?
I'VE GOT A FEW THEORIES.
COULD BE THAT I WASN'T SUPPOSED TO DO THE SHOW AND SHE PULLED BACK. I'VE THOUGHT ABOUT THAT A LOT.

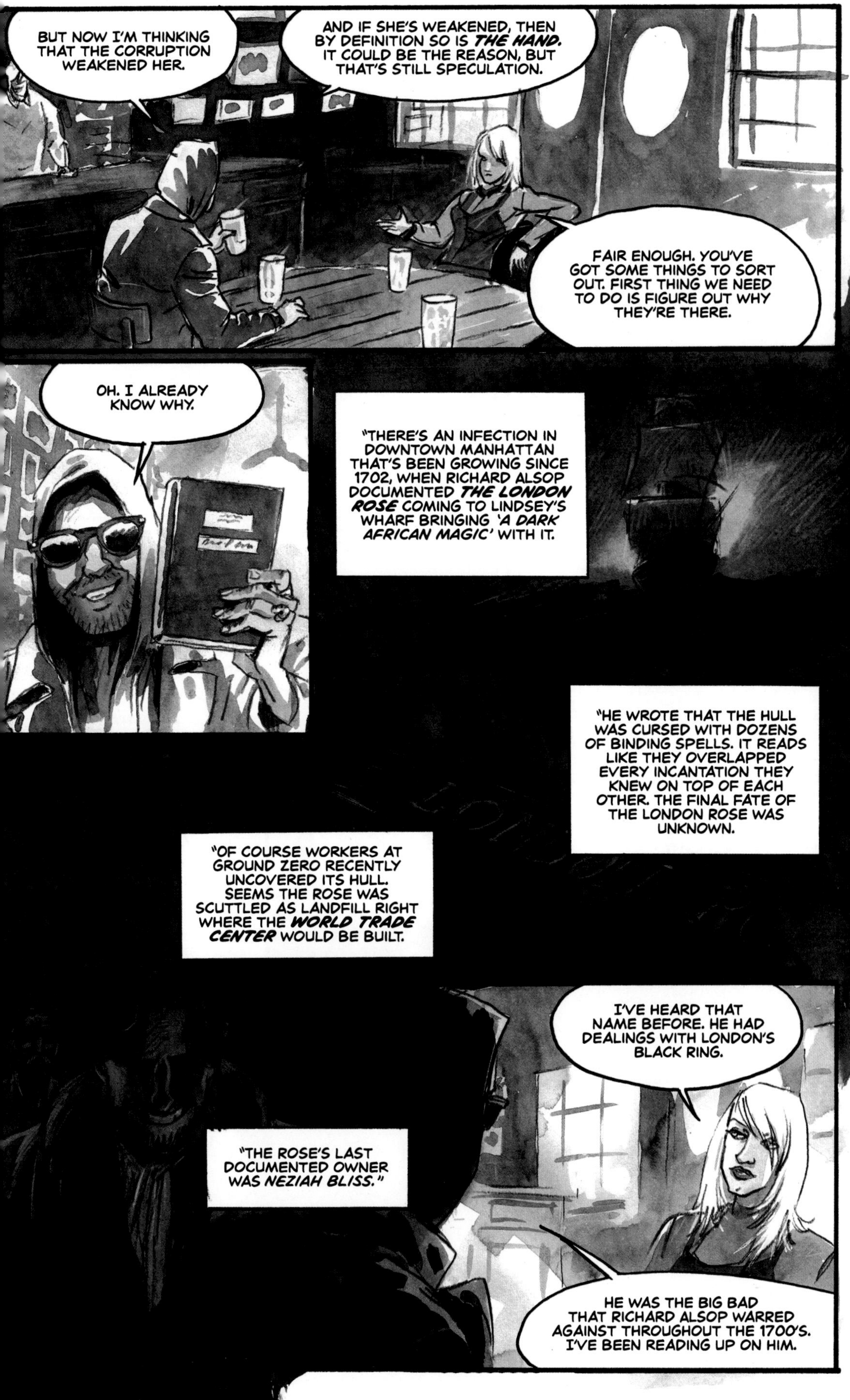
BUT NOW I'M THINKING THAT THE CORRUPTION WEAKENED HER.
AND IF SHE'S WEAKENED, THEN BY DEFINITION SO IS THE HAND. IT COULD BE THE REASON, BUT THAT'S STILL SPECULATION.
FAIR ENOUGH. YOU'VE GOT SOME THINGS TO SORT OUT. FIRST THING WE NEED TO DO IS FIGURE OUT WHY THEY'RE THERE.
OH. I ALREADY KNOW WHY.
"THERE'S AN INFECTION IN DOWNTOWN MANHATTAN THAT'S BEEN GROWING SINCE 1702, WHEN RICHARD ALSOP DOCUMENTED THE LONDON ROSE COMING TO LINDSEY'S WHARF BRINGING 'A DARK AFRICAN MAGIC' WITH IT.
"HE WROTE THAT THE HULL WAS CURSED WITH DOZENS OF BINDING SPELLS. IT READS LIKE THEY OVERLAPPED EVERY INCANTATION THEY KNEW ON TOP OF EACH OTHER. THE FINAL FATE OF THE LONDON ROSE WAS UNKNOWN.
"OF COURSE WORKERS AT GROUND ZERO RECENTLY UNCOVERED ITS HULL. SEEMS THE ROSE WAS SCUTTLED AS LANDFILL RIGHT WHERE THE WORLD TRADE CENTER WOULD BE BUILT.
"THE ROSE'S LAST DOCUMENTED OWNER WAS NEZIAH BLISS."
I'VE HEARD THAT NAME BEFORE. HE HAD DEALINGS WITH LONDON'S BLACK RING.
HE WAS THE BIG BAD THAT RICHARD ALSOP WARRED AGAINST THROUGHOUT THE 1700'S. I'VE BEEN READING UP ON HIM.

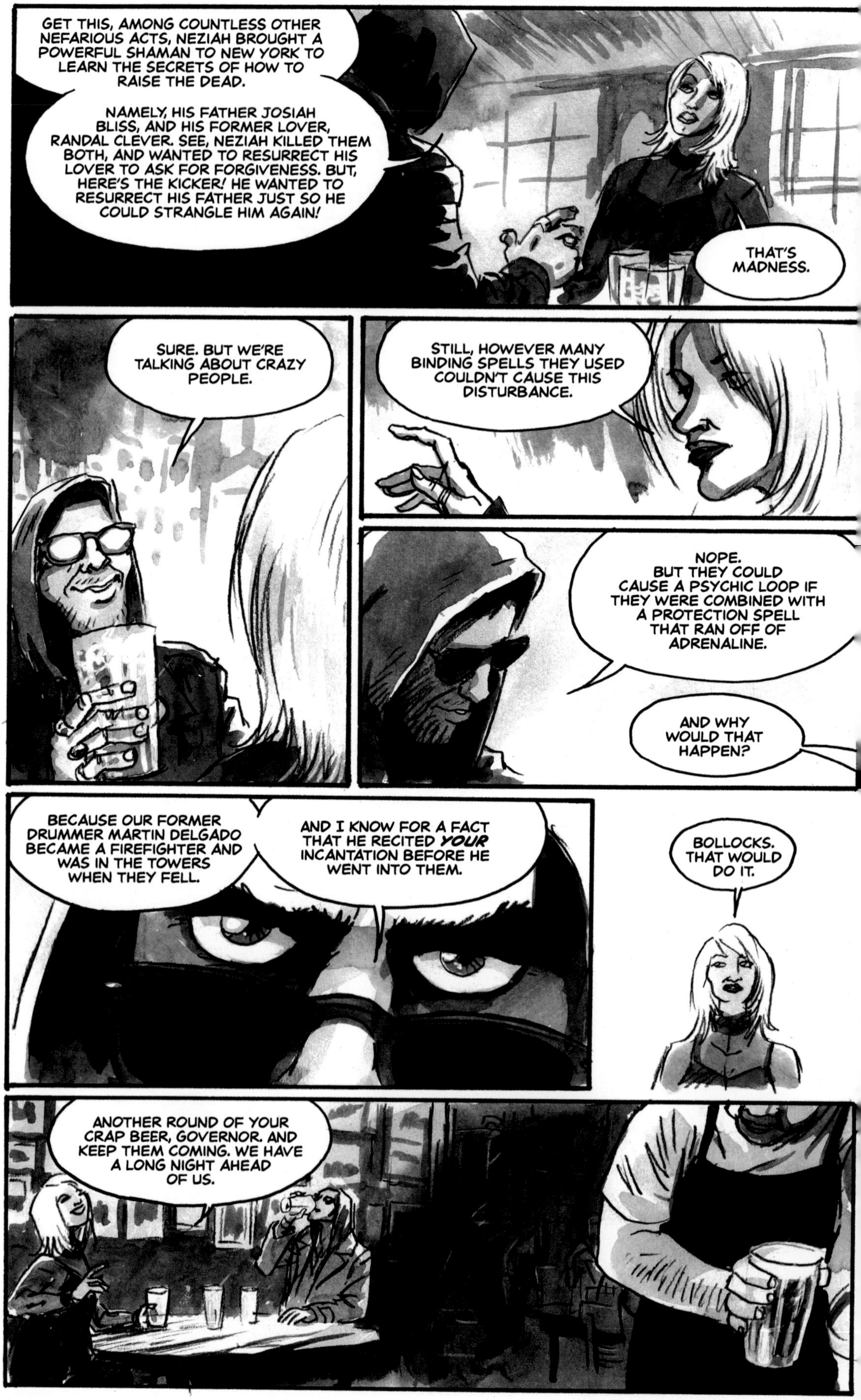
GET THIS, AMONG COUNTLESS OTHER NEFARIOUS ACTS, NEZIAH BROUGHT A POWERFUL SHAMAN TO NEW YORK TO LEARN THE SECRETS OF HOW TO RAISE THE DEAD.
NAMELY, HIS FATHER JOSIAH BLISS, AND HIS FORMER LOVER, RANDAL CLEVER. SEE, NEZIAH KILLED THEM BOTH, AND WANTED TO RESURRECT HIS LOVER TO ASK FOR FORGIVENESS. BUT, HERE'S THE KICKER! HE WANTED TO RESURRECT HIS FATHER JUST SO HE COULD STRANGLE HIM AGAIN!
THAT'S MADNESS.
SURE. BUT WE'RE TALKING ABOUT CRAZY PEOPLE.
STILL, HOWEVER MANY BINDING SPELLS THEY USED COULDN'T CAUSE THIS DISTURBANCE.
NOPE. BUT THEY COULD CAUSE A PSYCHIC LOOP IF THEY WERE COMBINED WITH A PROTECTION SPELL THAT RAN OFF OF ADRENALINE.
AND WHY WOULD THAT HAPPEN?
BECAUSE OUR FORMER DRUMMER MARTIN DELGADO BECAME A FIREFIGHTER AND WAS IN THE TOWERS WHEN THEY FELL.
AND I KNOW FOR A FACT THAT HE RECITED *YOUR* INCANTATION BEFORE HE WENT INTO THEM.
BOLLOCKS. THAT WOULD DO IT.
ANOTHER ROUND OF YOUR CRAP BEER, GOVERNOR. AND KEEP THEM COMING. WE HAVE A LONG NIGHT AHEAD OF US.

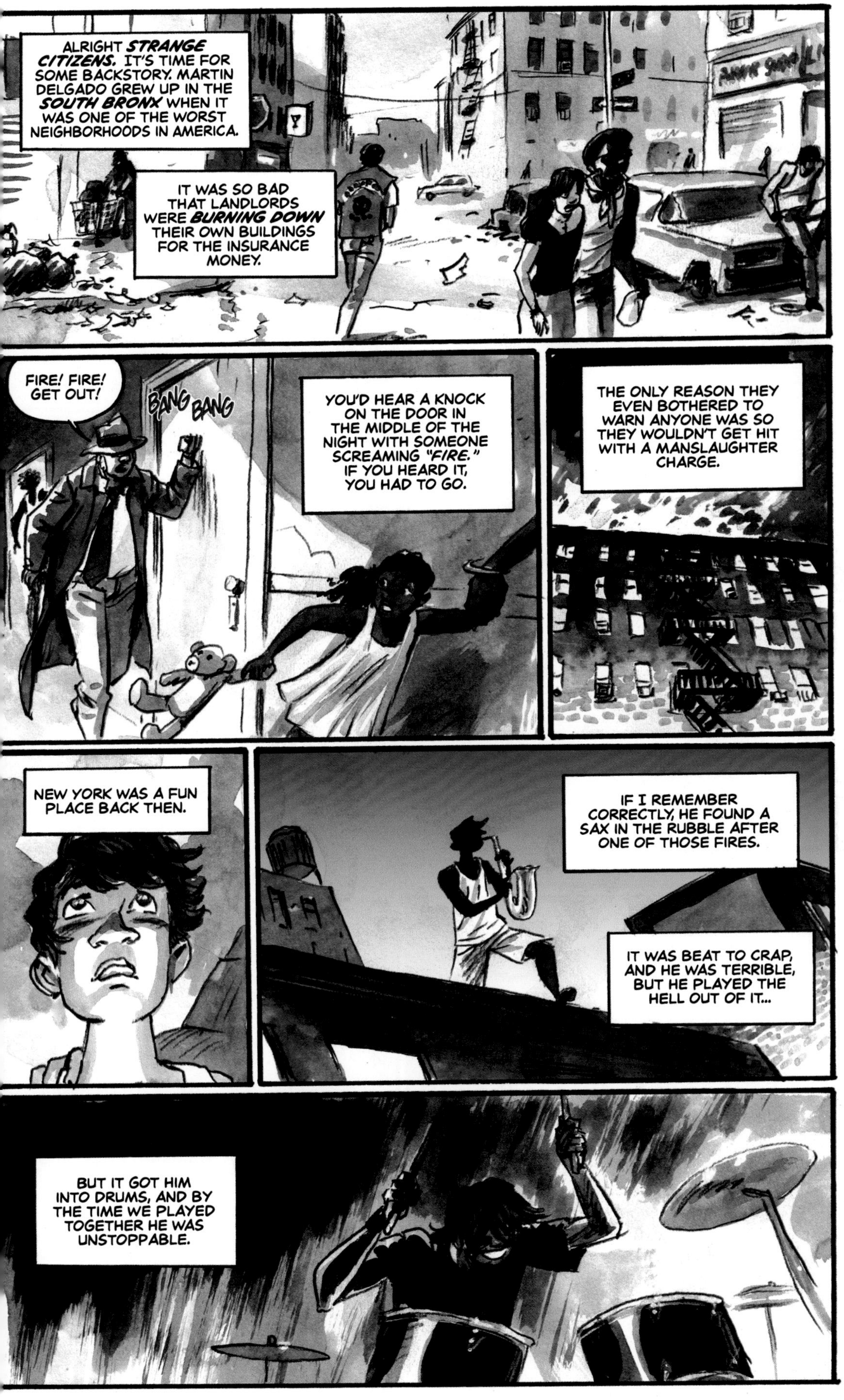
ALRIGHT STRANGE CITIZENS. IT'S TIME FOR SOME BACKSTORY. MARTIN DELGADO GREW UP IN THE SOUTH BRONX WHEN IT WAS ONE OF THE WORST NEIGHBORHOODS IN AMERICA.
IT WAS SO BAD THAT LANDLORDS WERE BURNING DOWN THEIR OWN BUILDINGS FOR THE INSURANCE MONEY.
FIRE! FIRE! GET OUT!
BANG BANG
YOU'D HEAR A KNOCK ON THE DOOR IN THE MIDDLE OF THE NIGHT WITH SOMEONE SCREAMING "FIRE." IF YOU HEARD IT, YOU HAD TO GO.
THE ONLY REASON THEY EVEN BOTHERED TO WARN ANYONE WAS SO THEY WOULDN'T GET HIT WITH A MANSLAUGHTER CHARGE.
NEW YORK WAS A FUN PLACE BACK THEN.
IF I REMEMBER CORRECTLY, HE FOUND A SAX IN THE RUBBLE AFTER ONE OF THOSE FIRES.
IT WAS BEAT TO CRAP, AND HE WAS TERRIBLE, BUT HE PLAYED THE HELL OUT OF IT...
BUT IT GOT HIM INTO DRUMS, AND BY THE TIME WE PLAYED TOGETHER HE WAS UNSTOPPABLE.

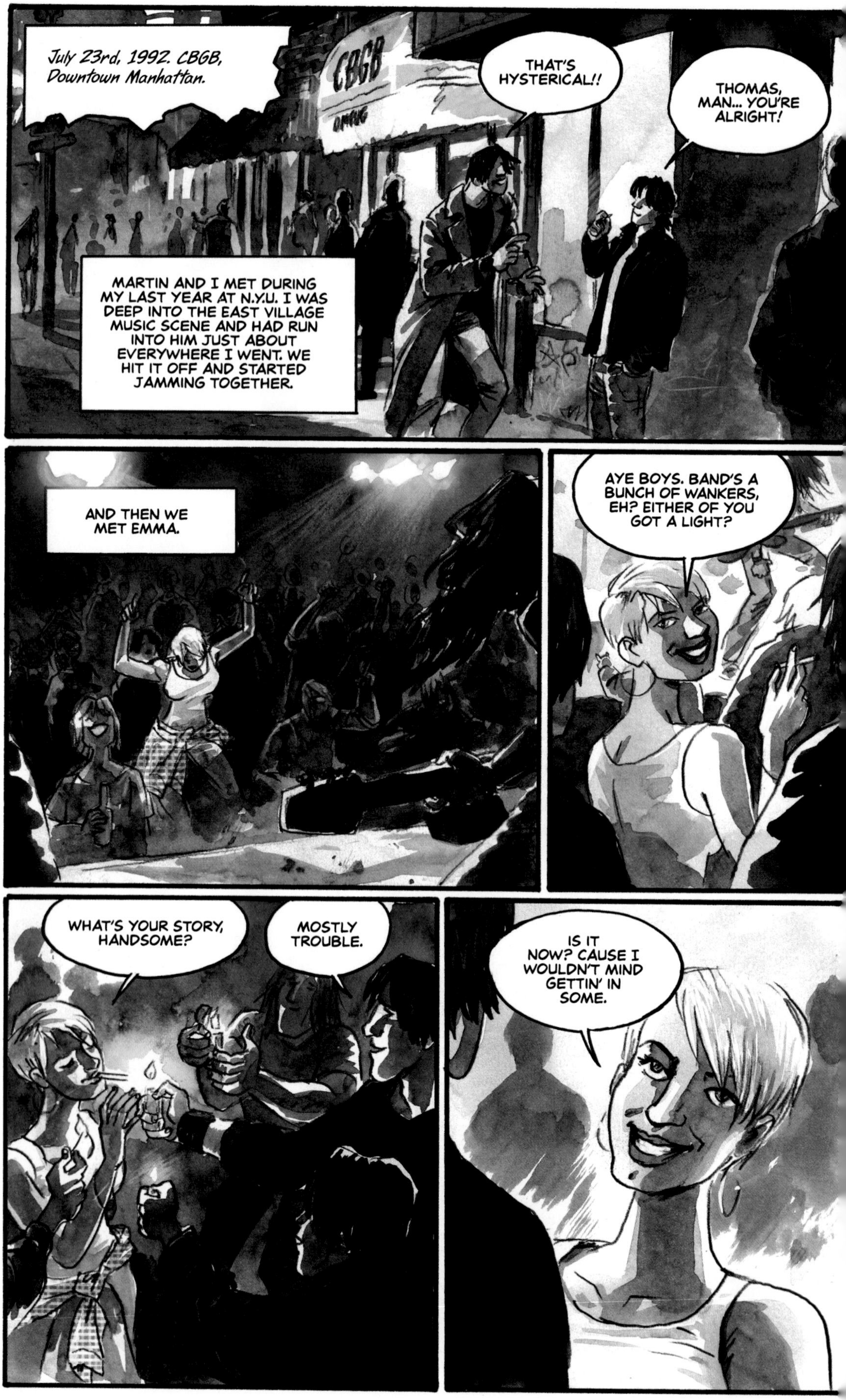
July 23rd, 1992. CBGB, Downtown Manhattan.
CBGB
THAT'S HYSTERICAL!!
THOMAS, MAN... YOU'RE ALRIGHT!
MARTIN AND I MET DURING MY LAST YEAR AT N.Y.U. I WAS DEEP INTO THE EAST VILLAGE MUSIC SCENE AND HAD RUN INTO HIM JUST ABOUT EVERYWHERE I WENT. WE HIT IT OFF AND STARTED JAMMING TOGETHER.
AND THEN WE MET EMMA.
AYE BOYS. BAND'S A BUNCH OF WANKERS, EH? EITHER OF YOU GOT A LIGHT?
WHAT'S YOUR STORY, HANDSOME?
MOSTLY TROUBLE.
IS IT NOW? CAUSE I WOULDN'T MIND GETTIN' IN SOME.

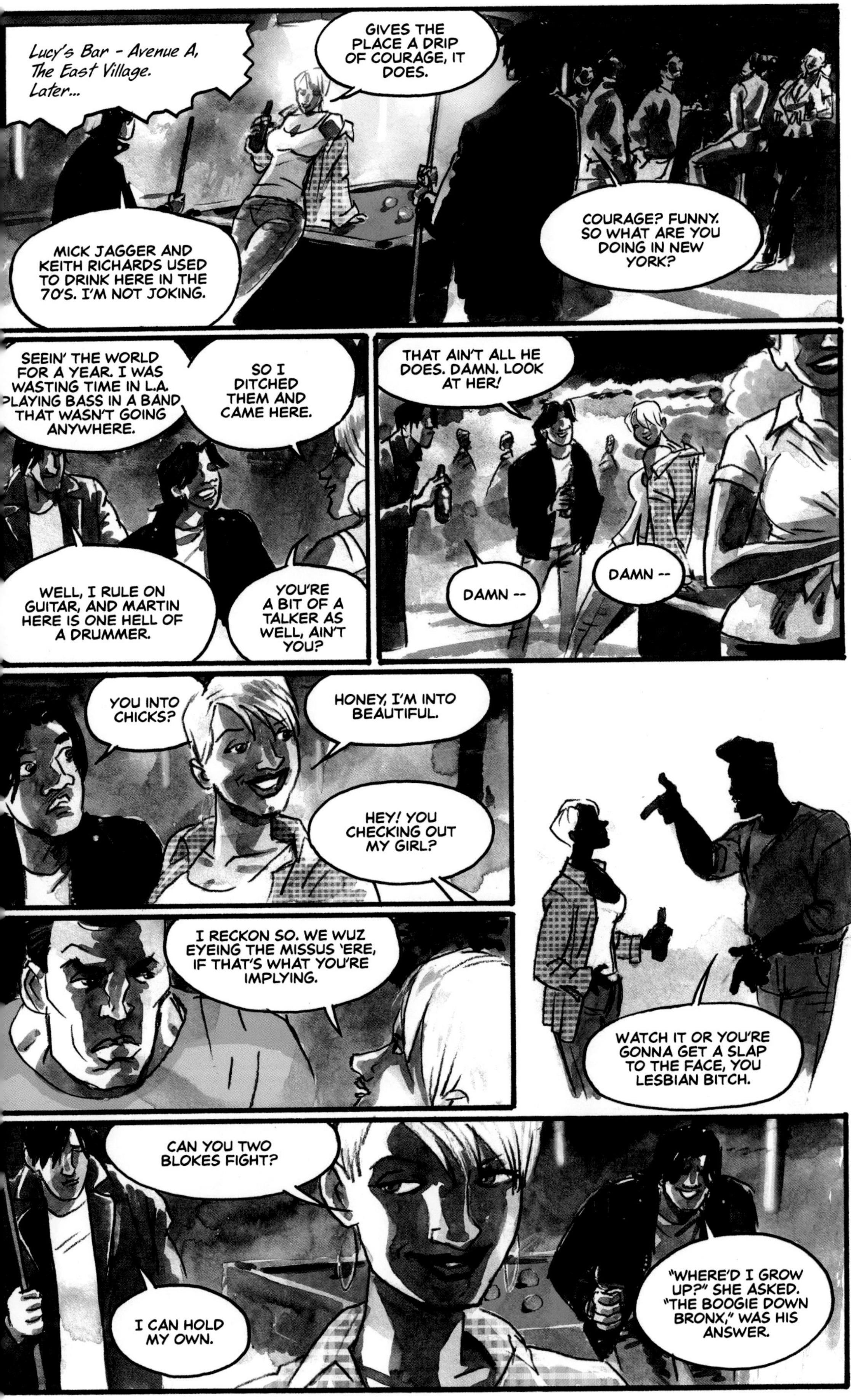
Lucy's Bar - Avenue A, The East Village. Later...
GIVES THE PLACE A DRIP OF COURAGE, IT DOES.
MICK JAGGER AND KEITH RICHARDS USED TO DRINK HERE IN THE 70'S. I'M NOT JOKING.
COURAGE? FUNNY. SO WHAT ARE YOU DOING IN NEW YORK?
SEEIN' THE WORLD FOR A YEAR. I WAS WASTING TIME IN L.A. PLAYING BASS IN A BAND THAT WASN'T GOING ANYWHERE.
SO I DITCHED THEM AND CAME HERE.
WELL, I RULE ON GUITAR, AND MARTIN HERE IS ONE HELL OF A DRUMMER.
YOU'RE A BIT OF A TALKER AS WELL, AIN'T YOU?
THAT AIN'T ALL HE DOES. DAMN. LOOK AT HER!
DAMN --
DAMN --
YOU INTO CHICKS?
HONEY, I'M INTO BEAUTIFUL.
HEY! YOU CHECKING OUT MY GIRL?
I RECKON SO. WE WUZ EYEING THE MISSUS 'ERE, IF THAT'S WHAT YOU'RE IMPLYING.
WATCH IT OR YOU'RE GONNA GET A SLAP TO THE FACE, YOU LESBIAN BITCH.
CAN YOU TWO BLOKES FIGHT?
I CAN HOLD MY OWN.
"WHERE'D I GROW UP?" SHE ASKED. "THE BOOGIE DOWN BRONX," WAS HIS ANSWER.

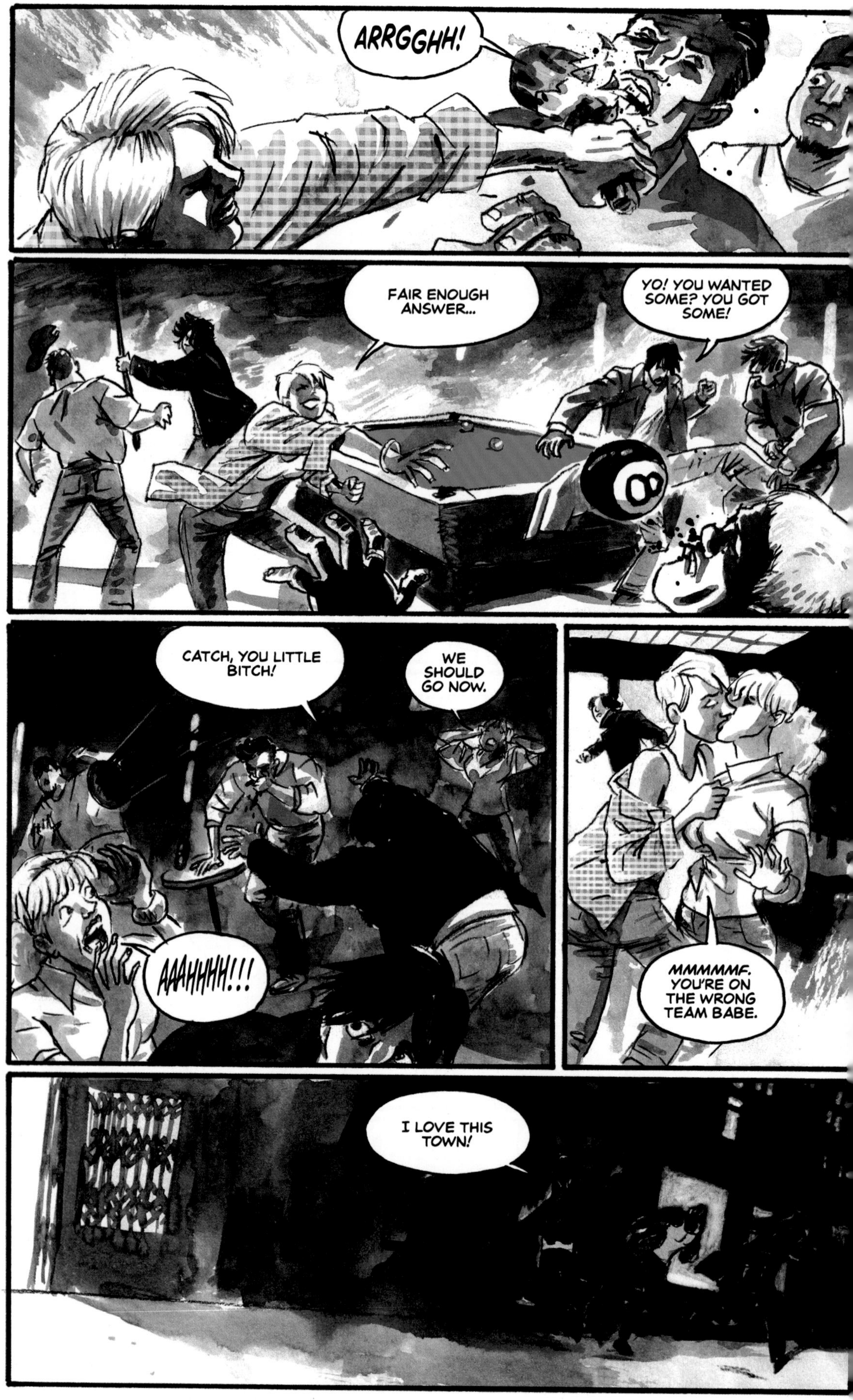
ARRGGHH!
FAIR ENOUGH ANSWER...
YO! YOU WANTED SOME? YOU GOT SOME!
CATCH, YOU LITTLE BITCH!
WE SHOULD GO NOW.
AAAHHHH!!!
MMMMMF. YOU'RE ON THE WRONG TEAM BABE.
I LOVE THIS TOWN!

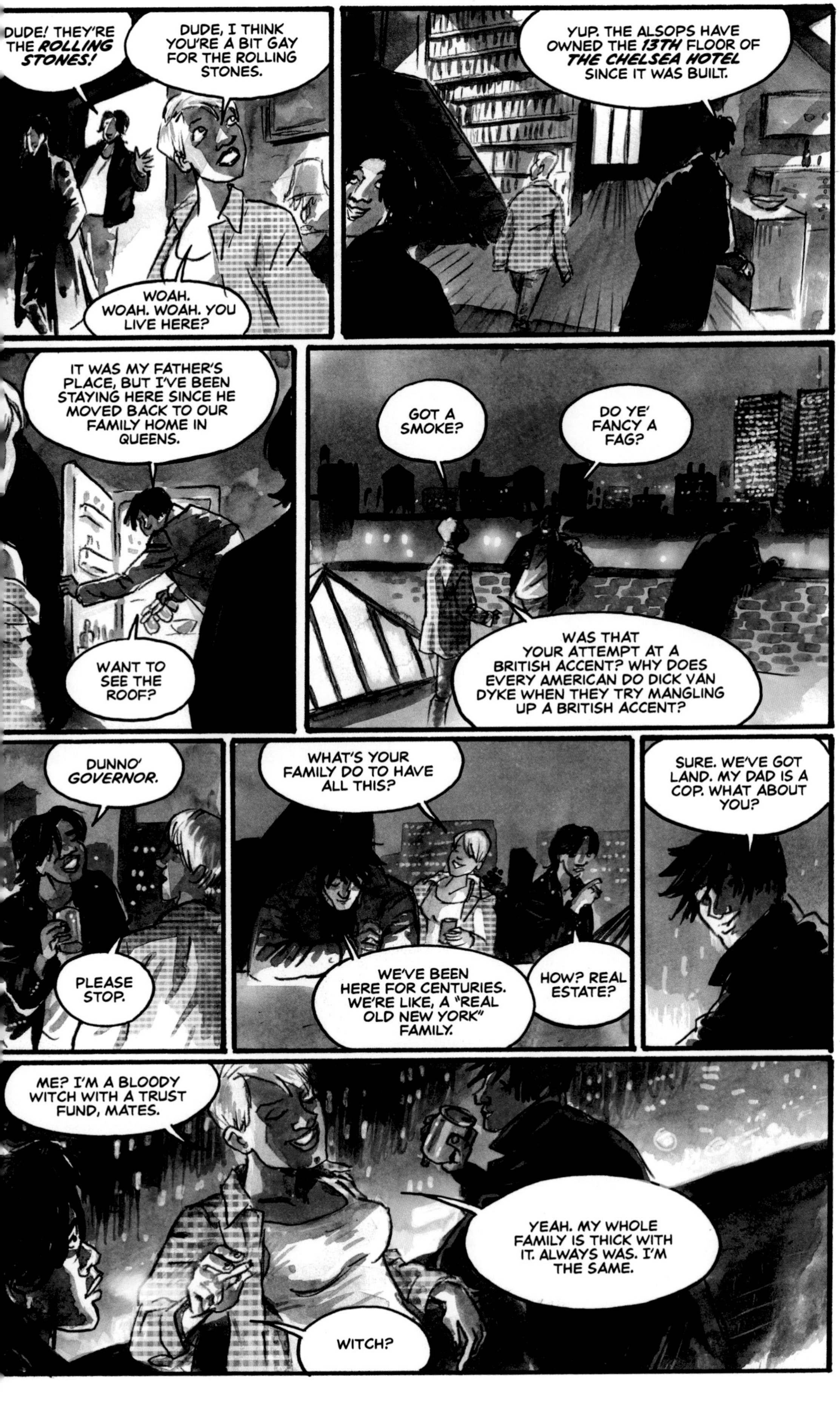
DUDE! THEY'RE THE ROLLING STONES!
DUDE, I THINK YOU'RE A BIT GAY FOR THE ROLLING STONES.
WOAH. WOAH. WOAH. YOU LIVE HERE?
YUP. THE ALSOPS HAVE OWNED THE 13TH FLOOR OF THE CHELSEA HOTEL SINCE IT WAS BUILT.
IT WAS MY FATHER'S PLACE, BUT I'VE BEEN STAYING HERE SINCE HE MOVED BACK TO OUR FAMILY HOME IN QUEENS.
WANT TO SEE THE ROOF?
GOT A SMOKE?
DO YE' FANCY A FAG?
WAS THAT YOUR ATTEMPT AT A BRITISH ACCENT? WHY DOES EVERY AMERICAN DO DICK VAN DYKE WHEN THEY TRY MANGLING UP A BRITISH ACCENT?
DUNNO' GOVERNOR.
PLEASE STOP.
WHAT'S YOUR FAMILY DO TO HAVE ALL THIS?
WE'VE BEEN HERE FOR CENTURIES. WE'RE LIKE, A "REAL OLD NEW YORK" FAMILY.
HOW? REAL ESTATE?
SURE. WE'VE GOT LAND. MY DAD IS A COP. WHAT ABOUT YOU?
ME? I'M A BLOODY WITCH WITH A TRUST FUND, MATES.
YEAH. MY WHOLE FAMILY IS THICK WITH IT. ALWAYS WAS. I'M THE SAME.
WITCH?

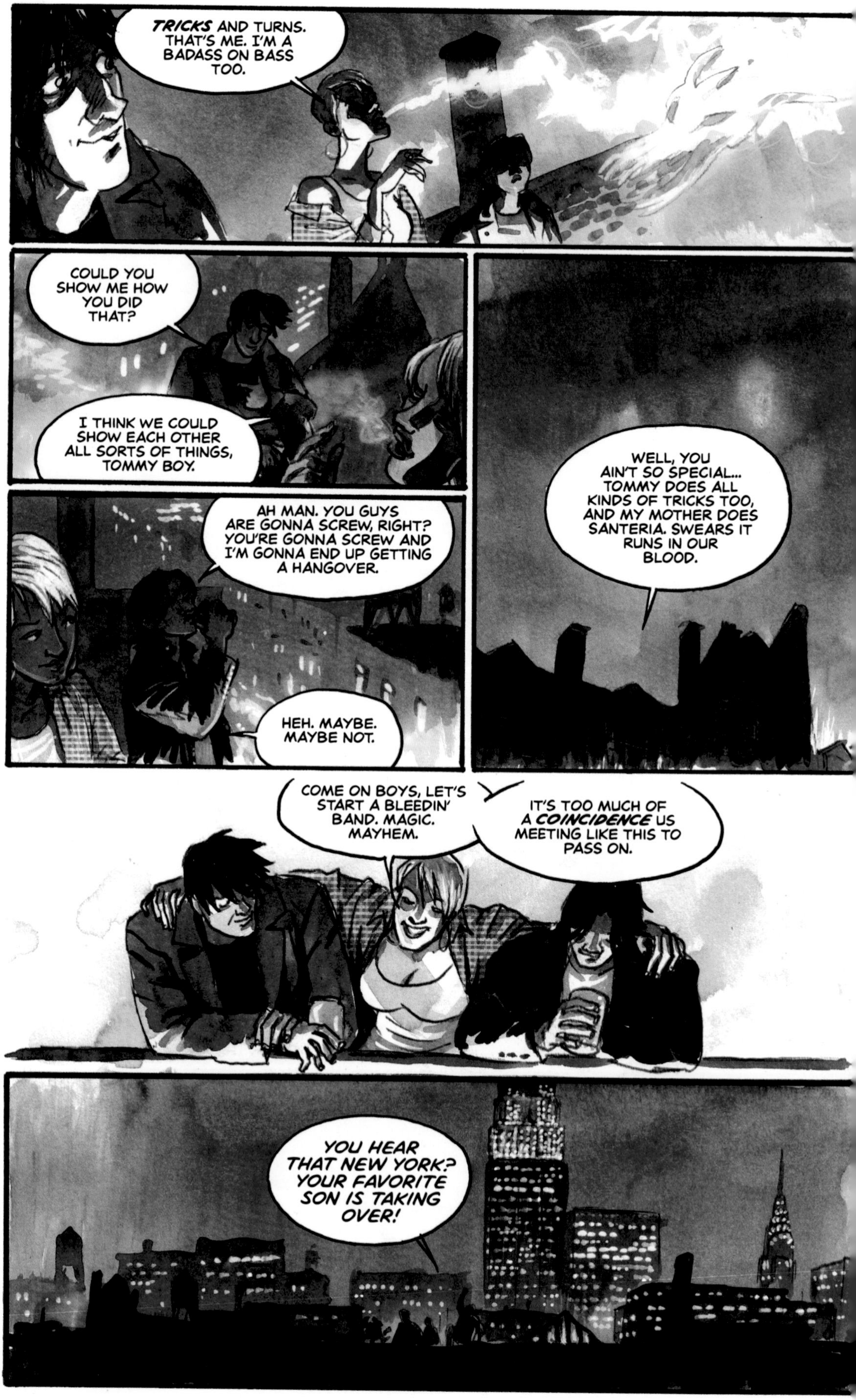
TRICKS AND TURNS. THAT'S ME. I'M A BADASS ON BASS TOO.
COULD YOU SHOW ME HOW YOU DID THAT?
I THINK WE COULD SHOW EACH OTHER ALL SORTS OF THINGS, TOMMY BOY.
AH MAN. YOU GUYS ARE GONNA SCREW, RIGHT? YOU'RE GONNA SCREW AND I'M GONNA END UP GETTING A HANGOVER.
HEH. MAYBE. MAYBE NOT.
WELL, YOU AIN'T SO SPECIAL... TOMMY DOES ALL KINDS OF TRICKS TOO, AND MY MOTHER DOES SANTERIA. SWEARS IT RUNS IN OUR BLOOD.
COME ON BOYS, LET'S START A BLEEDIN' BAND. MAGIC. MAYHEM.
IT'S TOO MUCH OF A COINCIDENCE US MEETING LIKE THIS TO PASS ON.
YOU HEAR THAT NEW YORK? YOUR FAVORITE SON IS TAKING OVER!

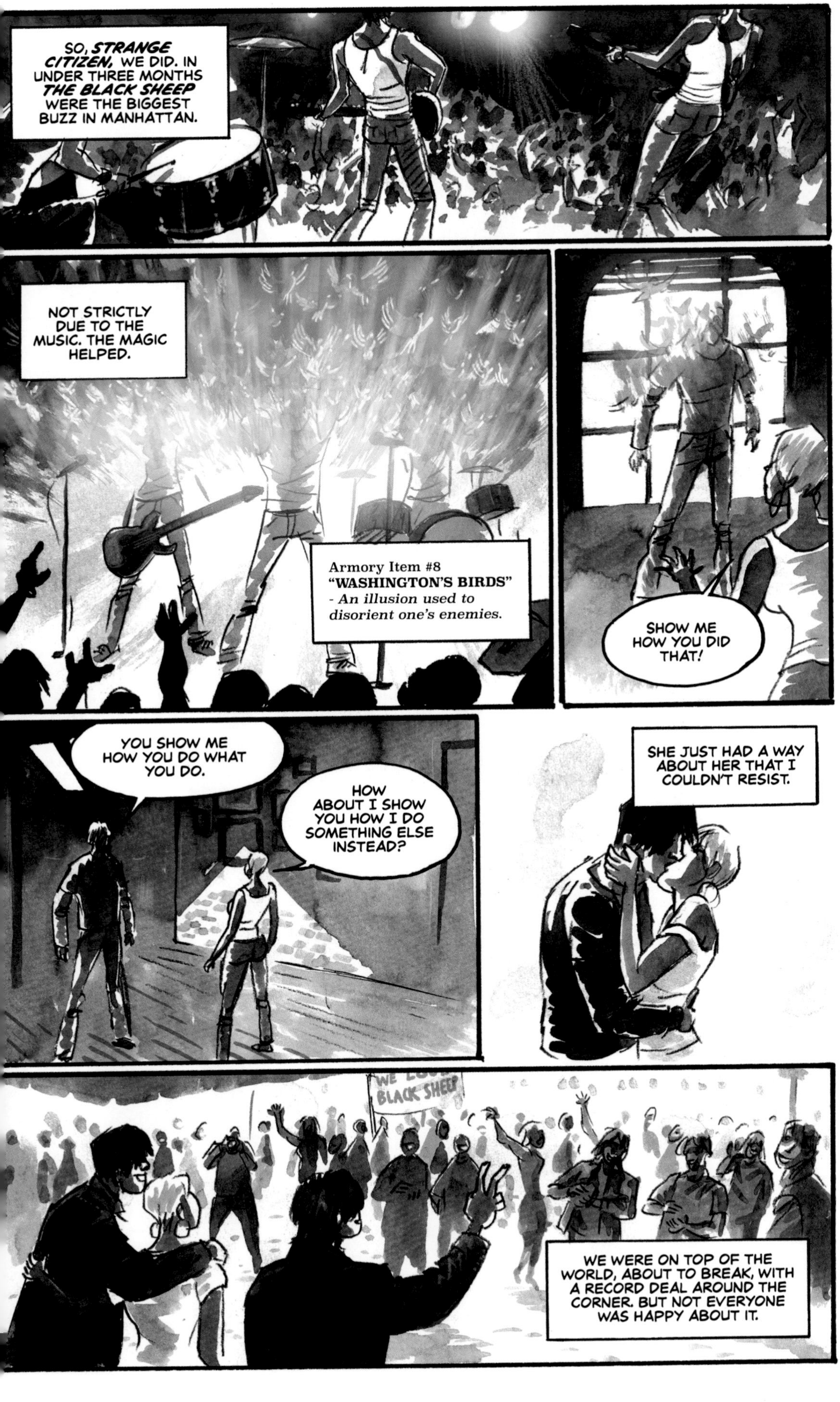
SO, *STRANGE CITIZEN,* WE DID. IN UNDER THREE MONTHS *THE BLACK SHEEP* WERE THE BIGGEST BUZZ IN MANHATTAN.
NOT STRICTLY DUE TO THE MUSIC. THE MAGIC HELPED.
Armory Item #8 **"WASHINGTON'S BIRDS"** *- An illusion used to disorient one's enemies.*
SHOW ME HOW YOU DID THAT!
YOU SHOW ME HOW YOU DO WHAT YOU DO.
HOW ABOUT I SHOW YOU HOW I DO SOMETHING ELSE INSTEAD?
SHE JUST HAD A WAY ABOUT HER THAT I COULDN'T RESIST.
BLACK SHEEP
WE WERE ON TOP OF THE WORLD, ABOUT TO BREAK, WITH A RECORD DEAL AROUND THE CORNER. BUT NOT EVERYONE WAS HAPPY ABOUT IT.

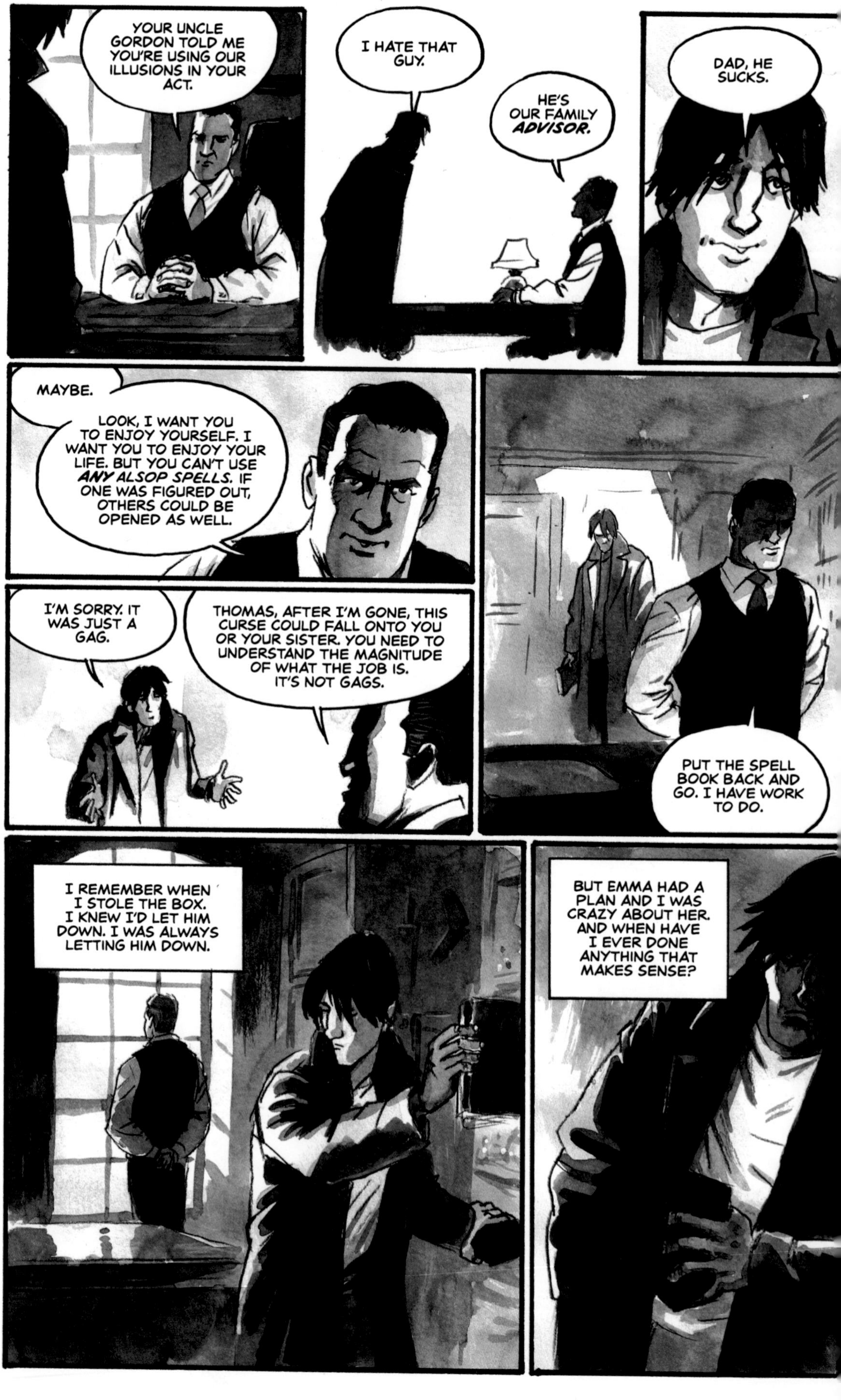
YOUR UNCLE GORDON TOLD ME YOU'RE USING OUR ILLUSIONS IN YOUR ACT.
I HATE THAT GUY.
HE'S OUR FAMILY *ADVISOR.*
DAD, HE SUCKS.
MAYBE.
LOOK, I WANT YOU TO ENJOY YOURSELF. I WANT YOU TO ENJOY YOUR LIFE. BUT YOU CAN'T USE *ANY ALSOP SPELLS.* IF ONE WAS FIGURED OUT, OTHERS COULD BE OPENED AS WELL.
I'M SORRY. IT WAS JUST A GAG.
THOMAS, AFTER I'M GONE, THIS CURSE COULD FALL ONTO YOU OR YOUR SISTER. YOU NEED TO UNDERSTAND THE MAGNITUDE OF WHAT THE JOB IS. IT'S NOT GAGS.
PUT THE SPELL BOOK BACK AND GO. I HAVE WORK TO DO.
I REMEMBER WHEN I STOLE THE BOX. I KNEW I'D LET HIM DOWN. I WAS ALWAYS LETTING HIM DOWN.
BUT EMMA HAD A PLAN AND I WAS CRAZY ABOUT HER. AND WHEN HAVE I EVER DONE ANYTHING THAT MAKES SENSE?

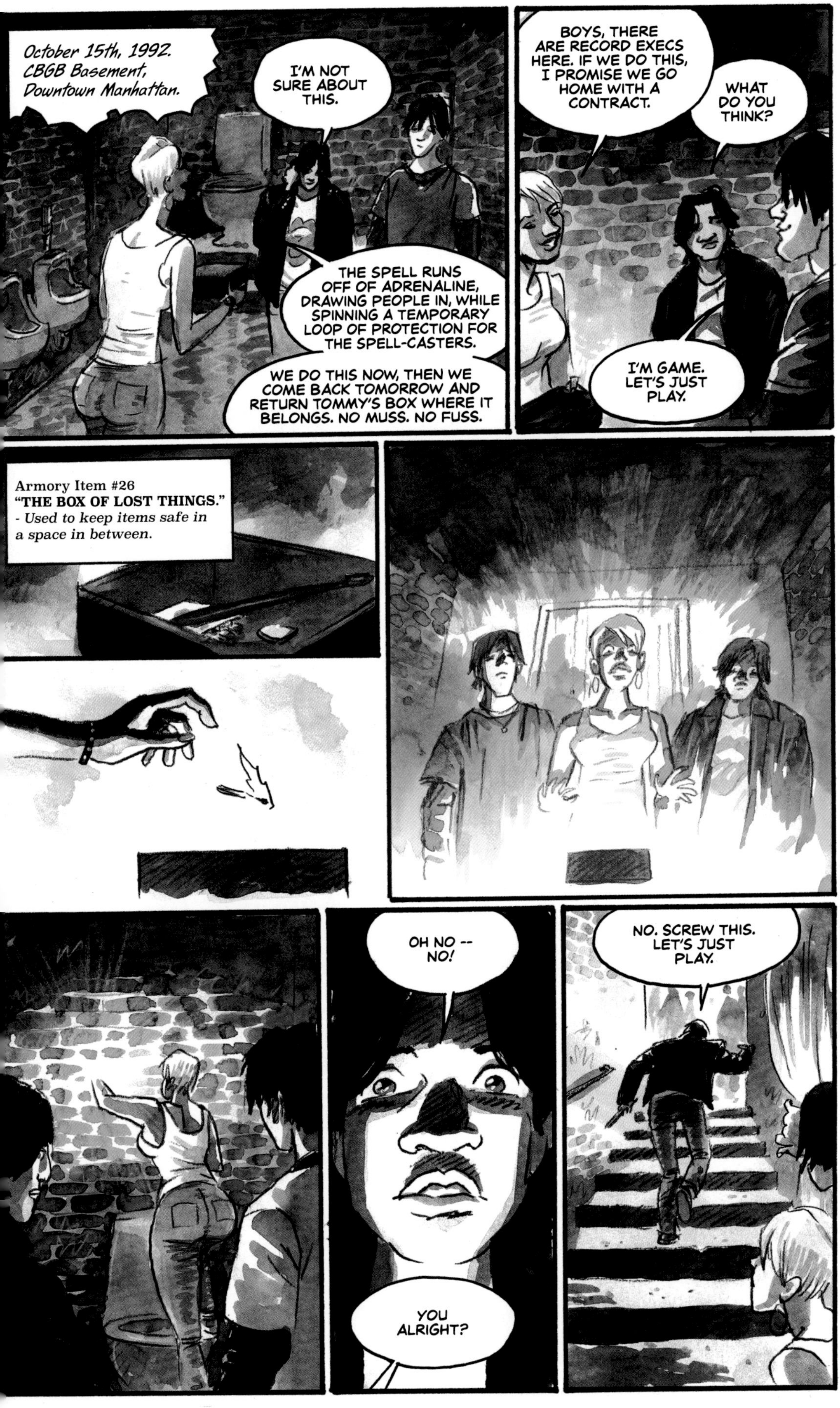
October 15th, 1992. CBGB Basement, Downtown Manhattan.
I'M NOT SURE ABOUT THIS.
THE SPELL RUNS OFF OF ADRENALINE, DRAWING PEOPLE IN, WHILE SPINNING A TEMPORARY LOOP OF PROTECTION FOR THE SPELL-CASTERS.
WE DO THIS NOW, THEN WE COME BACK TOMORROW AND RETURN TOMMY'S BOX WHERE IT BELONGS. NO MUSS. NO FUSS.
BOYS, THERE ARE RECORD EXECS HERE. IF WE DO THIS, I PROMISE WE GO HOME WITH A CONTRACT.
WHAT DO YOU THINK?
I'M GAME. LET'S JUST PLAY.
Armory Item #26
"THE BOX OF LOST THINGS."
- Used to keep items safe in a space in between.
OH NO -- NO!
YOU ALRIGHT?
NO. SCREW THIS. LET'S JUST PLAY.

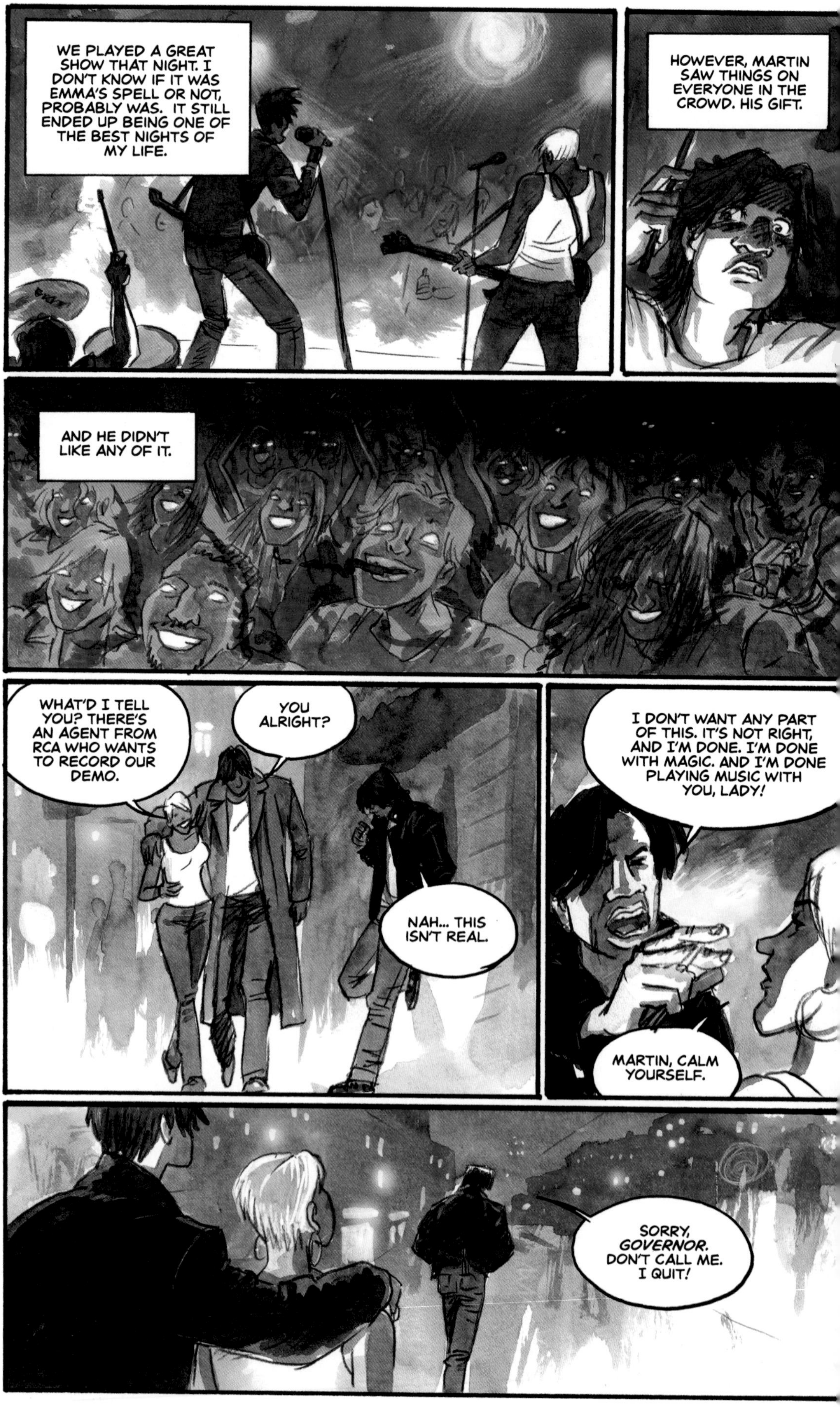
WE PLAYED A GREAT SHOW THAT NIGHT. I DON'T KNOW IF IT WAS EMMA'S SPELL OR NOT, PROBABLY WAS. IT STILL ENDED UP BEING ONE OF THE BEST NIGHTS OF MY LIFE.
HOWEVER, MARTIN SAW THINGS ON EVERYONE IN THE CROWD. HIS GIFT.
AND HE DIDN'T LIKE ANY OF IT.
WHAT'D I TELL YOU? THERE'S AN AGENT FROM RCA WHO WANTS TO RECORD OUR DEMO.
YOU ALRIGHT?
NAH... THIS ISN'T REAL.
I DON'T WANT ANY PART OF THIS. IT'S NOT RIGHT, AND I'M DONE. I'M DONE WITH MAGIC. AND I'M DONE PLAYING MUSIC WITH YOU, LADY!
MARTIN, CALM YOURSELF.
SORRY, *GOVERNOR*. DON'T CALL ME. I QUIT!

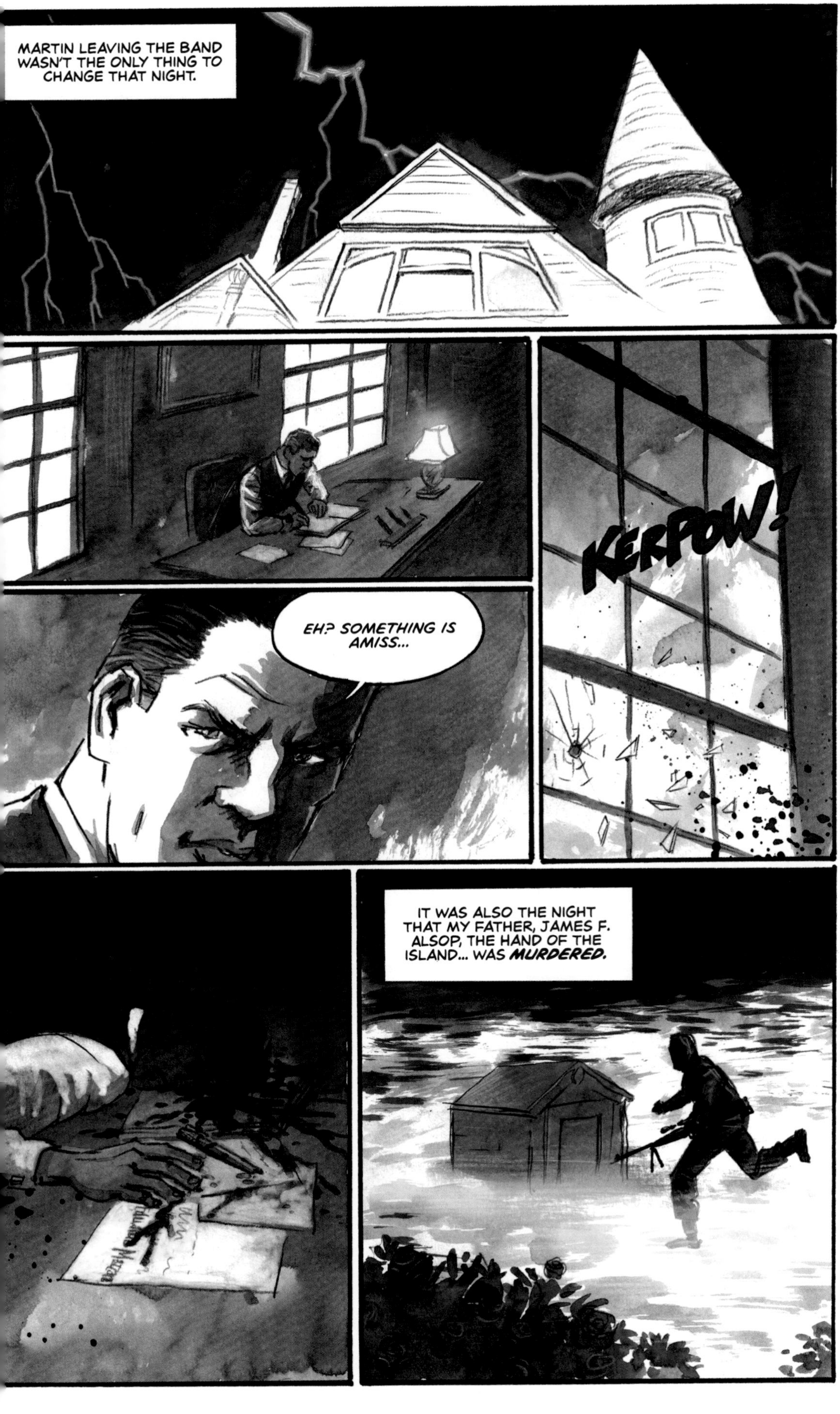
MARTIN LEAVING THE BAND WASN'T THE ONLY THING TO CHANGE THAT NIGHT.
KERPOW!
EH? SOMETHING IS AMISS...
IT WAS ALSO THE NIGHT THAT MY FATHER, JAMES F. ALSOP, THE HAND OF THE ISLAND... WAS *MURDERED.*

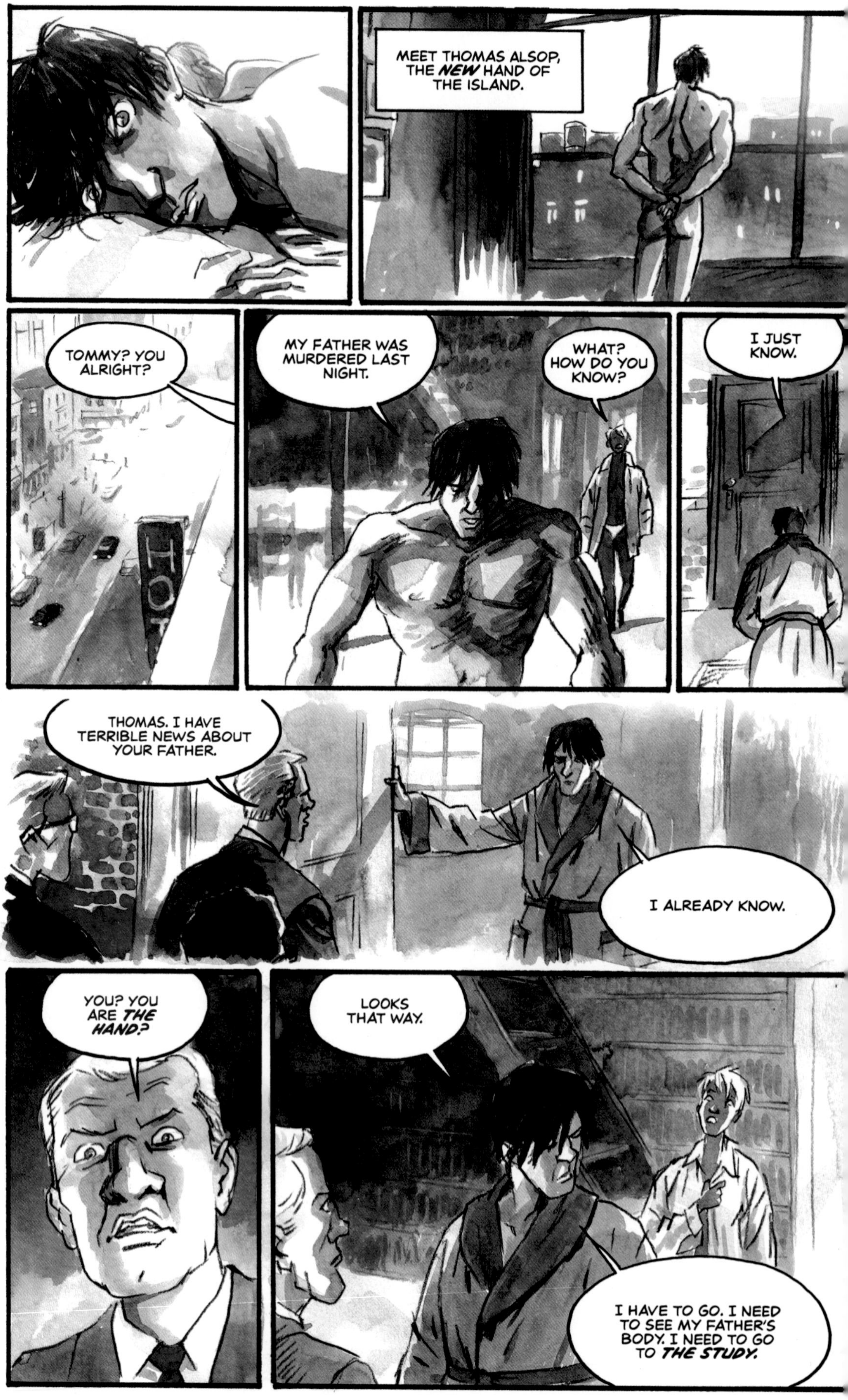
MEET THOMAS ALSOP, THE NEW HAND OF THE ISLAND.
TOMMY? YOU ALRIGHT?
MY FATHER WAS MURDERED LAST NIGHT.
WHAT? HOW DO YOU KNOW?
I JUST KNOW.
THOMAS. I HAVE TERRIBLE NEWS ABOUT YOUR FATHER.
I ALREADY KNOW.
YOU? YOU ARE THE HAND?
LOOKS THAT WAY.
I HAVE TO GO. I NEED TO SEE MY FATHER'S BODY. I NEED TO GO TO THE STUDY.

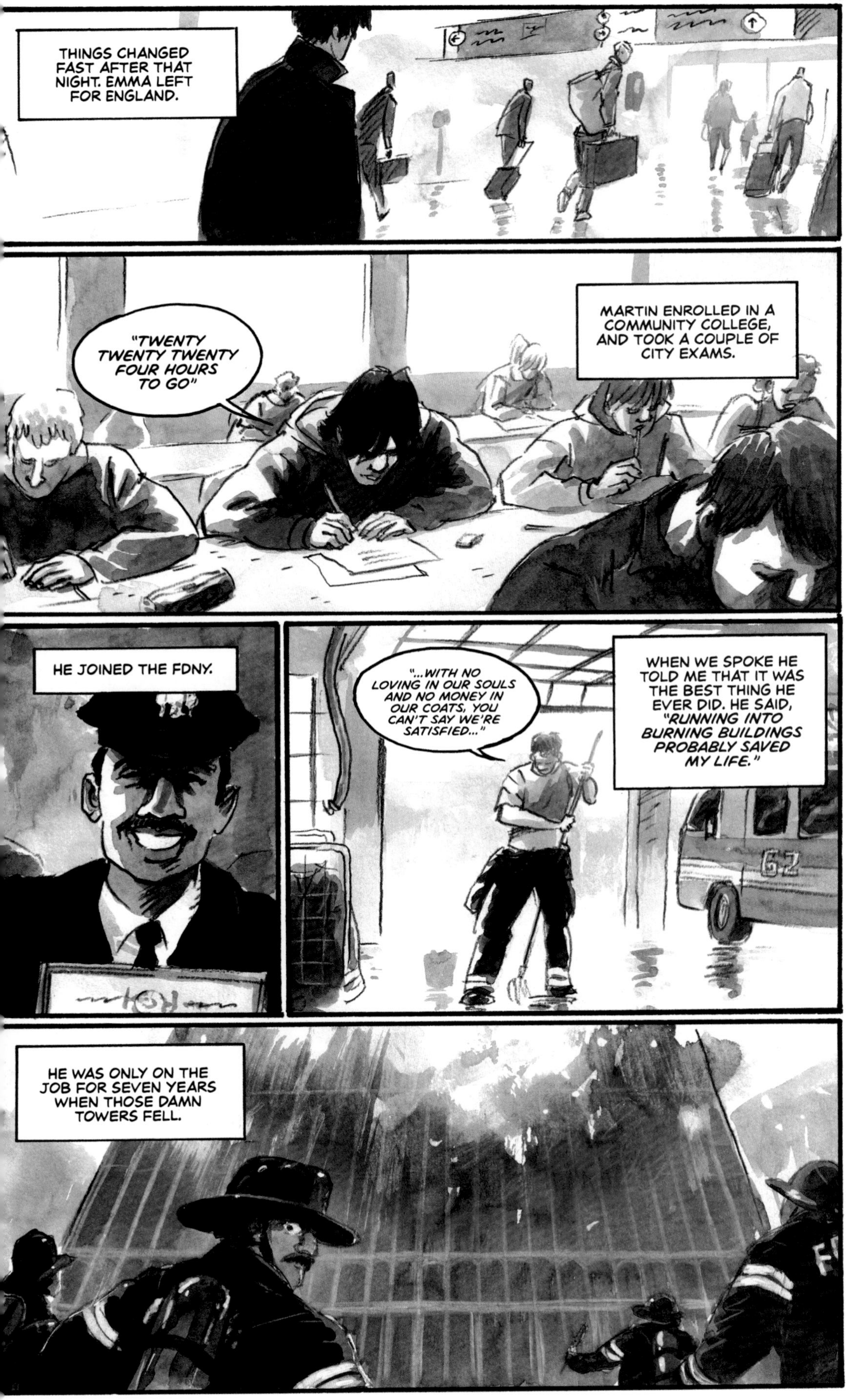
THINGS CHANGED FAST AFTER THAT NIGHT. EMMA LEFT FOR ENGLAND.
"TWENTY TWENTY TWENTY FOUR HOURS TO GO"
MARTIN ENROLLED IN A COMMUNITY COLLEGE, AND TOOK A COUPLE OF CITY EXAMS.
HE JOINED THE FDNY.
"...WITH NO LOVING IN OUR SOULS AND NO MONEY IN OUR COATS, YOU CAN'T SAY WE'RE SATISFIED..."
WHEN WE SPOKE HE TOLD ME THAT IT WAS THE BEST THING HE EVER DID. HE SAID, "RUNNING INTO BURNING BUILDINGS PROBABLY SAVED MY LIFE."
62
HE WAS ONLY ON THE JOB FOR SEVEN YEARS WHEN THOSE DAMN TOWERS FELL.

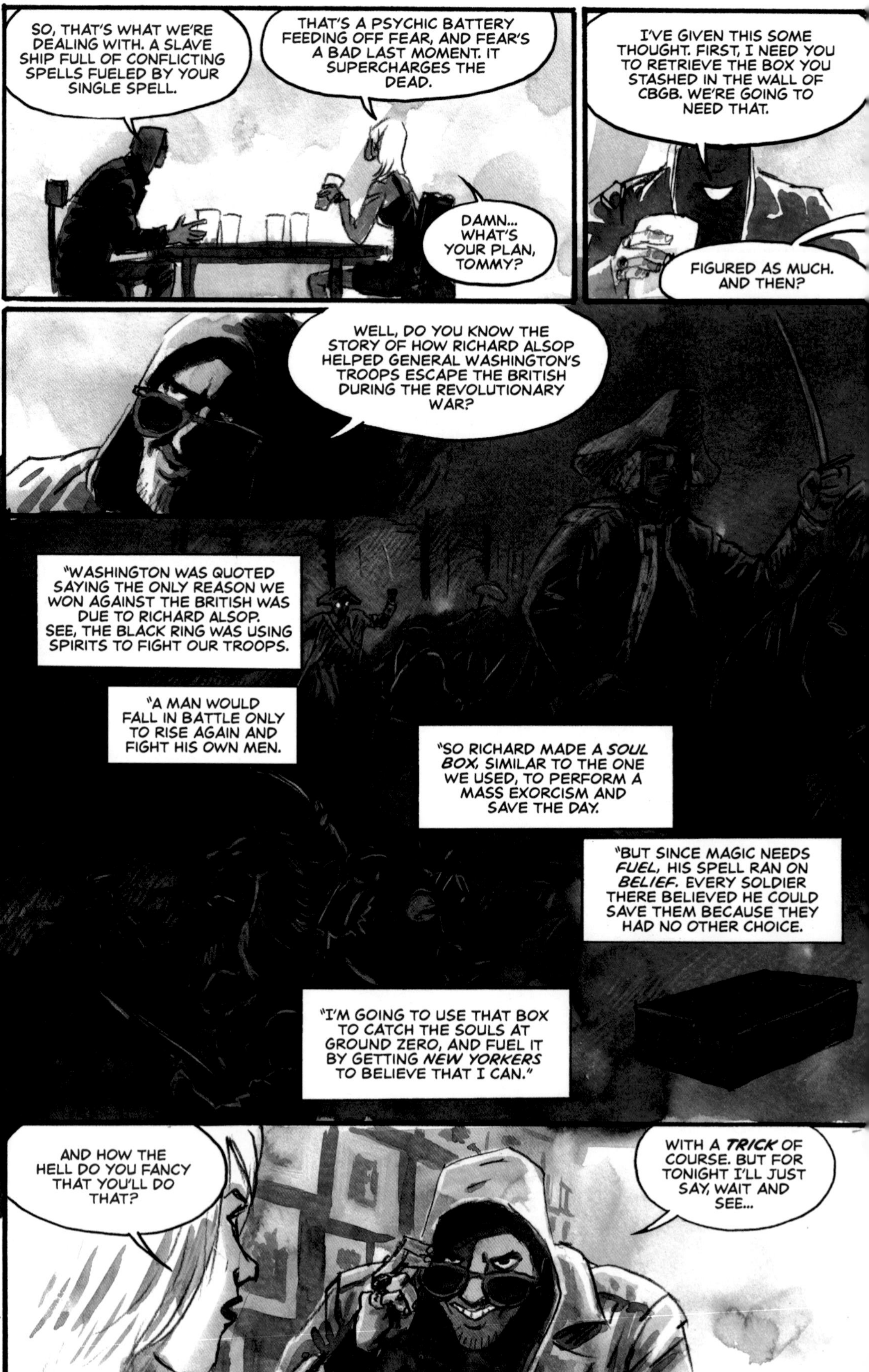
SO, THAT'S WHAT WE'RE DEALING WITH. A SLAVE SHIP FULL OF CONFLICTING SPELLS FUELED BY YOUR SINGLE SPELL.
THAT'S A PSYCHIC BATTERY FEEDING OFF FEAR, AND FEAR'S A BAD LAST MOMENT. IT SUPERCHARGES THE DEAD.
DAMN... WHAT'S YOUR PLAN, TOMMY?
I'VE GIVEN THIS SOME THOUGHT. FIRST, I NEED YOU TO RETRIEVE THE BOX YOU STASHED IN THE WALL OF CBGB. WE'RE GOING TO NEED THAT.
FIGURED AS MUCH. AND THEN?
WELL, DO YOU KNOW THE STORY OF HOW RICHARD ALSOP HELPED GENERAL WASHINGTON'S TROOPS ESCAPE THE BRITISH DURING THE REVOLUTIONARY WAR?
"WASHINGTON WAS QUOTED SAYING THE ONLY REASON WE WON AGAINST THE BRITISH WAS DUE TO RICHARD ALSOP. SEE, THE BLACK RING WAS USING SPIRITS TO FIGHT OUR TROOPS.
"A MAN WOULD FALL IN BATTLE ONLY TO RISE AGAIN AND FIGHT HIS OWN MEN.
"SO RICHARD MADE A *SOUL BOX*, SIMILAR TO THE ONE WE USED, TO PERFORM A MASS EXORCISM AND SAVE THE DAY.
"BUT SINCE MAGIC NEEDS *FUEL*, HIS SPELL RAN ON *BELIEF*. EVERY SOLDIER THERE BELIEVED HE COULD SAVE THEM BECAUSE THEY HAD NO OTHER CHOICE.
"I'M GOING TO USE THAT BOX TO CATCH THE SOULS AT GROUND ZERO, AND FUEL IT BY GETTING *NEW YORKERS* TO BELIEVE THAT I CAN."
AND HOW THE HELL DO YOU FANCY THAT YOU'LL DO THAT?
WITH A *TRICK* OF COURSE. BUT FOR TONIGHT I'LL JUST SAY, WAIT AND SEE...

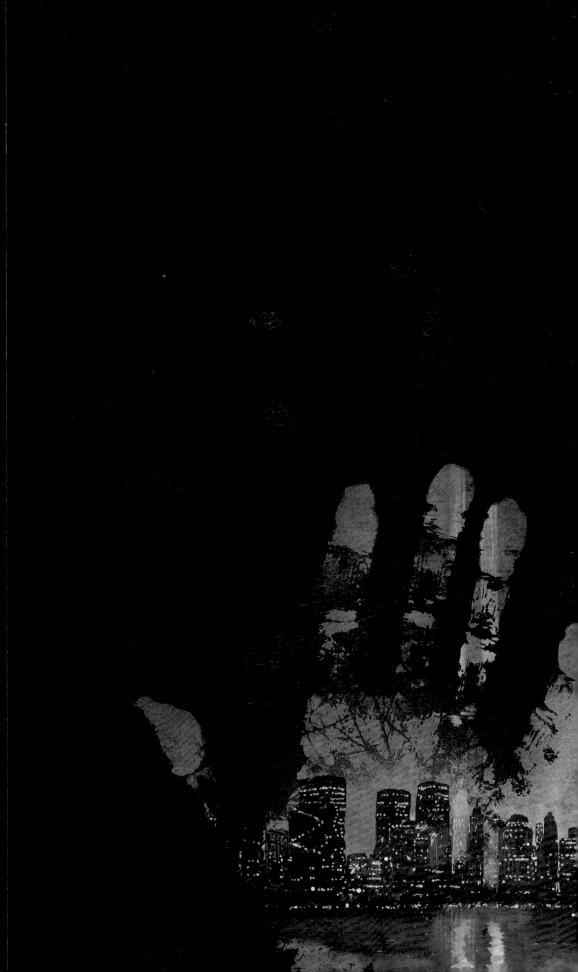

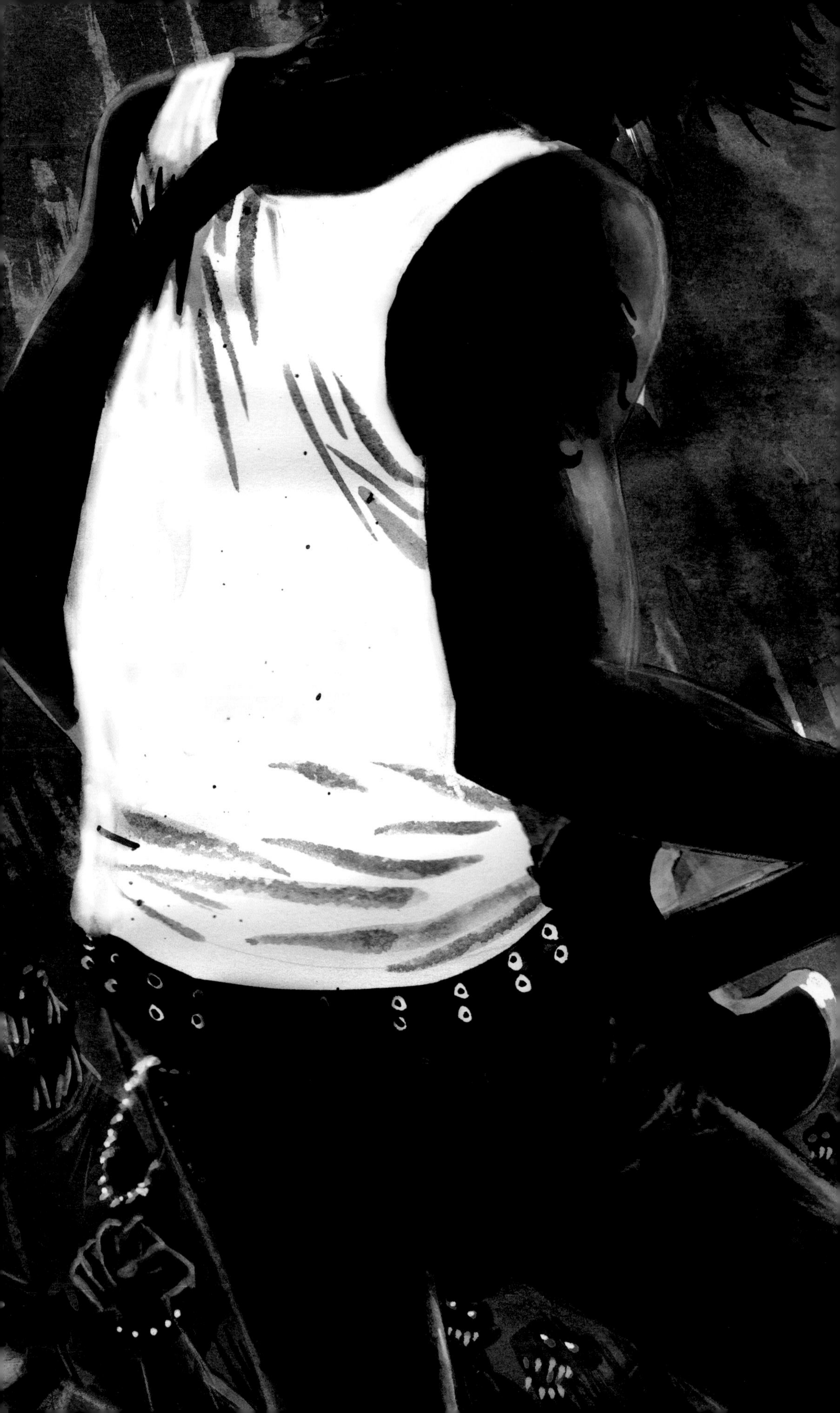

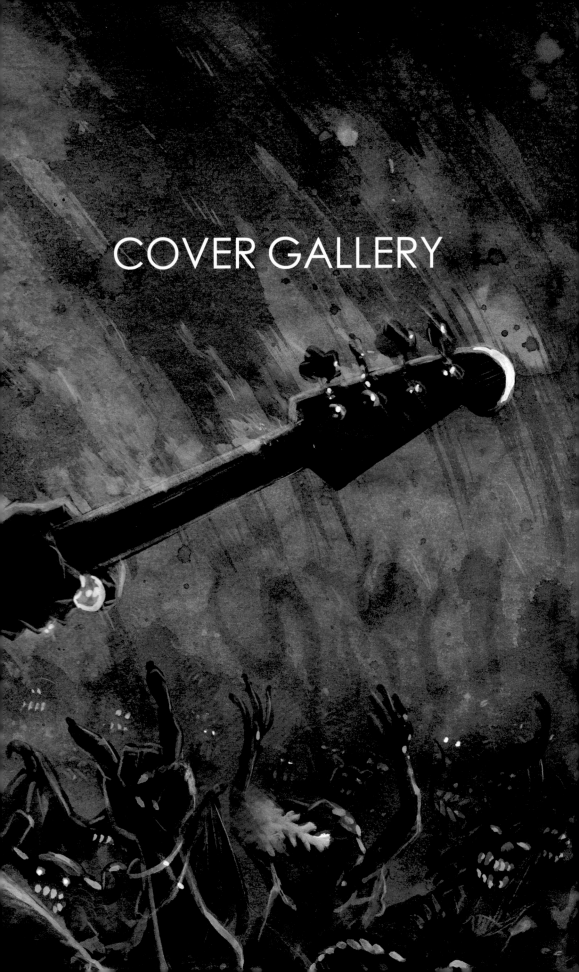

COVER GALLERY

ISSUE ONE COVER
PALLE **SCHMIDT**

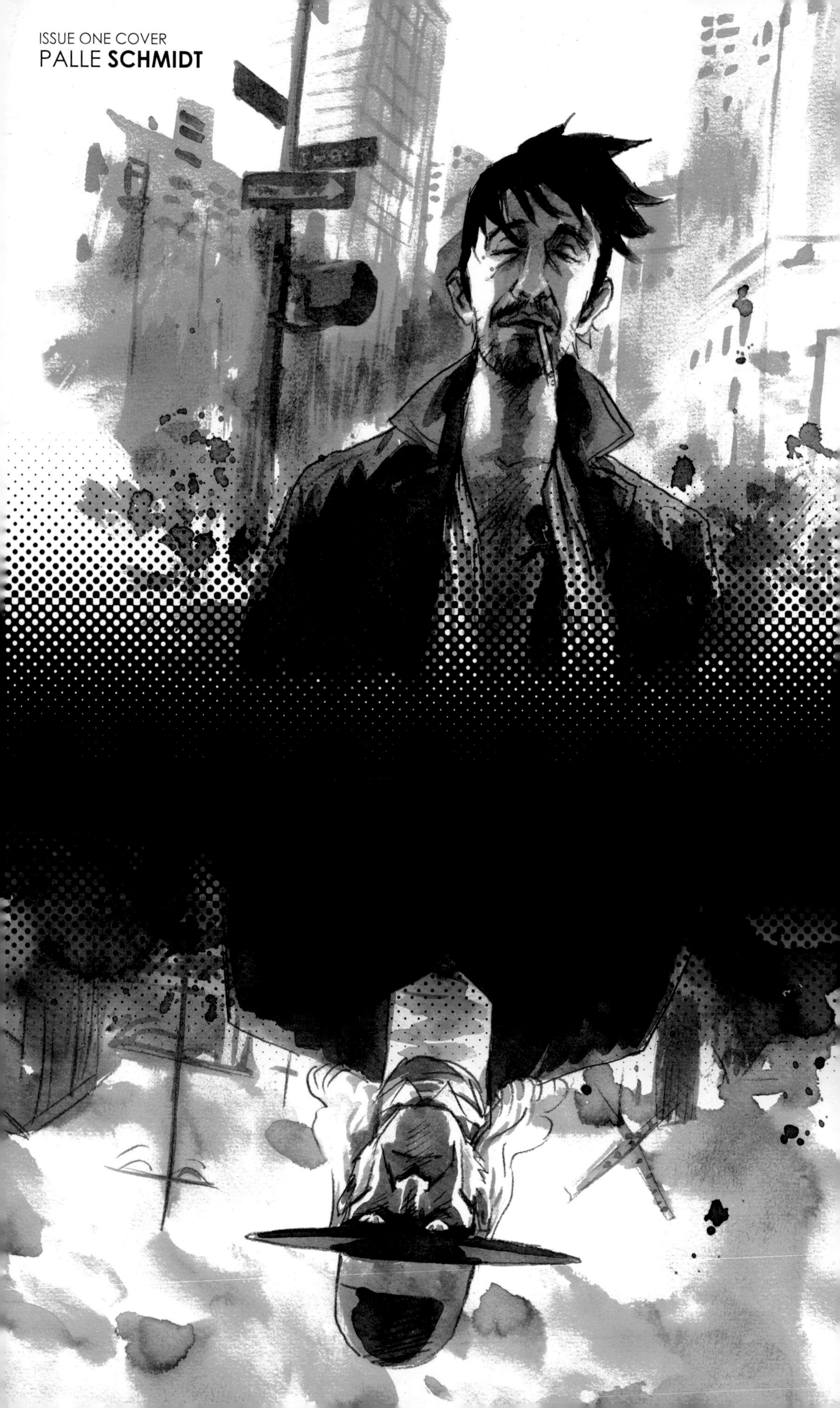

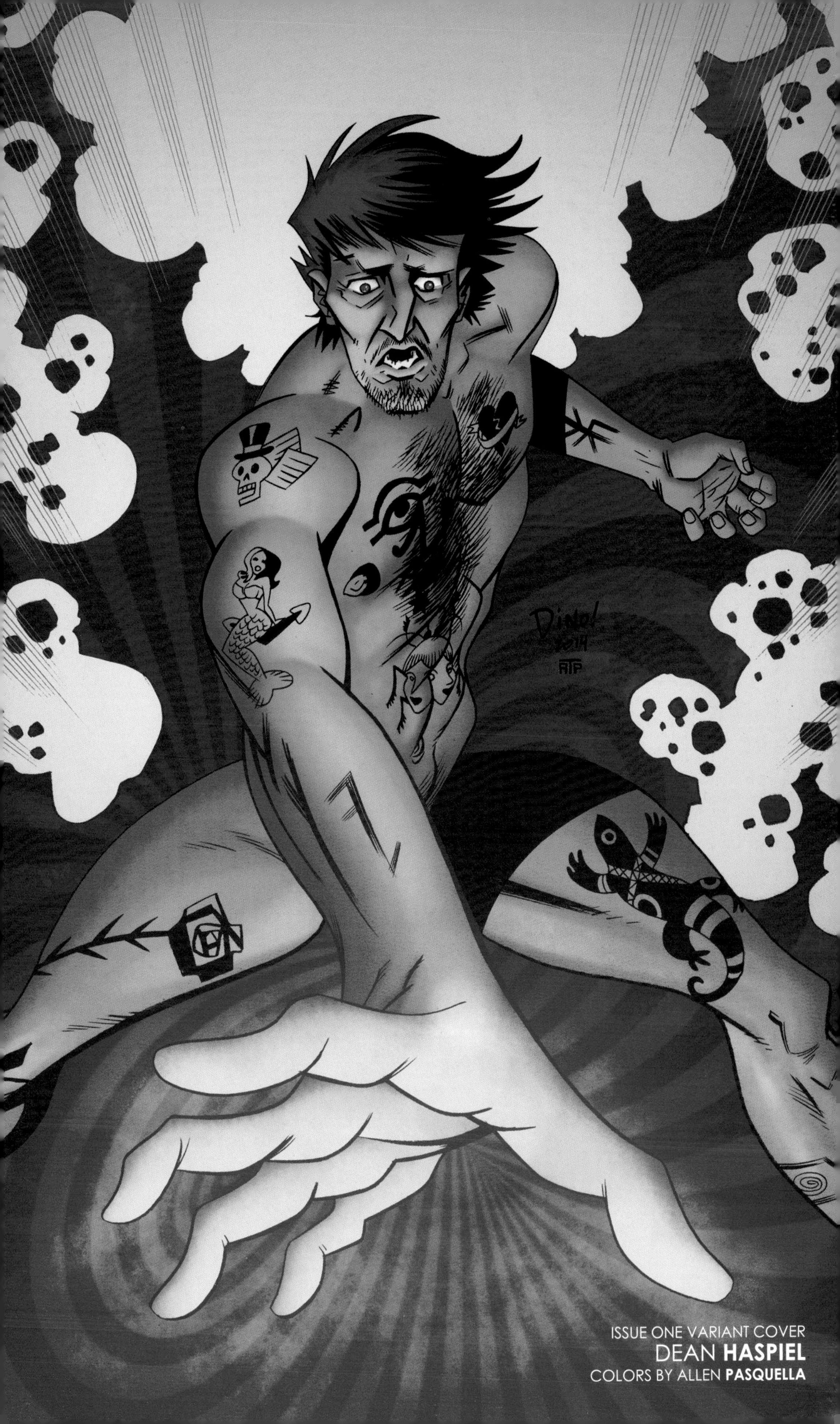

ISSUE ONE VARIANT COVER
DEAN **HASPIEL**
COLORS BY ALLEN **PASQUELLA**

ISSUE ONE NYCC EXCLUSIVE
PETER **SNEJBJERG**

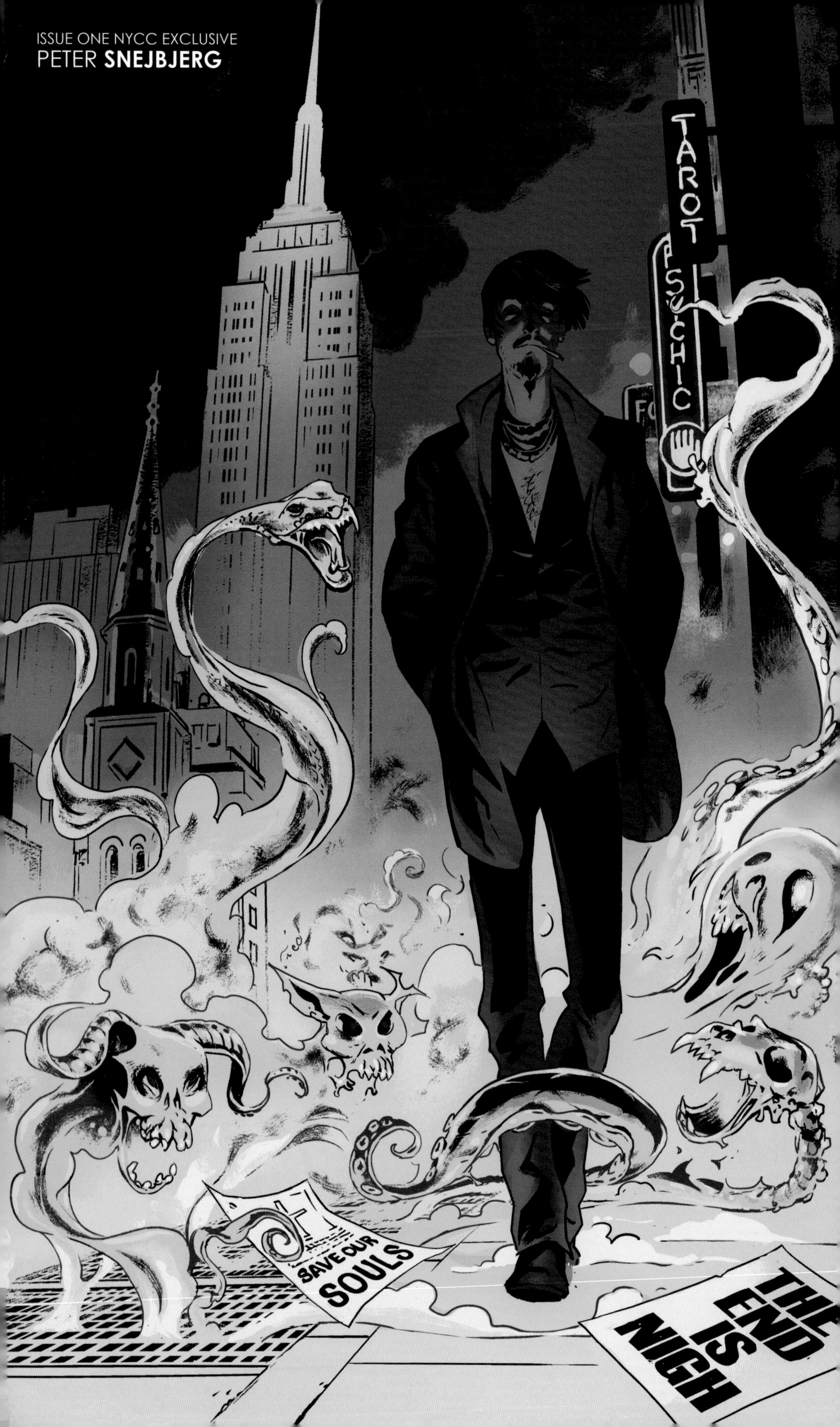
TAROT
PSYCHIC
SAVE OUR SOULS
THE END IS NIGH

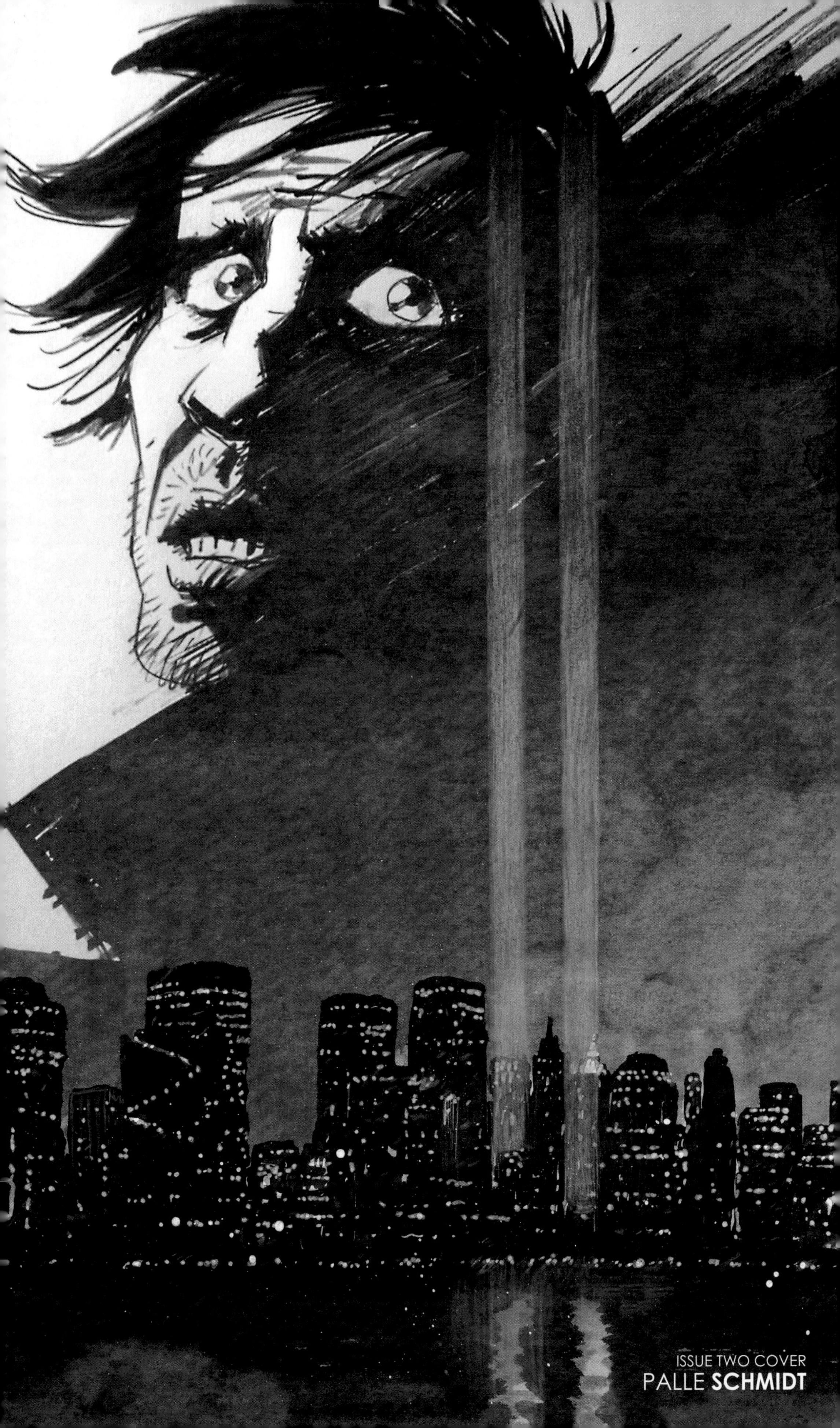

ISSUE TWO COVER
PALLE **SCHMIDT**

ISSUE THREE COVER
PALLE **SCHMIDT**

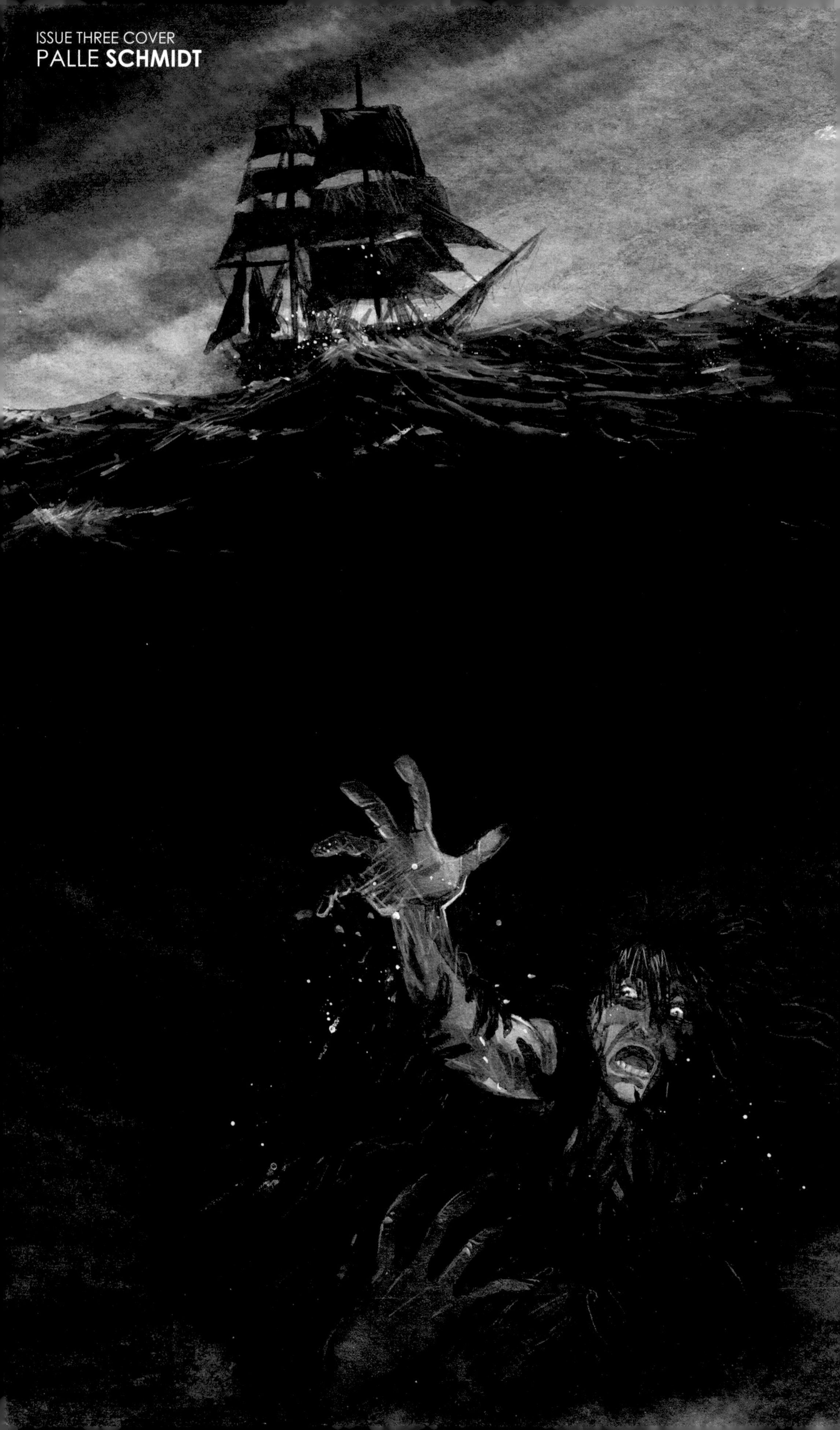

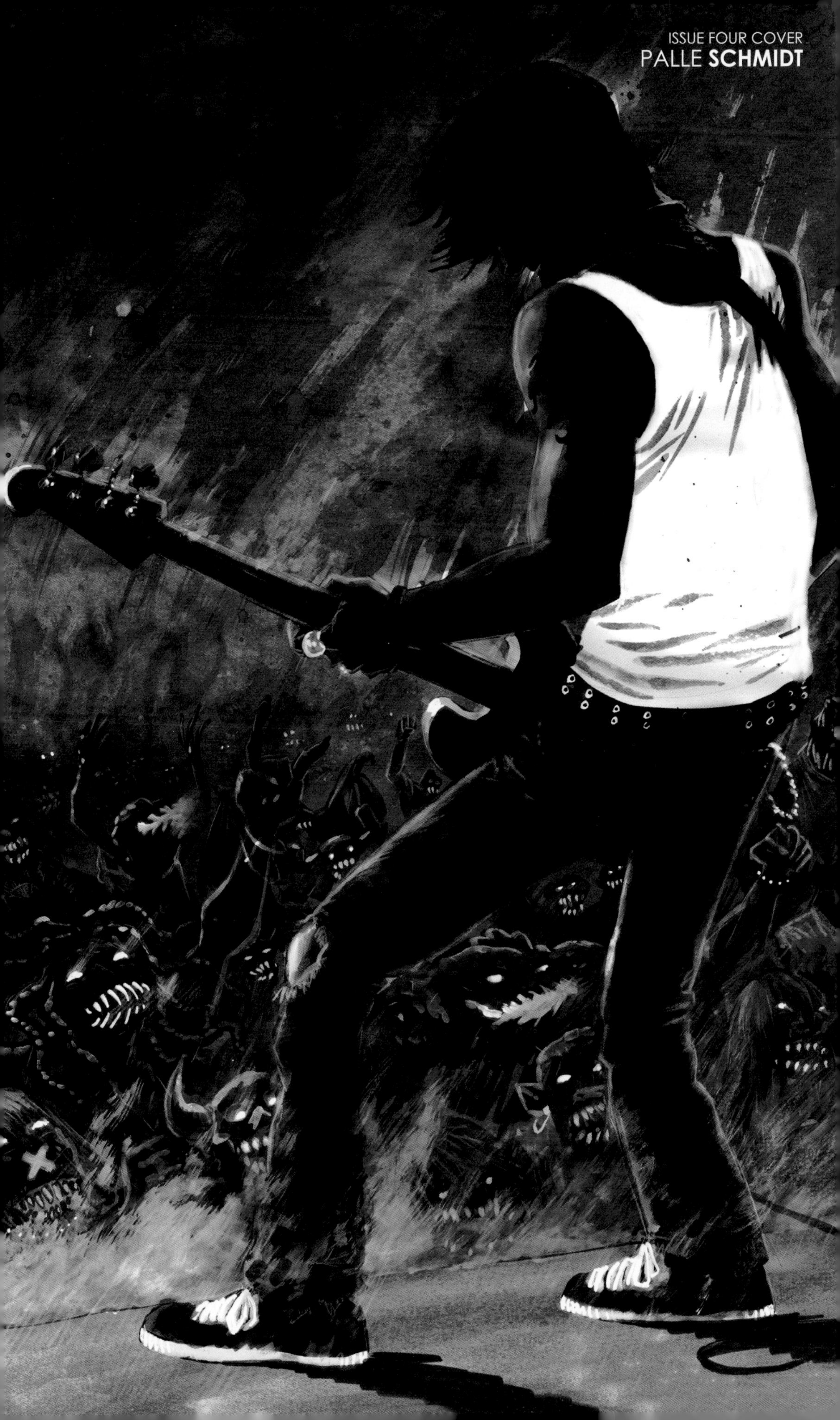

ISSUE FOUR COVER
PALLE **SCHMIDT**